The Last Freedom

THE LAST FREEDOM

Religion from the Public School to the Public Square

Joseph P. Viteritti

PRINCETON UNIVERSITY PRESS

PRINCETON AND OXFORD

Copyright © 2007 by Princeton University Press
Published by Princeton University Press, 41 William Street,
Princeton, New Jersey 08540
In the United Kingdom: Princeton University Press, 3 Market Place,
Woodstock, Oxfordshire OX20 1SY
Requests for permission to reproduce material from this work should be sent to
Permissions, Princeton University Press.

Library of Congress Cataloging-in-Publication Data

Viteritti, Joseph P., 1946–
The last freedom : religion from the public school
to the public square / Joseph P. Viteritti.
p.   cm.
Includes bibliographical references and index.
ISBN-13: 978-0-691-13011-8 (cloth : alk. paper)
1. Church and state—United States. 2. School choice—
United States. I. Title.
BR516.V58 2007
322′.10973—dc22
2006034332

British Library Cataloging-in-Publication Data is available

This book has been composed in Goudy

Printed on acid-free paper. ∞

press.princeton.edu

Printed in the United States of America

1   3   5   7   9   10   8   6   4   2

To the Memory of My Parents

John Viteritti and Catherine LaFroscia

CONTENTS

PREFACE

WRITING ABOUT religion at the beginning of the twenty-first century is something like writing about race at the beginning of the twentieth. I don't mean to suggest that the consequences of religious bias are as grave now as the effects of racial bigotry were then, but the manifestations are similar. Most Americans are not mindful of the problem because they are not affected by it; those who bear the heaviest burdens from it are not positioned to correct it; and the people who feed its malice have convinced themselves that they are justified, even righteous, in what they do.

Religion is among the most fragile of our freedoms. Through the latter half of the twentieth century, the governmental actors who assumed responsibility for interpreting and enforcing the American Constitution gave freedom of religion a relatively low priority. They did so at a time when the nation was becoming increasingly sensitive to human rights and the needs of minority populations.

Even in the best of circumstances, religion, like any freedom, is not absolute. It must be reconciled with other individual rights, and competing definitions of religious liberty itself. As a result, it is virtually impossible to grant devout religious observers the degree of legal protection they need to live their lives in harmony with the dictates of conscience. That is a serious shortcoming in itself. Beyond that, we can be doing a better job protecting them than we now are.

It may seem counterintuitive to speak of the erosion of religious freedom in America in the year 2007, when the so-called blue states are scrambling to take the White House back from the red states, and the composition of the Supreme Court seems to be growing more conservative. The ascendancy of the religious Right in American politics carries its own problems, to be sure. Among others, it has fed a backlash against religion, making the most religious among us more vulnerable.

In any case, the story of religious freedom in America is older than the last presidential election. Religious controversy has a way of reinventing itself in the United States. Who would have thought that, more than eighty years after the famous Scopes "monkey trial," school boards would be fighting over the teaching of evolution in the public schools?

Or that an offshoot of the Mormon church would be stealing headlines in Utah for practicing polygamy? Then again, not so long ago it would have been inconceivable that marriage between two people of the same sex would become a major social issue of the day; and even the best informed among us could not have comprehended the meaning of stem-cell research. Yet the larger questions behind these issues are timeless: How can people of different persuasions live in harmony? What role can the government play in mediating their differences? How can public authority be exercised judiciously so that it becomes part of the solution rather than part of the problem? On the American continent, these questions have been with us since before the founding of the republic.

When we look back on that definitive moment in our nation's history, it seems all too apparent now that the men who shaped it were better equipped to deal with the dilemmas of religious diversity than is the present political leadership—in either party. As a group, they were smarter. Their understanding of what it meant to promote democracy in a plural society was better reasoned. Their approach to the larger questions may be even more applicable to our present circumstances than it was to their own. That being said, this is more a book about our time than theirs. This is a book that hopes to use the lessons of history and the wisdom of the past to help us define the proper role of religion in American public life.

This won't be easy. The instincts that drive men and women to practice religion and the instincts that drive them to practice democracy can be contentious. Religious conviction, which is morally based, sometimes demands that believers be steadfast and immutable about their lives. Democratic government requires compromise in order to work; and in the process, it must also protect religious freedom. No, not at all easy; but as I said before, we could be doing better.

It seems only natural, when considering the role of religion in American public life, to start with the Supreme Court. Surely there is no other branch of the government that plays so important a role in sorting out the meaning of our basic rights. The Supreme Court, however, is not the only important player in the contest over the Constitution. The other branches of the government weigh in with their own interpretations. There are also the American people, whose priorities are supposed to be reflected in the popular organs of government.

While the Supreme Court seems to speak in the most authoritative voice, constitutional interpretation is really a dialogue between the Court, the popular branches, and, especially in the era of rapid polling, the American populace. In some periods of time the Court has acted in accord with popular sentiment; at other times it has asserted itself to reverse the popular course. We will come back to this point later, and discuss which is the lesser of two evils, and under what conditions. Suffice it to say for now, that at times the Court has stumbled in its efforts to help resolve the religion problem. To put it more bluntly, the Supreme Court itself has often been a part of the problem. And it may again.

In its more reflective moments, when the facts of a particular case are so peculiar or confounding, better judgment requires the Court to make hairsplitting decisions, which can only serve as a vague guide to future policy. As an institution, apart from the individuals who compose it, the High Court can appear ambivalent about religion. Take, for example, a recent pair of five-to-four rulings concerning the Ten Commandments.

Derived from the Old Testament, the Decalogue is a centerpiece of the Judeo-Christian tradition and the moral code it establishes. Should it be displayed on government property? On the final day of the 2004–5 term, the Supreme Court, after careful deliberation, decided, "Sometimes, maybe." In separate rulings, the Court approved two six-foot-high granite tablets mounted on the grounds of the state capitol in Texas and disapproved framed copies of the Commandments that appeared on the walls of two Kentucky courthouses. Was bigger better?

The first case had been brought by Thomas Van Orden, a homeless man who was offended by the monuments, which he passed frequently on his way to the library. The decision must have come as a surprise to Judge Roy S. Moore, the former chief justice of Alabama, who was driven from office in 2003 when he defied a federal court order to remove a similar two-and-a-half-ton stone monument he had installed in his courthouse. What was the difference?

The Texas monolith was one of twenty-one historical markers, including seventeen monuments situated on twenty-two acres around the capitol grounds to "commemorate the people, ideals, and events" of Texas. It had stood there for some forty years. The Court never denied its religious significance, but determined that "promoting a message consistent with a religious doctrine does not run afoul of the Constitution."

Writing one of his last opinions, the late chief justice William Rehnquist emphasized that the assemblage was designed to trace several strands of political and legal history, of which religion was just one part. Several justices differentiated the *Van Orden* case from a 1980 case in which the Court struck down a Kentucky law requiring the Ten Commandments be posted in every schoolroom in the state, noting that public schools and the impressionable children who attend them must be afforded special protection from religious indoctrination.

Justices Breyer and Stevens asserted in separate opinions that the purpose of the religion clauses was to avoid religious animosity; however, the former interpreted this to mean that the monument should be left in place, while the latter urged that it be taken away. Aside from the attention to principle and precedent, there was a strong current of pragmatism that ran through the majority opinions. What would it mean for the rest of the country if Texas were told to remove the giant sheets of granite?

Chief Justice Rehnquist noted that a portrait of Moses, holding the two tablets inscribed with the Commandments, appears in the company of other lawgivers on the south frieze of the very courtroom where he and his colleagues heard the case. Moses also sits with tablets in hand on the east façade of the Supreme Court building, and representations of the Decalogue adorn the metal gates that line the courtroom and the doors through which people enter.

In fact, if a careful observer were to take a stroll through the nation's capitol, he or she would discover representations of the Ten Commandment at the Library of Congress, the House of Representatives, the Department of Justice, the National Archives, and the Ronald Reagan Federal Office Building, as well as the federal district and appeals courts. One can only imagine how many federal and state buildings there are throughout the country where the Commandments might be seen. One can also imagine miles of scaffolding raised throughout the land to remove the offensive images, ringed by political protesters, if the Court had decided *Van Orden* differently.

Circumstances also dictated the outcome of the second case, this one brought by the American Civil Liberties Union. In the *McCreary* case, two Kentucky counties had posted copies of the commandments in their courthouses, and twice modified the displays to include other historical documents after a federal court issued an injunction against their posting. The additional exhibits also included religious references, such as the words "endowed by their Creator" from the Declaration of Independence, and "In God We Trust," which appears on our currency. This led the Supreme Court to conclude that the main purpose behind the exhibition was to convey a religious message—similar to what the federal court had found in Judge Moore's case in Alabama.

In conflicting opinions across the two rulings, several justices referred to the "borderline" nature of the cases, the lack of clear constitutional guidelines for addressing them, and even "confusion" with regard to the law. Justice Scalia argued that intent was irrelevant in the second case because the Constitution has always allowed government to recognize the religious heritage of the American people. Justice Stevens had dissented in the first case, contending that the Judeo-Christian teaching conveyed in the Ten Commandments excludes nonbelievers and people of other faiths, such as Hindus and Buddhists.

The pair of closely decided rulings underscored the fact that such disputes over the meaning of religious freedom are not easily resolved. The debate would continue in the political and legislative arenas, and the court of public opinion. They simultaneously signified the highly suspect nature of anything connoting religion in American public life, and the central role that religion has always played in that life—how religion has been viewed as both foundational and fractious in American politics.

Aside from the debate over high principle, pragmatism plays a role in determining what is right. Let's face it, some religious monuments are just tougher to remove than others. Finally, adults do not always need the same level of protection from religion as do schoolchildren, who are more vulnerable to its potentially offensive messages, or at least the messages that offend their parents. This partially explains why the preponderance of our political and legal battles over religion has involved school-related issues.

• • •

Chapter 1 outlines the main argument of the book, a concern that I
would define as the legitimization of religious bias within an influential
segment of the American population, all the while recognizing the
real threats posed by religious extremists in contemporary American
politics. Chapter 2 further structures the larger discussion. It briefly
describes the current political environment in the United States, and
the unseverable connections that exist between politics, morality, and
religion. It also examines polling data as a way to better understand
public attitudes with regard to key issues. These attitudes are not entirely consistent in their leanings, which is one reason why we tend to
fight over them.

Chapter 3 presents two education case studies, one involving the
famous Scopes "monkey trial" from 1925, the other being the less-
known *Mozert* case from 1986, which involved a group of parents who
refused to let their children read an assigned textbook that offended
their religious sensibilities. There is already much written about the
Scopes trial, but because it has become part of the folklore of the evolution controversy, there are many misperceptions that surround it. More
importantly, reading about it in concert with the *Mozert* case highlights
a central point I want to make about the vulnerability of religious minorities in a secular culture. It also illustrates the inherent problems
that majority rule poses for individuals and groups that find themselves
part of a religious and political minority. These stories are positioned
at the front end of the book to remind readers that there are more than
abstract principles at stake in the discussion about religion. These are
human stories in which there are winners and losers, in which parties
to a dispute may be forced to act against their will.

Educators have long been aware that schools convey social values,
and indeed reflect the values of the larger society. Chapter 4 explains
that schools also reflect the biases of the larger society. It is difficult to
appreciate this in the society in which we live. We are just too close
to it, really a part of it. For this reason a historical perspective can be
especially informative. So in this chapter I examine the thoughts of
three significant thinkers on education within their own historical context and ours: Thomas Jefferson, Horace Mann, and John Dewey. The
remainder of the chapter focuses on educational politics from the eigh-

teenth and nineteenth centuries, once again documenting how the
rights and interests of religious minorities can be compromised by the
self-righteous prejudices of political majorities. I hope this chapter will
alert more open-minded readers to the possibility that perhaps we have
our own biases to overcome. The other option is for us to convince
ourselves that we are the only generation in American history to have
no such biases.

Chapter 5 brings us to the twentieth century. It focuses on the interaction between law and politics around several key education issues:
textbook content, religious instruction on and off public school property, school prayer, the use of public school facilities for religious purposes, and aid to religious schools. This brief historical overview traces
the secularization of education in the United States, and explains how
the school debates provide a window on a larger societal trend.

Chapter 6 more specifically concentrates on Supreme Court case
law. It shows how the Establishment Clause of the First Amendment
was applied to overpower the Free Exercise Clause, resulting in a jurisprudence that enforced a freedom *from* religion rather than a freedom
of religion. This examination of First Amendment case law takes us
beyond education issues, and serves as a segue back to the larger discussion from which the book began.

There is a general misperception about the founding era that suggests
that the philosophical influence of the European Enlightenment
turned the writing of the Constitution into a secular project. I would
interpret the project somewhat differently, as an attempt to define religious freedom in a society steeped in religion, or at least many Protestant versions of it. This is different from our present task, which might
be described as an attempt to define religious freedom in a predominantly secular society. Nevertheless, the thinking behind the original
project remains instructive to us today. Chapter 7 examines the religious beliefs of the founding generation. We will review the thoughts
and actions of several of the major players, beginning with Benjamin
Franklin, George Washington, and John Adams. We will finally take
up the important work of Thomas Jefferson and James Madison, the
latter because he wrote the Constitution, the former because so many
of our contemporaries rely on him to interpret it.

Chapter 8 surveys the present religious landscape in the United
States. It portrays an ongoing process of diversification—not only in

denominational affiliation, but also in the ways people choose to practice their faith. It explores what churches and other houses of worship
do, and the role religious institutions play in civil society. Chapter 9
draws on the thinking of the Founders and information on the present
religious landscape to frame a discussion on the proper role of religion
in American public life. It distinguishes between private life and public
life, political speech and political action, politics and government, the
special place of schools, and the distinct role the Supreme Court plays
in mediating our differences.

ACKNOWLEDGMENTS

THIS PROJECT was generously supported by grants from the John M. Olin Foundation and the Achelis and Bodman Foundations. Jack Coons, Chris Eisgruber, Rick Garnett, Nathan Glazer, Diane Ravitch, Rosemary Salomone, Jesse Choper, Robert Putnam, and Alan Wolfe took time from busy schedules to read all or part of the manuscript. Thomael Joannidis, Jennifer Panicali, and Jalean Anthony provided valuable research assistance. At Princeton University Press, Chuck Myers embraced the project before a word was put to paper, Peter Dougherty gave it personal attention that was beyond the call of duty, and Meera Vaidyanathan saw it to completion. I am grateful to all, and accept full responsibility for the final product.

The Last Freedom

1

FEAR AND LOATHING

As it happens, I started thinking about this book while writing another. The earlier project was on a similarly controversial topic, school vouchers. When I began my research in the mid-1990s, national opinion was divided over the proposition that public money might be used to pay tuition for children to attend religious schools, as already was happening in Milwaukee and Cleveland. White liberals and Democrats had lined up against the idea in near unison for a variety of reasons, one being an abiding demand for the constitutional separation of church and state. As someone who had studied urban education for more than twenty years, I saw the issue somewhat differently. I was impressed with polls that were showing strong support among African-American and Hispanic parents for school choice in general and vouchers in particular. Such support was a major reason why voucher bills were passed by the state legislatures in Wisconsin and Ohio.

Poor parents in Milwaukee and Cleveland, as in most cities across the country, were desperate to find alternatives to the failing public schools to which their children were routinely assigned. When I spoke to these same parents about the constitutional problems that vouchers raised with regard to religion, they would look at me rather quizzically as if I were just another fuzzy-headed academic. They had real problems to face. Generation upon generation of their children had been forced to attend neighborhood public schools that were unsound and unsafe. For years, politicians had been promising these parents education reform, but there were no visible signs of change. The same politicians had sent their own children to private schools or public schools that bore no resemblance to schools in the inner city. To these parents, the concept of church-state separation was an irrelevant abstraction, a white middle-class hang-up that had no connection to their reality-packed lives.

At the time I started writing on the subject, school choice and vouchers were widely understood to be conservative issues. For economic conservatives, choice was a way to impose competition and market discipline on underperforming public schools. For religious conservatives, vouchers were a mechanism for channeling public dollars into sectarian schools. Again, I saw the issue differently. I understood school choice primarily as a matter of social justice.[1] Education has always been an essential part of the American dream, so much so that every state constitution defines it as both an individual right and a parental obligation. As long as middle-class parents have the means to remove their children from undesirable schools—either by selecting private schools or by moving to high-priced communities with better public schools—we owe poor parents similar opportunities to control the education of their children. It is morally indefensible to confine poor students to schools that middle-class families would never consider for their own children, especially when other educational options exist that poor parents prefer.

I began my earlier book with an assumption. Knowing that many of those on the political left who opposed vouchers genuinely cared about the plight of poor and minority children, I assumed that if I explained school choice in the context of an egalitarian agenda, I could at least get them to pay attention, to be open-minded. I tied the demand for choice to the moral mandate that Chief Justice Earl Warren, writing for a unanimous Supreme Court, had set down in the landmark *Brown* decision of 1954, declaring that education "must be made available to all on equal terms."[2] I explained that a needs-based choice program targeted at poor families is a form of redistributive public policy. It was not my intention to dismiss separationists' long-held concerns about the First Amendment, but to remind them that there may be more compelling social demands that need to take precedence over their legal challenges. I also disagreed with their strict interpretation of the Establishment Clause, which is probably already apparent to anyone who has gotten this far in the book.

I think my assumption was correct. I don't know how many minds I changed, but I do know that advocates and academicians on the left whom I later encountered in public forums conceded that my argument had merit, that I had offered a perspective on the voucher question worthy of consideration. Many had spent years working for education reform and trying to improve the lives of disadvantaged populations. They got the point. A targeted voucher plan directed at poor underserved populations, which I proposed, was different from the universal voucher schemes advocated by free market economists like Milton Friedman.[3]

Choice advocates on the right also got the point, and ran with it. On the day the United States Supreme Court decided that the Cleveland voucher program was permissible under the First Amendment,[4] Clint Bolick, then the very able litigation strategist for the Washington-based Institute for Justice, a libertarian public interest law firm, declared the 2002 ruling to be the most important education decision since *Brown*. Four days later President George W. Bush drew the same analogy, followed shortly by conservative columnist George F. Will.

While I had linked the plea for choice to the egalitarian mandate sounded in *Brown*, I had never taken the step of planting the Cleveland decision on the same sacred ground where *Brown* stood in the civil rights community. The comparison angered some African-American leaders, including officials at the NAACP whose lawyers had argued the *Brown* case, and who did not support vouchers.

Clint Bolick, who has represented black parents and children in more voucher cases than any other litigator in the country,[5] had a broader strategy in mind. Bolick appreciated the symbolic value of a landmark case in which liberal civil rights groups were attempting to strike down a law that was expanding the range of educational opportunities available to low-income children in Cleveland. He wanted to steer public discussion of the case in a particular direction. As he explained to Linda Greenhouse of the *New York Times*, "We wanted to make sure that this was seen not as a case about religion but education. If the court perceived it as a religion case, then we would be in serious trouble. If they saw it as an education case, then we would win."[6] I believe that Bolick's insight on the case was correct. In this book I want to explore why. I want to explain why this negative predisposition toward religion in the courts is a symptom of a larger problem worthy of our attention.[7]

Religion evokes deep passions in people. Those who practice it devoutly use it as a guidepost to their lives. Many of those who do not hold such fervent beliefs view it as divisive and potentially dangerous. I am troubled by the animosity that so many good people exhibit towards religious observers and institutions. Granted, living in New York and working in a university setting exposes me to a peculiar slice of life that is not entirely representative of the American psyche. Manhattan, with all its creative energy, can also be the narrowest slip on the planet. Yet the cosmopolitans who inhabit it influence the way many others think. They are opinion leaders.

Many individuals who describe themselves as "multiculturists," who sincerely support the causes of racial minorities, women, gays, immigrants, and other groups that have been the victims of discrimination, exhibit a genuine hostility towards the devoutly religious. They are not ashamed to say it. Their sentiment is proudly worn as a badge of sophistication, yet it is nothing but a form of prejudice, a snobbish bigotry. The underlying premise of this book is that if American liberalism is in trouble, the threats against it are coming from the left as well as the right.

Like all forms of prejudice, religious bias is rooted in fear—in this instance a fear concerning cherished values that are targeted by religious activists who aggressively pursue their political agenda. Like all forms of prejudice, it is based on ignorance. Those who are most susceptible to it don't know very much about the people they dislike. They rarely bother with deeply religious people; so they only know what they read, and they prefer reading material that confirms their own prejudices.

Like all forms of prejudice, religious bias has serious consequences for those against whom it is directed. It undermines values that are fundamental in a liberal democracy, the same values that perpetrators of this sentiment so dearly want to protect for themselves. It is especially harmful when those carrying the bias employ the Constitution as a tool for acting on it. Reasonable men and women can argue over the meaning of the First Amendment; we can be certain, though, that the framers did not write the Bill of Rights to indulge individual bias.

It may seem fanciful to write a book about antireligious bias as we find ourselves in the second term of President George W. Bush. Political analyst Kevin Phillips has written forcefully about the rise of an "American theocracy," brought on by religion's surge of political prowess in the last two presidential elections. Phillips traces public policy towards Iraq, Israel, abortion, gays, stem-cell research, and sex education to a "religiously correct" worldview that is the mirror image of the political correctness of the political Left.[8] His vision is ominous, and not without merit.

Bush, after all, presented himself to the country as a born-again Christian, and successfully cultivated the support of evangelical groups to win reelection. His comfortable margin of victory in 2004 cast popular sentiment about religion and the fears associated with it in bold relief. His public remarks brought things to a fever pitch. I will say more about him later. Here I want to make a more central point about what the discussion that framed the 2004 election told us about ourselves.

My point is illustrated in a cover story by Ron Suskind that appeared in the *New York Times Magazine* weeks before the election. Suskind, a former national reporter for the *Wall Street Journal*, had coauthored Paul O'Neill's memoir of his experience as secretary of the treasury in the Bush administration. In the *Times* article, the well-regarded journalist depicted the Bush White House as a "faith-based presidency," shaped by religious belief rather than reasoned judgments.[9] He repeats a claim lodged in the O'Neill memoir, that the circle of decision makers in the Oval Office was a closed one, averse to dissenting opinions. The point of the article was to show that this alleged close-mindedness is a function of religious conviction. What I found interesting about the piece is that it devoted less attention to substantiating that claim than it did to drawing a portrait of the kind of person who supported the president's bid to stay in office. It read as if it were a warning posted to voters on the eve of the election.

Suskind describes a December 2000 meeting where the president-elect met with thirty ministers in an Austin church to explore how he could "speak to the soul of the nation," and better understand poor people. He reminds us how Bush had reached out in 1985 to the Reverend Billy Graham for help to overcome his abuse of alcohol and turn his life around. As if to alert the reader to the dangers ahead, Suskind cites a statistic indicating that 42 percent of all Americans identify themselves as evangelical or "born again" (a figure that also includes African-Americans, who do not seem to concern him).

We then are introduced to a few of these worrisome types. Gary Walby is a retired jeweler who once told Bush during a meeting at a high school gymnasium in Destin, Florida, "This is the first time that I have felt that God is in the White House." Walby didn't actually think Bush was God, he just admired the president's open identification with his faith. Then we meet Hardy Billington, a social conservative from Popular Bluff, Missouri, who is quoted as telling a rally of twenty thousand Bush supporters gathered at a Labor Day rally, "I love my president. I love my country. And most important of all, I love Jesus Christ."

We then meet Mark McKinnon, a media advisor to the Bush campaign. He tells Suskind that the individuals being profiled love Bush, and detest people like Suskind who read the *New York Times*, the *Washington Post*, and the *Los Angeles Times*. Suskind interprets the statement to distinguish these folks from the "entire reality based community." The article ends with a comment by Joseph Gilderhorn, a Jewish contributor to the Bush campaign, who respects Bush's religion but expresses dismay that "he turn(s) to prayer or God rather than digging in and thinking things through." This is the punch line of the article.

Of course, most religious people do not see praying and thinking as mutually exclusive, and many do pray. Nor is politics the domain of pure reason. As with religion, politics also can be animated by vision, zeal, and demagoguery. Suskind's portrait is part of a larger picture that intellectuals and opinion leaders share of people who take religion seriously—that they are irrational and uninformed, a stupid lot who must be treated with suspicion.

The stammering Bush, who got the nation involved in a seemingly irresolvable global conflict on the basis of false information, fits the picture nicely. The big scare that hovered over the Iraqi conflict during the 2004 election could be summarized in one word—Vietnam. What if Iraq became Vietnam, the endless war that brought a generation to political maturity, cost thousands of lives, and ended in national humiliation? Those who make the comparison should be reminded that the ordeal in Southeast Asia was not attributed to religious zeal, or a God-struck chief executive. Vietnam was the handiwork of well-trained minds, the "best and brightest" that universities and expert think tanks could muster.

The picture Suskind draws is bolstered in a best-selling book that appeared at about the same time, in which the author, Sam Harris, asserts, "Religious faith represents so uncompromising a misuse of the power of our minds that it forms a kind of perverse, cultural singularity—a vanishing point beyond which rational discourse proves impossible."[10] There are no subtleties in the book. Harris exploits the devastating attack on the World Trade Center as proof positive of how monstrous religious fanaticism can be, warning that the worst may lie ahead in a world where maniacs have access to weapons of mass destruction. American leaders and commentators have exercised restraint in separating the suicide bombers from the teachings of Islam. Harris argues that the murderers were representative of mainstream Islamic beliefs recorded in the Koran.

For Harris, the boundaries between moderation and extremism are a blur, no matter what the religion. Whether Muslims, Hindus, Christians, or Jews, we are each intoxicated with our own irrational faith. Belief in the existence of one true God dictates an encyclopedic ignorance of the human experience. Religious moderation requires us to challenge the core dogmas of faith—including the existence of God—if it is to lead us out of the wilderness. The one thing that most Americans share with Osama bin Laden and the nineteen hijackers who carried out his deadly mission is that certain fantastic propositions can be taken as a matter of faith without the benefit of tangible evidence.

Harris's irreverence for what believers hold as sacred is truly ecumenical. Catholics are derided for accepting the doctrine of the Virgin birth, Jews for believing in a benevolent God after experiencing the Holocaust. The objective of Harris's book is unambiguous; it is to "close the door to a certain style of irrationality."[11] The reader is treated to a litany of historical travesties that have been committed in the name of God: feudalism, the caste system, slavery, execution, castration, chastity belts, human sacrifice, cannibalism, all sorts of sexual taboos. He might have mentioned pedophilia, too. In Harris's mind, faith and reason are irreconcilable. His vision of a better world, I would add, is difficult to reconcile with a vibrant notion of religious freedom. This is how far the American conversation has come. Kevin Phillips, the author of *American Theocracy*, concedes, "In the 1960's and 1970's, to be sure, secular liberals grossly misread American and world history by trying to push religion out of the public square, so to speak. In so doing they gave faith-based conservatism a legitimate basis for countermobilization."[12]

There are important substantive issues that separate secularists from the devout. These issues involve risks to other cherished freedoms, which we will begin to take up in the next chapter. These differences, however, are not a justification for the kind of intolerance that comes to the surface when mainstream liberals dismiss religious observers as being otherworldly or irrational. Many deeply religious people are not politically active, and most do not identify with the so-called religious Right. For most religious observers, prayer and love of God gives meaning to the practice of faith. Some are more vocal about religion than others. Such exuberance, however, should not be used against individuals or communities to disqualify them from full participation in democratic life, no matter how odd it may appear to the majority.

The true measure of religious freedom is the tolerance it affords those whose behavior is most out of step with the rest of us. At the same time, religious organizations should not be permitted to impose their faith on nonbelievers or those who follow a different religious tradition. The trick has always been to find a proper balance between protecting an individual's right to practice religion to the fullest, and guarding against the use of state power to endorse or sanction religion.

Despite the alarm sounded over the Bush presidency, much of which is legitimate, I will argue that the balance has been, and will continue to be, weighed against those who are deeply religious, whose day-to-day existence is shaped by their faith. This is not merely a legal question that pits the Free Exercise Clause against the Establishment Clause, or a citizen's right to practice religion against a citizen's right to not. Constitutional law, as interpreted by the Supreme Court over our two-hundred-year history, is in no small way a reflection of larger political forces. These political tides flow from a deeply felt public philosophy, one imprinted on the minds of the American people, that reinforces and is reinforced by public policy. This confluence of the legal, political, and social is the source of the problem that I identify. It is the full measure of religious freedom, or the lack of it.

This is not to say that Americans are contemptuous towards religion. The United States is among the most religious countries in the Western world. But our religiosity on the whole does not reflect the intensity of belief that characterizes the most religious among us. It is wider than it is deep. It is not at the heart of our lives as it is for the deeply religious. Many Americans who believe in God and attend church regularly are enmeshed in a ubiquitous secular culture that defines their morals and their mores. They are out of touch with the sentiments and values of people whose life is defined by their faith.

The great majority of the American people who inhabit the center of political life, whom I will later describe nonpejoratively as the *hollow middle*, are uncomfortable with extremists on both the right and the left. They do not want religion to be used as a guide to govern the country, nor do they want the public square to be rid of it. They are troubled by the activists who have enjoyed a disproportionate measure of influence in the two major political parties. They are not satisfied with the answers these operatives have offered us on the "religion question."

But since the lifestyle of most Americans has more in common with the secular minority than the deeply religious minority, they are more prone to overlook the needs of the latter. Since opinion leaders make the false assumption that the so-called religious Right speaks for most people of faith, these influential writers and thinkers exaggerate the threats posed from the right. That being said, we need to guard against the dangers posed from all sides of the political spectrum. Before I get to that, let me say more about what I mean by "extreme secularism" and what it might produce.

The French come to mind. On March 15, 2004, President Jacques Chirac signed a law that made it illegal for students in elementary, middle, and high schools to "wear symbols or clothes through which students conspicuously (*ostensiblement*) display their religious affiliation." In Paris coffeehouses, Article 141-5-1 became known as the *la loi contre le voile* because it was directed at young Muslim women who wore headscarves to school as an expression of their religious beliefs and identity. The veil issue had always been a sensitive one in French schools. It found new meaning after 9/11, as immigration swelled the ranks of the Arab minority to an estimated 5 or 6 million, about 10 percent of the population. Chirac, who is usually a cautious politician on domestic issues, decided to take a tough stance as the spring elections approached. France, after all, had defined itself as a secular state for more than one hundred years.

As Jane Kramer explained it in the *New Yorker* after interviewing Chirac, "France is an idea of citizenship, an identity forged in the neutral space of its public schools," referred to by the secular educator Jules Ferry as *ecole sanctuaire*.[13] There was no place for religious expression or exceptionalism in these institutions, although it should be mentioned that the French government pays 85 percent of the costs for religious schools that meet specified academic standards. Article 14-5-1 implied that there was an inherent tension between being French and being Muslim, or being a practitioner of any faith, for that matter. While the law was prompted by animosity towards the Arab community, it banned all forms of religious expression. A student could be expelled from school for wearing a Jewish yarmulke, a Christian cross, or a Sikh turban.

Could this happen here in the United States, where the idea of the hyphenated American has been taken for granted by so many for so long? Well, yes and no. Like the French, our public school system was also founded on the premise that education could serve as a mechanism for converting a diverse body of people, mostly immigrants, into a single populace. As we say on our currency, *E Pluribus Unum*. It is unclear what we mean by that today. Is our much celebrated pluralism a myth? Is it more about race and ethnicity than about religion? Or does it mean different things to different people: race and ethnicity for those on the political left, religion for those on the political right?

That approach to diversity, if taken to its logical conclusion, could easily degenerate into a notion of tolerance that holds, "If we like them, they're welcome; if not, then not. We just can't agree on whom we like." Fortunately, life in America is more complicated than that. An examination of present immigration patterns will show that race, ethnicity, and religion are bound together. We also have laws, based on lofty aspirations, that tell us that we need to learn to tolerate other people whether or not we agree with the way they live their lives, even if we do not like them a whole lot. How we as individuals view each other, nevertheless, has as much to do with guaranteeing freedom or equality as laws and constitutions do. How opinion leaders and the media deal with such sensitive issues matters as well. Since this book is about religion, let me draw on another foreign example to explain the point further.

In the fall of 2005, violent protests broke out in cities around the world when a Danish newspaper published a dozen political cartoons that Muslims found to be blasphemous towards the prophet Mohammed. One drawing portrayed Mohammed wearing a bomb as a turban. Another pictured him in heaven greeting suicide bombers. Muslims believe that it is sacrilegious to produce any representation of their holy Prophet. This collection of illustrations was especially offensive in the way it portrayed Islam as an intrinsically violent religion. The Western press was, nonetheless, taken by surprise by the rioting carried out by angry Muslims.

Aside from the indefensible violence that occurred, there was a notion of civility behind the reaction of many Muslim leaders that was somewhat incomprehensible to Western journalists. As Prime Minister Anders Fogh Rasmussen of Denmark explained, "I personally have such respect for people's religious feelings that I personally would not have depicted Mohammed, Jesus, or any other religious figures in such a manner that would offend other people."[14] Western journalists saw the incident primarily as a free press issue, but because no government authority was exercised either to encourage or discourage the publication of the cartoons, it really was not about freedom. This imbroglio was about the exercise of discretion.

Flemming Rose, the editor of *Jyllands-Posten*, the newspaper that printed the cartoon, insisted that his decision to do so was an "an act of inclusion" towards the two hundred thousand Muslims living in his country. He wrote, "By treating a Muslim figure the same way I would a Christian or Jewish icon, I was sending an important message: You are not strangers, you are here to stay, and we accept you as an integrated part of our life. And we will satirize you too."[15]

The difference between Prime Minister Rasmussen's notion of multiculturalism and Mr. Rose's is striking. I personally favor the prime minister's conception, believing that mutual respect is more effective way for fostering good fellowship in a diverse setting than wholesale antagonism. Disagreement is essential in a free society, but it is not necessary for the press, or anyone for that matter, to denigrate a group when being critical of it. Yet Mr. Rose, in his appeal for equal treatment, has a point also, perhaps best appreciated when comparing the reaction of the Danish press to the violence with that of the American.

Ordinarily, mainstream American journalists would agree with their Western colleagues, who are inclined to operate under the assumption that the more exposure given to a controversial subject, the better. Newspaper editors said as much when the riots broke out, then refrained from printing the controversial cartoons out of respect for the religious sensibilities of Muslims. Their restraint was remarkable. The American press is not usually inclined to treat religion with such deference. In this situation, reproducing the controversial drawings would have allowed the reading public to draw its own conclusions about the Muslim reaction, but the press held them back. They rarely exercise such restraint when mainstream religions are concerned. Does this suggest a double standard?

All too often, Americans turn to government, especially the courts, to function as an impartial referee in the famous "culture wars" over religion. This inclination to invoke government authority does not always serve democracy well. Especially when the press is concerned, democracy is better served when the government lets private matters remain private matters, as it did with the Danish cartoon episode. In other situations the boundary between the private and the public spheres is more vague, and thereby invites governmental intervention.

In no sphere is the overlap between the private and the public more apparent than in education. There are several reasons for this. Since its inception in the early part of the nineteenth century, the public school has been the place where we have defined our aspirations as a nation, indeed the very definition of what it means to be an American.[16] The school is the institution through which society passes on its values from one generation to the next. But the question has always been, whose values?

Discord over controversial political issues commonly finds its way into the schoolhouse—not just education-related fights like desegregation and affirmative action, but hot-button social controversies like abortion, birth control, stem-cell research, and same-sex marriage—all of which have religious implications. These disputes inevitably need to be decided, if not resolved, by some governmental authority, whether it is a school board, a legislative body, or the courts. Because religion also involves fundamental values, it has always been at the center of the more contentious debates. The intensity of these conflicts, and their outcomes, shed light on the larger problem that Americans confront today on the role of religion in public life.

That these disputes over religion inevitably end up in the courts is fortuitous for the student of public policy, because judicial opinions provide us with a record of well-reasoned, if contested, arguments that explain why public authorities have acted as they have. These opinions are also a window for peeking into the mind of the nation at particular periods in our history, including the present one. The record has not always been encouraging. At different times religion has been both oppressed and oppressive. Nonetheless, as a close observer to this unfolding saga, I remain a pragmatic optimist.

My optimism flows from a confidence in the capacity of our democratic form of government to mediate the most heart-wrenching disputes, even when the outcome leaves contestants feeling not entirely satisfied. This institutional capacity is a testimony to the genius of the men who designed our governmental system, how they both anticipated our divisions over religion and constructed a framework for accommodating it. It is virtually impossible to give this voluminous subject its due without conversing with the likes of Thomas Jefferson, James Madison, and the talented individuals who made up the founding generation. If the shelves at the local bookstore are any indication, Americans have an endless fascination with these giant personalities. One reason for this is that they can help us work through our ongoing anxieties.

My pragmatism flows from an understanding that political conflict, when it is so passionate, can be ugly. It is troubling when those who describe themselves as liberals are unable to distinguish between disagreement and disdain. It is equally disturbing when public officials are unable to reconcile the dictates of their conscience with their power to exercise public authority. I believe that the risks inherent in the outpour of antireligious sentiment now outweigh the risks that emerge form the outbreaks of religious zealotry that have dotted the political landscape; to put it more bluntly, the threats from the left are more dangerous than those from the right.

That, I am sure, appears unfathomable to some readers in the era of George W. Bush. They have let their fears outpace the protections the Founders have given us in the evolving experiment called American democracy. In the end, even a fair settlement of the dispute over the role of faith in American public life will require the most religious among us to make the greatest concessions. In the final analysis we must define a constitutional standard that inhibits government from using its power to force an individual to act against the dictates of his or her conscience, whether its source is religious or not.

While I am not inclined to invoke the Founders to support my views on the Constitution, I am fairly confident that this basic proposition is not inconsistent with the ideals they had in mind when they wrote the First Amendment. In order to make sense of it, we need to adapt their eighteenth-century context into ours. It was virtually inconceivable for even the most able minds of the founding generation to divorce the notion of conscience from religion, or Christianity, to be more precise. Our notion of conscience and the need to protect it must be more inclusive. It must be appropriated to the religious and the nonreligious alike.

2

RELIGION AND PUBLIC LIFE

SENATOR JOHN KERRY is a Roman Catholic from Boston who attends Mass regularly. He likes to recall his days as a young altar boy, and tells audiences that he wore rosary beads around his neck as a combat officer in Vietnam. When he became the presidential candidate of the Democratic Party in 2004, he declared that his stance on political questions would not be guided by his religious beliefs. He said that while he opposes abortion personally, he supports a woman's right to choose as a matter of public policy. This announcement disturbed leaders in the Catholic Church, who believe that abortion is the taking of an innocent life.

Some clergy members said that Senator Kerry should not be permitted to receive Holy Communion because his public position violated church teaching on a matter of life and death; it was sinful. In separate editorials, the *Boston Globe* and the *New York Times* denounced these religious leaders for their intrusion into the election, alarmed by what they saw as a dangerous mixing of politics and religion.[1] In the final weeks of the campaign, Archbishop Charles J. Chaput of Colorado, a swing state, told a group of college students that a vote for Kerry could constitute "cooperation with evil" and require Catholics to go to confession before receiving Holy Communion.[2]

Catholic theologians could disagree over whether Senator Kerry's stance on abortion is a "mortal sin," disqualifying him from receiving the sacrament of Communion; and Cardinal Chaput's attempt to classify a vote for Kerry as an act requiring penance is out of step with the usual church practice of telling parishioners to vote their consciences. But if the Catholic Church has a moral position on abortion, why shouldn't it inject that position into a national debate? Should the position be barred from public discussion because it is derived from religious dogma? Who are the *Boston Globe* and the *New York Times* to tell the Catholic Church how to resolve a dispute within its own house with one of its own members? Do the opinions of editorial writers need to be considered by religious leaders when they deliberate on matters of faith?

Senator Kerry was not the first Catholic politician to defy the teachings of the church when speaking at the public podium. John F. Kennedy, the only Catholic ever to be elected president, made a habit of assuring audiences that he would not take his instructions from Rome. New York governor Alfred Smith, the first Catholic to receive the presidential nomination of a national political party, felt compelled to assure voters in 1927, "I recognize no power in the institutions of my Church to interfere with the operations of the Constitution of the United States or the enforcement of the law of the land."[3] In an attempt at ecumenical patriotism, the New Deal Democrat then closed his remarks by confirming his "belief in the common brotherhood of man under the common fatherhood of God." He finally added, "I join with fellow Americans of all creeds in a fervent prayer that never again in this land will any public servant be challenged because of the faith in which he has tried to walk humbly with his God."

In 1984, in the heat of the Reagan-Mondale contest for the White House, Governor Mario Cuomo of New York gave an address on religion and public morality at Notre Dame University that has since become the mantra for Roman Catholic office-seekers.[4] By then the nation had more than a decade to digest *Roe v. Wade*,[5] wherein the U.S. Supreme Court upheld a woman's right to an abortion. In his talk, Governor Cuomo acknowledged his agreement with Catholic teachings on abortion, and declared that "as a matter of conscience" he believed "fetal life in the womb should be protected even if five of nine Justices of the Supreme Court and my neighbor disagree with me." He then went on to explain that as an elected official in a pluralistic society he has an obligation to obey the law and refrain from imposing his religious views on other people.

The late archbishop John O'Connor of New York responded to the Notre Dame speech with an article in *Catholic New York*, a diocesan newspaper, stating that he "could not see how any Catholic could vote for a candidate who actively supports abortion."[6] The archbishop's remarks raised questions that he himself may not have been prepared to address at the time. Specifically, the moral conundrum might better be defined as whether a Catholic who agreed with the position of the church on abortion could vote for a candidate who supports it, or more to the original point, how a politician who espoused such Catholic views as a matter of conscience (since not all do) could sanction abortion under any conditions.

The Notre Dame speech laid out a number of important questions on the role of religion in public life that are still with us. Supreme Court Justice Antonin Scalia, a practicing Catholic who is not ordinarily predisposed to positions embraced by the more liberal former governor of New York, took a similar stance when he wrote that as a public official he had a responsibility to follow the law when opining on the death penalty, despite the fact that capital punishment is opposed by church leaders.[7] Justice Scalia himself does not oppose the death penalty on moral grounds, and points out that while church officials object to it politically, they have not taken a dogmatic position on capital punishment, as they have on abortion. Moreover, judges have a different role in the governmental process than do legislators and executives. The job of elected officials is to make policy; the job of a judge is to interpret existing laws.

The question remains, however, under what circumstances should faith-based considerations override legal considerations for those in public office? If an individual truly believes that an action by the government is immoral, how could he or she in good conscience go along with it, even as a government official? Is one expected to take leave of one's conscience upon entering public life? Or is it only religious convictions that one is obliged to leave behind in the name of church-state separation? People in public life have some choices when confronted with such a dilemma.

First, one could disobey the law and live with the consequences. Chief Justice Roy Moore of Alabama did just that in 2003 when he refused to remove the Ten Commandments from his courtroom, and subsequently was driven from office. Or a public official could refuse to enforce a legal mandate that he believes is immoral and respectfully resign from office, as Solicitor General Archibald Cox famously did during the Watergate episode (although the ethical issue there was not intrinsically religious). There are estimable consequences that flow from such actions that cannot be easily disregarded. As former Health, Education and Welfare secretary Joseph Califano pointed out in the context of the Notre Dame debate, if Catholic leaders resigned their offices every time they were required to enforce a law that was contrary to church teaching, Catholics would suffer a significant loss of voice in government.[8] Secretary Califano's point provides the foundation for a moral argument based on pragmatic considerations. It has merit. Cardinal O'Connor, nonetheless, saw the argument as a cop-out, a bow to political ambition, holding that many Catholic politicians had already surrendered their voice voluntarily. But there are other options.

As Governor Cuomo explained, an elected official could follow the legal requirements of his or her governmental position, while at the same time speaking out on an issue in the public forum. This separation of the governmental role from the political seems like a reasonable compromise; it is also politically expedient. The fact of the matter is that many Catholic politicians who have distinguished their religious convictions from their political positions spend more airtime promoting the latter. Vice presidential candidate Geraldine Ferraro, Mr. Mondale's running mate, was a case in point. As a Catholic, she opposed abortion personally; as a candidate she devoted much of her energy to defending a woman's right to choose. On the political stage, her identity as a woman seemed to overshadow her identity as a Catholic (though many Catholic women do not oppose abortion, and many non-Catholic women do).

This dilemma is not the sole province of Catholic office-seekers. Senator Joseph Lieberman, an observant Orthodox Jew, made a similar distinction between his religious and political convictions on abortion when he sought the vice presidency in 2000. So what does it mean, then, when a politician says that she or he has a religious conviction? What does it mean for anybody, for that matter? Polls consistently show, for example, that a majority of Catholics support legalized abortion,[9] though they are not as inclined as politicians to distinguish their political view from their personal ethics.[10] When pushed, they are more prone to defend their position on moral grounds and disagree with church leaders. This raises a larger question: Are matters of faith of any consequence in American public life?

Well of course they are. Consider the president, George W. Bush. When once asked if he sought the counsel of his father, the former president, on world matters, he responded that he drew strength from a "Higher Father." President Bush has been unambiguous about the way his religious convictions inform his policy choices. His efforts to channel social funding through faith-based institutions has rankled First Amendment separationists. President Bush also opposes abortion and stem-cell research because he believes they violate the sanctity of human life, a view he closely aligns with his Christian faith. When asked about his position on embryonic research during the campaign, he referred to human life as "a sacred gift from our Creator."[11] Senator Kerry and other Democratic leaders criticized the president's introduction of religion into the political campaign as divisive, verging on un-American.

President Bush also opposes gay marriage. He underscored this opposition in the middle of his 2004 reelection campaign when he proposed a constitutional amendment that would ban it. The religiosity of the gay marriage issue, however, is distinguishable from that of abortion or stem-cell research in at least one significant way. Aside from religious orientation, the ethics of the abortion and stem-cell issues turns largely, though not entirely, on a central empirical question to which we do not have a definitive answer. This question concerns nothing less than the genesis of human life; that is, whether it begins with an embryo or at some later time during gestation. Individual responses to this elementary question are informed by religious beliefs and turn on a moral calculation of when the fetus reaches legal personhood deserving of state protection. Nonetheless, the "veil of ignorance" that overshadows it provides a basis for those who might adopt a "pro-life" position on purely ethical grounds. It is arguable that so long as the possibility of life exists, we have a moral obligation to protect it. This position is logical, it is reasonable, and it is humanly responsible—apart from any religious grounding.

Of course there are ways to look at the abortion question in less absolute terms. One might argue that the level of risk to life increases during pregnancy as the embryo develops into a fetus, entirely separating the abortion question from stem-cell research. The circumstances under which an abortion is performed are also pertinent, such as in a pregnancy resulting from rape, or when the mother's life is in danger. Factoring in the right of a woman to make a personal decision about terminating a pregnancy, or the right of her mate to have a say, further complicates the ethical calculation.[12]

One might also argue that the right of a woman to control her body and its functioning is so basic that it is inviolable even when the loss of an innocent life might be involved. This is regarded as an extreme position by those who care about protecting the rights of a fetus or an unborn child, and many "pro-choice" advocates are reluctant to measure the merits of abortion in those terms. Nonetheless it is morally arguable. The point to be made here is that taking a firm pro-life stance on abortion is not as extreme as other positions one might adopt on the basis of a religious orientation. The rights of several individuals are at stake when one confronts abortion as a matter of public policy, and there is an irresolvable question about the beginning of human life that hangs over the entire debate.

The issue of gay marriage is quite different in a number of respects. It turns not on an empirical question but on a disagreement over assumptions and values. Many of those who oppose gay marriage, including President Bush, believe that marriage is an institution meant to involve, in his words, "one man and one woman." Underlying this position are two more fundamental claims: That sex between people of the same gender is unnatural, therefore sinful; and that the purpose of marriage is to procreate. Indeed, the Catholic position against birth control is premised on the proposition that procreation is the primary purpose of sex, and that the higher purpose of the act ought not to be interfered with by artificial or unnatural means.

These claims have deep religious roots and are difficult to anchor empirically or rationally, though natural law theorists would argue to the contrary.[13] Based on human behavior, it is evident that most sexually active people are more attracted to individuals of the opposite gender than their own. Yet heterosexuality is far from universal. How common does homosexuality need to be in order for it to be considered normal, or at least not abnormal or unnatural? Obviously what repels some in the bedroom, delights others.

As Bush and Kerry were crisscrossing the country gathering votes, bookstores from coast to coast were stocking their shelves with a best-selling memoir by a former dancer from the New York City Ballet.[14] The intimate journal is a reflection on her "spiritual journey," which begins and ends, according to her account, with an obsession she has with anal intercourse. She obviously did not consider the act unnatural. Taking on the literary persona of a college coed, Tom Wolfe, in his most recent work of fiction cum social commentary, tells in vivid detail how oral sex is a preferred way to go among the campus generation.[15] Wolfe's claim is corroborated by a University of Michigan survey, which found that the great majority of adolescents (88 percent of boys, 83 percent of girls) who have had sexual intercourse have also had oral sex.[16]

Who should decide what is preferable or permissible in the privacy of one's domicile? Why should sex be a matter of government regulation at all? Are governmental controls legitimately triggered only when homosexuals are involved? Here again the right of an individual to choose is at stake, but unlike the abortion issue there are no conflicting legal claims posed from the other side, at least insofar as individual rights are concerned. When the U.S. Supreme Court struck down the Texas antisodomy law in 2003, the majority viewed the case essentially as a matter of individual rights for homosexuals.[17] The moral arguments offered in defense of antisodomy laws are less persuasive than those against abortion. The fact that Mrs. Jones finds her gay neighbor's sexual behavior repulsive is less compelling than Mrs. Jones's concern for what she believes to be the loss of an innocent life. The former confuses sense with sensibility; the latter erupts from the individual conscience.

The implications are somewhat different with regard to gay marriage. Beyond individual rights of privacy and association, marriage requires positive legal action by the state if the union is to carry all the usual privileges for the partners. Nonetheless, there must be some legal or moral justification for excluding homosexuals from marrying, and this returns us to assumptions that traditionalists hold about the institution itself, particularly those concerning sexuality and the purpose of marriage. Once again the central claim, based loosely on natural law theory, is that the function of marriage, and indeed sexual activity itself, is the procreation of the human race.[18] Here the evidence is not especially persuasive either. Most people who marry plan to have children, but not all. Increasingly people well beyond their childbearing years marry for love and companionship. Given the birth rate in modern society, it is also evident that most fertile married couples have effectively severed sexuality from reproduction, the latter increasingly understood as a deliberate decision, not something that might result from every physical encounter.

The truth is that, as a matter of public policy, government authorities have never established procreation as a condition of sex or marriage. Sex and marriage mean different things to different people, whether they are straight or gay: an expression of love or affection, physical gratification, the formation of a family. Indeed, because of the availability of children for adoption and technological advances in medicine, child rearing is no longer limited to married heterosexual couples. In a world where so many children of heterosexual couples go unloved and uncared for, it is unreasonable to exclude homosexual couples from parenting solely on the basis of their sexual orientation. Given the laws of adoption, it is easier for the state to enforce a standard for parental quality in adoption than it is in natural birth, where public authorities have no discretion. The government has no say in whether two people can have children together, whether or not they are married.

While the majority of Americans hold traditional views about marriage, most arguments against single-sex unions do not hold up to reason. These traditional views, based on customs that have always been in a state of flux, have their roots in religious conventions. The Supreme Court said as much in upholding a Georgia antisodomy law in 1986, when Chief Justice Warren Burger concurred, "Condemnation of those practices is firmly rooted in Judeo-Christian moral standards."[19]

President Bush's proposal to enact a constitutional amendment banning same-sex unions was bold in several respects. It was one of the clearest manifestations in recent times of a political action undertaken by an incumbent president that was conspicuously linked to his religious beliefs. Moreover, it was put forward at a time when legal questions over the constitutional rights of homosexuals were unsettled, occasioned not only by the *Lawrence* decision on a federal level, but by state supreme court decisions in Hawaii, Vermont, and Massachusetts that were sympathetic to civil rights claims by gays and lesbians.[20] The latter struck down a state law outlawing same-sex marriages, and was a motivating factor behind the president's proposal.[21] If the federal amendment were adopted, it would effectively preempt judicial policymaking at either level of government, which in Bush's mind was a win for the democratic process.

President Bush's proposal for a federal constitutional amendment also had all the markings of political opportunism. Although eleven state referenda supported similar bans in 2004, the conventional political wisdom gave the federal amendment a low probability for success.[22] It was a keen gesture for rallying his base among the religious Right. Many politicians on the left, including Senator Kerry, had ducked the issue by endorsing a traditional view of marriage while holding that the policy was a matter of state discretion. Both Bush and Kerry supported civil unions between people of the same gender, the Republican splitting with his own party's platform in doing so. President Bush introduced the constitutional proposal again in 2006, when his popularity ratings reached an all-time low and the Republicans were on the verge of losing control of Congress in the midterm elections. Once again, the election year squabble reinforced the fact that religion and morality remain essential features of American politics.

In 2006, New York's highest court upheld the "opposite sex" provision of the state marriage law, denying that a homosexual right to marry could be found in the state constitution.[23] Later that year, the New Jersey Supreme Court held that homosexual couples must be afforded the same rights as heterosexuals, but left it to the state legislature to decide whether these rights would be defined as marriage or civil unions.[24] The legislature subsequently chose the latter. During the 2006 elections, seven out of eight state ballot measures designed to ban same-sex marriage passed, with Arizona being the exception.

MORALITY AND POLITICS

From the very beginning, religion, morality, and politics have been linked together in the American psyche. On the day of his inauguration, President George Washington stood on the second-floor balcony of Federal Hall in New York, placed his hand on the Holy Bible borrowed from a nearby Masonic temple, and calling on God to witness the event, began a lasting American tradition. As he took the oath of office, and swore to faithfully execute its duties, the first president instinctively uttered the words "So help me God," thereby initiating another time-honored tradition. The inaugural address that he later

delivered in the Senate chamber was filled with references to the Deity,
"the Great Author of every public and private good."[25] After speaking,
the president, accompanied by the vice president and members of Congress, walked over to St. Paul's Chapel in lower Manhattan to attend
services conducted by Rev. Samuel Provoost, the Episcopal bishop of
New York, and newly appointed congressional chaplain. Churches
throughout the city were opened for prayers, and bells rang from their
high steeples to celebrate the birth of the new nation.

Later that year, shortly after Congress approved the First Amendment
to the Constitution, a delegation of its members paid a visit to Mr.
Washington and urged him to designate "a day of public thanksgiving
and prayer" acknowledging the "many and signal favors of Almighty
God." The president willingly complied, establishing yet another American tradition, proclaiming, "It is the duty of all nations to acknowledge
the providence of Almighty God, to obey His Will, to be grateful for
his benefits and humbly to implore His protection and favor."[26] Eight
years later, when Washington delivered his Farewell Address, he told
the country, "Of all the dispositions and habits which lead to political
prosperity, religion and morality are indispensable supports."[27]

Washington was not an avid churchgoer, nor was he the sole author
of the farewell statement. In drafting the address the president had
sought the help of James Madison and John Jay. The words about religion are usually attributed to Alexander Hamilton, a close advisor who
was not especially known for his religious devotion. Washington was
embracing a widely held disposition shared by his generation that tied
the success of their great democratic experiment to a notion of civic
virtue. Notwithstanding a shared Madisonian realism about the role of
interest in politics, civic virtue, it was hoped, would allow men to elevate public life to the pursuit of a higher good that would benefit all
citizens. It would focus national aspirations on the sense of commonal-
ity essential to cooperative social interaction, rather than the individu-
ality that divides people of different backgrounds.[28]

The selflessness inherent in such civic mindedness could not be severed from a larger morality that was associated with religion, or more
specifically Christianity at the time. Thus even Thomas Jefferson, an
avowed separationist, was moved to concede, in a letter to John
Adams, that Christ's ethical teachings of universal brotherhood were

the "most sublime and benevolent code of morals which has ever been offered to man," without which life in society would not be possible.[29] Later Tocqueville would declare religion "the first" American political institution. He observed, "The Americans combine the notions of Christianity and liberty so intimately that it is impossible to make them conceive of one without the other."[30]

For better or worse, the connection between religion, virtue, and politics has persisted as a recurring theme in the American historical narrative. These morality plays are well known to us all, once a common feature of the grade school curriculum. At one end of the spectrum was the social gospel of Jane Addams, who sought to fight deprivation in the slums of Chicago in the late nineteenth century; at the other end were the Salem witch trials that resulted in public burnings at the stake during the seventeenth century.[31] Both could be traced to the Christian pulpit.

The story of race, perhaps the country's most indelible moral catastrophe, is more complex to unravel. White churches in the South had been complicit in concocting a moral justification for slavery on the pretense that the horrible institution was beneficial for blacks, deemed to be incapable of caring for themselves, while asserting that support for the practice could be found in the Bible. Meanwhile, the beginnings of the abolition movement could also be traced to the Christian teaching.[32] In his first inaugural address, Abraham Lincoln urged his countrymen to put their trust in divine providence, calling forth "Intelligence, patriotism, Christianity and firm reliance on Him, who has never forsaken this favored land." In his second inaugural address, delivered toward the end of the Civil War, Lincoln, citing the Scriptures, told the nation that "the judgments of the Lord are true and righteous altogether." The president mentioned God fourteen times in the speech, and quoted directly from the Bible four times. Lincoln had also invoked the phrase "under God" in his Gettysburg Address.[33]

Nearly a century later, after the Supreme Court handed down its momentous decision in 1954 outlawing racial segregation in public schools,[34] white churches in the South split on the issue of segregation. Southern Presbyterians and the Southern Baptist Convention overwhelmingly passed resolutions supporting desegregation.[35] Most white pastors stayed neutral, some falling back on arguments for church-state separation as an excuse for not taking a stance on the burning issue confronting their congregations. Thus, while local politicians resented the clergy's reluctance to lend support to their racist agenda, black religious leaders like Martin Luther King Jr. castigated the ministers for their lack of moral courage.

African-American churches, surprisingly, also played a mixed role in the movement towards racial equality. As far back as the plantation days of the Old South, religious gatherings had been a source of psychological strength and comfort for those oppressed by slavery. Historians of the civil rights movement, however, have criticized African-American religious leaders for their otherworldliness—a reluctance to take on the issue of segregation, instead preaching complacency and promising the faithful that true salvation would come in the next life.[36] What distinguished leaders like Martin Luther King was a capacity to convert faith into political militancy.

Taking a fresh look at the defeat of Jim Crow in the South, historian David Chappell explains it this way: White liberals reluctant to alienate southern Democrats who gave them commanding majorities in Congress convinced themselves that human reason would eventually move the civil rights campaign forward, permitting them to take a gradualist position; King and other black preachers embraced the prophetic message of the Bible to demand immediate justice, believing that God was truly on their side.[37] From then on the black church would play a distinct role in the political and social life of the African-American community, one that has no parallel in the white community.[38] To divorce religion from politics in the African-American community would leave it barren, might I say without a soul. There is no separation of church and state in the world of black politics.

President Ronald Reagan's election in 1980, with the activist support of the Moral Majority, put a new face on the role of religion in American public life. The ability of the coalition to effectively promote its conservative agenda and the commensurate swing of the country to the political right (or at least the middle) distracted mainstream liberals from recognizing the significance of religion in the lives of racial minorities, opening a cleavage in the liberal consensus that would only become apparent much later. In the latter part of the twentieth century, fear of Christian fundamentalism became a driving force behind demands for church-state separation, much as fear of Catholicism had been in the nineteenth century. George W. Bush's ascendancy to the White House in 2000 would only serve to accentuate these fears. As Catholics had swelled the ranks of the Democratic Party in the earlier century, evangelical Protestants would now emerge as a power base within the Republican Party.

According to the most recent census, conservative churches experienced more rapid growth in the last decade of the twentieth century than all other denominations.[39] The trend continues. A variety of new groups have come into being to make sure that moral issues demand the attention of elected officials and candidates for office. Focus on the Family, the Family Research Council, and Concerned Women for America, for example, have lobbied the government on matters concerning gay rights, family values, abortion, and violence in the media. Other organizations, such as the Rutherford Institute and the American Center for Law and Justice, have used litigation as a strategy to influence public policy.[40]

Despite these developments, Paul Weyrich, a supporter of the Moral Majority who was instrumental in linking the religious conservative cause to the fortunes of the Republican Party, announced in 1999 that he was near ready to give it all up in frustration. As he explained, "I no longer believe that there is a moral majority. I believe we have lost the culture war."[41] Of course many would beg to differ with Mr. Weyrich's assessment of his own movement. Organizations such as the American Civil Liberties Union, Americans United for the Separation of Church and State, and People for the American Way have devoted enormous resources and energy to stem what they see as a dangerous intrusion of religion into the political life of the country. The truth is somewhere in between. Americans have conflicting views on the role of religion in public life.

On the basis of a variety of measures, Americans are among the most religious people in the Western world. According to a Gallup poll, 96 percent believe in God, 90 percent believe in heaven, and 69 percent claim membership in a church, synagogue, or other religious congregation.[42] Americans also report high rates of church attendance, though some experts believe that self-reporting may lead to overreporting by respondents who feel compelled to give the impression that they are in church more frequently than they actually are. But such exaggeration is itself a measure of how important Americans think religion is. That being said, there is strong evidence that since 1965 church attendance has actually declined among Catholics and mainstream Protestants.[43] The single notable exception to this pattern is among black Protestants, for whom church attendance has increased, indicating how strong a factor religion remains in the African-American community.

The Washingtonian vision of good citizenship, built on a foundation of morality and religious conviction, is very much alive in the contemporary United States. According to a poll conducted by Public Agenda, the great majority of Americans believe that there is a close connection between faith and personal morality, with 69 percent saying that religion strengthens family values and good behavior.[44] Commensurate with this view, 85 percent agree that religious leaders have as much a right as anyone to speak out on political issues, and 63 percent feel that increased involvement by church leaders would not have a detrimental effect on the political process. Nearly half the people polled (49 percent) think that politicians would act with more honesty and integrity if they were more religious.

Seventy-four percent, however, say that when politicians talk about their religious beliefs publicly, they are just saying what people want to hear. Furthermore, an overwhelming 84 percent hold that public officials who are deeply religious must be willing to set their convictions aside in order to get things accomplished in government. In other words, religion can have a positive influence on politics and society so long as it is not taken very far. They seem to agree with Governor Cuomo that politicians can and should separate their official positions on moral questions from their own faith-based convictions; although this dichotomy is apparently colored by suspicions about the sincerity of religious utterances made on the stump. All the while, Americans on the whole appear to be sanguine about the prospect of religion playing a larger role in public life—at least to a point.

In September 2004, as the Bush-Kerry contest was moving into high gear, the Pew Forum on Religion and Public Life released the results of a survey on religion and politics.[45] It was the fourth such survey Pew had completed in the middle of a presidential race since 1992. The results revealed strong support for the expression of religious view-

points by candidates and for faith-based institutions. Sixty-eight percent of the respondents said that it was important for the president to
have strong religious beliefs, and 63 percent disagreed with the statement that they felt uncomfortable when candidates discuss faith. Sev-
enty-six percent agreed that organized religious groups should stand up
for their beliefs. Traditionalist evangelical Protestants (90 percent),
black Protestants (89 percent), and traditionalist Catholics (88 percent) were most in accord with the latter point of view. As much as
47 percent of the total population indicated, however, that organized
religious groups should stay out of politics. When asked how much
religion influences their own thinking on politics, 39 percent admitted
it was "important," 24 percent said "somewhat important," and 37 percent said "not important." Evangelical Protestants (58 percent), black
Protestants (57 percent), and Latino Protestants (51 percent) were
most likely to indicate that religion was an important influence in
shaping their political viewpoints.

The Pew report highlighted deep partisan divisions between specifically defined groups, with traditionalist Christians and centrist Protestants leaning Republican, while modernist Christians, minority religious groups, non-Christians, and the unaffiliated favored Democrats.[46]
The former tended to describe themselves as conservative, the latter
as liberal. When it comes to hot-button issues, such as those that fit
into the pro-life or gay rights categories, Americans also seem quite
divided. For example, 51 percent oppose a ban on stem-cell research
(32 percent support, 17 percent no opinion), 51 percent oppose implementing life in prison over the death penalty, and 48 percent oppose
abortion. The greatest opposition to abortion came from evangelical
Protestants (69 percent), Latino Catholics (58 percent), and black
Protestants (54 percent). Only 48 percent of all Catholics opposed
abortion, once again indicating that a majority disagrees with the
teachings of the Vatican on this controversial issue. Fifty-seven percent
of the entire population polled expressed support for gay rights. However, on the question of marriage, 55 percent came out for traditional
marriage (a man and a woman), 53 percent for civil unions between
gays, and 36 percent for same-sex marriage. These views on gay marriage and civil unions were confirmed in a 2006 poll.[47]

It is notable that, except for traditionalist evangelical Protestants, all groups responding ranked domestic and foreign policy issues above cultural issues (abortion, stem-cell research, and same-sex marriage) in determining their voting preferences. There was a clear division on the question of government support for faith-based institutions, with 50 percent expressing support, 34 percent opposition, and 16 percent no opinion. An earlier study conducted by Pew in 2001 provides some insight on the latter issue.[48] In that bimodal survey, 75 percent said that they favored such support, compared to 21 percent who were opposed. When further queried, 68 percent expressed concern that faith-based initiatives would result in too much government involvement in religious institutions; 60 percent worried that religious organizations would proselytize among social service recipients; and 78 percent had a problem with the thought that faith-based institutions would only hire employees who shared their religious beliefs.

There are many conclusions one can draw from the rich array of polling data. For a start, Americans are comfortable with religion. They believe it makes citizens and politicians better people. They believe this strongly enough to welcome musings about religion from their political leaders, and are steadfast in allowing religious figures to engage in public debate about important issues of the day. But they seem to draw a line between words and action. Politicians are expected to compromise, as if to suggest that true moral conviction, at least the kind derived from religious teaching, is the price to be paid for taking public office.

Americans have historically embraced religion as a way to elevate politics. We now seem to feel that public life is unsuitable for the moral purist. But this seems to be the democratic way, and there is a point to it. In a pluralistic society, politics is about the clash of convictions—mine versus yours—not moral absolutism. We might appreciate having a president who approaches stem-cell research as an ethical question, but we don't necessarily want to be governed by his convictions. Many reasonably believe that such research could prove beneficial, protecting and enriching life rather than sacrificing it.

As suggested earlier, there are legal and extralegal ways available to governmental leaders who are inclined to stick to their convictions when acting in an official capacity, by just accepting the consequences of their actions, whether this means resigning from office, being driven from office, or even going to jail in an act of protest. Few do. Perhaps that is part of a larger problem. There is a limit to what we expect from our politicians when it comes to the big moral questions of the day, and most seem to live up (or down) to those expectations. The purpose of government, after all, is to process a cacophony of interests and values, and to sort them out in ways that we can all accept. As Michael Sandel has suggested, our government functions as a "procedural republic" absent an underlying sense of what is good.[49] This has become a common criticism of modern liberalism, yet it may be the best we can do in a government in a pluralistic setting.[50]

Politics among groups and people, divorced from the sanctions of government authority, is another matter. The point becomes more transparent when we consider the religious leader in contrast to the government official, or even the candidate for office who aspires to be one. Americans seem to be very protective of the rights of religious leaders to speak out on public issues, but at the same time they are uncomfortable when these leaders cross the line into politics. These are the same respondents who welcome politicians who speak out on religious issues. This suggests that most Americans, except for African-Americans and the deeply religious, are not receptive to having men or women of the cloth running for public office. They are not even comfortable with clergy members who use the pulpit to support one candidate or another. Theirs is a rather restrictive viewpoint. It is one thing to argue that elected officials should not let their religious convictions interfere with the way they use government authority to conduct public business; it is quite another to expect people in religious life to exercise self-restraint when going about their own personal business. Americans seem to be most tolerant of religious viewpoints when these opinions are without consequence. Even the clergy are expected to act like good secularists when entering the political sphere.

Responses to questions on aid to faith-based institutions shed further light on how Americans feel about religion. Even some of the respondents who supported government aid to such institutions joined the majority in registering concern with how it might be used. Most were worried that such institutions would continue to proselytize. Religious organizations tend to do that since they come together on the basis of common principles and teachings. If we follow the logic of most respondents to the Pew survey, the effect of government aid would be to neutralize these institutions, or, more accurately make them behave as though they were secular. Many respondents just assumed that would happen as a result of government funding, and were not happy with that outcome either.

The poll respondents also expressed concern that faith-based organizations receiving public funding would only hire employees who support their religious beliefs. That is ordinarily the case with religious institutions, and the practice is supported by federal law. Title VII of the Civil Rights Act permits religious institutions to show such preference in hiring.[51] The provision has been upheld unanimously by the United States Supreme Court, which ruled that religious organizations must be granted such prerogatives in order to protect their autonomy.[52] The level of protection provided by the law is what any organization formed around a particular set of principles would need in order to thrive. One would not expect a labor union to hire someone who is pro-management, or an environmental organization to employ someone who is unsympathetic to the protection of our natural resources. To do so would be self-defeating.

It is interesting that the same Pew respondents who expressed concern that public aid would lead to excessive government intervention in the affairs of faith-based institutions were also worried about the exercise of institutional prerogatives that the government would be inclined to protect, and most nonreligious organizations would take for granted. What is it about religious institutions acting on their principles that creates anxiety in people? What is it that makes aid to such institutions problematic at a time when government gives financial assistance to multitudes of other organizations that are formed around a particular philosophy or social agenda many citizens might oppose?

THE SECULAR STATE

As contemporary social conventions have it, well-mannered people are expected to treat religion much the same way they used to treat sex. It was not anything to be ashamed of, mind you, so long as it did not involve extreme measures. We assumed that most people did it, and it was generally known with whom; but what went on behind closed doors was meant to stay there. Polite people didn't discuss it in a social situation, especially in mixed company; which in first case referred to people of the other sex, and in the latter refers to people of another sect. It was to be kept a strictly private matter. We have become more open about sex these days, but religion, worse than politics, is a good subject to avoid if you want to get through a pleasant evening with casual, or not so casual, acquaintances. Mix religion with politics, and anything is fair game.

In the early 1990s Yale law professor Stephen Carter garnered a great deal of attention for a book he wrote titled *The Culture of Disbelief*.[53] While conservative observers like Father Richard John Neuhaus and William Bennett were dismayed that religion had been banished from the public square, Carter was concerned that religion had been trivialized in public life.[54] As he saw it, the political and legal culture had dictated that religious people were to act as though their faith were not so important to them, especially when in public, but at times even in private. The thought that faith could serve as both an anchor and a compass for one's life had become foreign to most people. In addition to the usual contempt with which many intellectuals and journalists treat devout observers, Carter took issue with the assumption that people of faith had nothing useful to contribute to the public dialogue. In the age of George W. Bush, it hardly seems appropriate to speak of "the naked public square," but there are still many who would prefer to have it that way, and they are working at it quite assiduously. As a matter of fact, their cause has had a great deal of success in the one American institution that is most responsible for the formulation and preservation of public values: the public school.

Americans for a time have been convinced that learning and religion are anathema. Their attitude has a long history. It is attributed to a post-Enlightenment notion that dichotomizes rationality and spirituality, the former associated with the realm of reason, the latter with superstition. This is not an altogether accurate understanding of what the Founders had derived from the European Enlightenment more than two centuries ago, but we will take that up later. The misconception is held widely enough by an influential number of thinkers and opinion

leaders that it is a reality in and of itself. John Dewey, the most influential educational philosopher of the twentieth century, hoped out loud
that education would disengage children from the religious teachings
of their own parents.[55] It is not uncommon for contemporary political
theorists to dismiss religiously based arguments as unpersuasive, nor is
it surprising, given their own disbelief.

In a democracy, however, all arguments deserve a hearing. The problem with contemporary secularists is their determination to disqualify
faith-based arguments from public discourse as an accommodation to
a normative framework on which we can all agree.[56] Their position
suggests that if they do not find a point of view persuasive, it does not
deserve to be included as a part of legitimate public debate. Taken to
its logical end, secularism would confine all expressions of religiosity
behind the church door. This is a particular view of religious freedom
that warrants further explication. A recent book by Susan Jacoby, *Freethinkers*, is instructive on what they have in mind.[57]

"Freethinkers" are a small but diverse group of contemporary secularists that runs the gamut from those who are genuinely antireligious,
to those who abide by an unconventional form of faith that rejects
traditional religious authority. Among their heroes is Robert Ingersoll,
"the Great Agnostic," who, on the centennial anniversary of the signing of the Declaration of Independence, praised the authors of the
Constitution for deliberately omitting any mention of God, declaring,
"We have retired the gods from politics."[58] It may be worth noting that
the Declaration itself is replete with references to the Deity, by whom,
it is said, all inalienable human rights are bestowed. Freethinkers also
count among their number Thomas Paine, the American revolutionary
propagandist and author of *The Age of Reason*, who denounced Christianity as an invention of man, not God. Their sense of religious freedom can better be described as freedom from religion, rather than freedom of religion.

Jacoby captures their sentiment nicely when she discusses her own
personal reaction to events surrounding 9/11. Like many New Yorkers
who walked the streets of their ravaged city in the aftermath of the
attack, she felt a sense of comfort from the expression of national unity
that greeted the event. But, she claims, this feeling of inclusiveness
was lost for her when President George W. Bush participated in an

ecumenical prayer service at the National Cathedral in Washington. Speaking to those assembled, the president read a passage from Paul's Epistle to the Romans, as a way to acknowledge the tragic loss of those departed, and to assure the survivors that God still loves us. In order to avoid offending those gathered who were of the Jewish and Muslim faiths, Mr. Bush omitted a reference to Jesus Christ contained in the passage. But, Jacoby protested, the president was perfectly comfortable ignoring Americans who like herself do not adhere to any faith, whose outlook is decidedly secular. There was no speaker at the service who represented her views.

My first reaction to Jacoby's complaint was one of . . . well, disbelief. Should atheists and agnostics have gotten an invitation to the prayer service? I can't imagine that anybody even thought of them. Would you invite the Sierra Club on a hunting trip, or a group of vegetarians to a pork roast? I really doubt secularists were purposely excluded from the event, and there were probably a few sprinkled through the crowd who just kept their thoughts to themselves. But would the die-hards really have wanted to go to a prayer service? I suppose that if the idea of inviting the secularists had come up, it would have been difficult to decide who might represent them, because they have no bishops or rabbis. They did hire a Washington lobbyist in 2005, but lobbyists, we all know, don't belong in church.[59] Maybe a spokesperson could have done it. Everybody seems to have one of those these days. Then again, should the atheists and agnostics be represented separately? What about plain old secularists? Where would they all sit? Inside the church, or on the outside? How would they take it either way?

After my initial reaction, I began to take Jacoby's point more seriously, and found that there are no easy answers to the problem she had raised. What she is telling us is that secularists, as religious groups, represent a particular worldview that needs to be taken into account when public officials measure the implications of actions that butt up against the wall of separation. The ceremony at the cathedral was an important national event designed to help a wounded national citizenry gather its thoughts, seek consolation in one another, and reassure themselves about the future. It was presided over by the nation's chief executive. There is a small number of Americans who might feel uncomfortable entering a house of God, even though they would have been welcomed. Some would be offended at the thought of their president leading a congregation in prayer.

According to Jacoby, 14 percent of the population has no formal ties to religion, but less than 1 percent describe themselves as atheist or agnostic. She did not perceive the turn to prayer as either a Bush phenomenon, or even a Republican phenomenon. She recalled how Jimmy Carter, the first born-again Christian to enter the White House, and Bill Clinton, the first chief executive to publicly ask God's forgiveness, also chipped away at the wall that stood between private faith and public officialdom. Speaking for a small, usually quiet, minority, Jacoby is put off by religion's way of creeping into public events that are in some way governmental in nature.

Certainly, the tendency on the part of public officials to engage the Deity was not the invention of Jimmy Carter and Bill Clinton, or a novelty of the twentieth century. As we saw earlier, the practice dates back to George Washington, with little interruption in between. In a country where more than 90 percent of the population expresses a belief in God, what are the alternatives? How might we accommodate the 10 percent who are agnostic about God, or the less than 1 percent who more pointedly renounce the existence of a Supreme Being? It is necessary to distinguish between the two because somewhere between the 1 percent and the 10 percent is a group of nonbelievers who do not care one way or another about God's presence in our public rituals. To the 1 (or more) percent who consider themselves conscious secularists, it is another matter. They have a particular worldview to which religion is repugnant, especially when it is mixed with the rites of government.

How might the preferences or needs of these various groups have been accommodated with regard to the 9/11 convocation presided over by President Bush? One alternative would be for the president to participate (which he actually did) in one or more public ceremonies that were religion-free, with no mention of God, the Bible, or an afterlife. This appears to be fair. Most constitutional scholars would agree that the First Amendment was designed to protect both freedom of religion and freedom from religion, although they might differ over what each entails. At a minimum, it should guarantee that no person be compelled to practice religion who chooses not to. Life is never that simple, though. At least a portion of the secularists whom Ms. Jacoby had in mind would not be entirely satisfied with the provision of an alternative service. Their consternation with the event that occurred at the National Cathedral is more basic. They are troubled by the fact that an elected public official participated in a religious event, even though the organizers, as Jacoby concedes, went to great lengths to include people of all religious persuasions, and not offend any. They are probably not too happy with the concept of a "National Cathedral" either, even though it is a private institution.

The only way to abide by such an absolutist position would be to disallow any accommodation between government and religion. This would involve an extreme standard of church-state separation out of step with common practices. Let's put aside, for the moment, the wording on our currency, public oaths, inscriptions on public buildings, and the like. Let us just consider the consequences for those present at the cathedral in the fall of 2002, or similar events. Let's agree that the event in question was religious in nature. Having people of all faiths stand shoulder to shoulder in common prayer is a powerful and consoling act. Why shouldn't they be allowed to do so? Wouldn't the denial of such an opportunity in the form of a legal prohibition infringe on their rights to practice religion as they choose to do?

Well, according to some secularists, yes and no. They surely have the right to commemorate a national tragedy any way they wish, with all the trappings of religion. The problem in this case is that they were joined by the president, who is a government official. That made the ceremony a public event. But what if the president himself is a religious person? Doesn't he have the right to participate in a religious ceremony if he wants to do so? Individuals are not required to shed their religious identity as a condition for taking office, at least as a matter of law (political practicality may dictate something else in some communities). The event did take place in a private cathedral belonging to the Episcopal Church.

What we have here are conflicting claims regarding the First Amendment definition of religious freedom: on the one hand the right of a majority to practice religion as they see fit, on the other the right of a small minority not to practice it at all. It would be facile to weigh the claims against the alternatives and conclude that the majority should not be so burdened to satisfy the peculiar demands of such a small minority, but our Bill of Rights was written for the purpose of protecting the rights of minorities. Were their rights compromised here?

One factor that seems to figure very largely in the calculation of fairness, aside from the fact that the occasion in question was a private event (or because of it), is that participation was voluntary. Nobody was required to attend. Nor were any public funds expended to support it. The aggrieved party (or parties) in this case was disturbed about what other people had decided to do, rather than what she (they) was required to do. Ms. Jacoby was unhappy with the event, for sure, but she suffered no loss or compromise of freedom. To have it the other way, to prohibit those assembled in the National Cathedral from seeking consolation and honoring the victims of the World Trade Center bombing in the manner they saw fit, would have involved a significant infringement on personal freedom.

Let us, for a moment, move the discussion to a different setting, from a private cathedral in Washington, D.C., to a public school in Elk Grove, California. In compliance with a state law that requires every public school to begin each day with "appropriate patriotic exercises," the district, as most throughout the country, has every elementary school class recite the Pledge of Allegiance. Michael Newdow, whose daughter attends school in the district, had a problem with this. An avowed atheist, he filed a suit alleging that, because the Pledge includes the words "under God," its recital in public school is a form of religious indoctrination in violation of the First Amendment of the Constitution, or more specifically his right to direct the religious education of his daughter.

Trained as a lawyer, Mr. Newdow argued his own case before the Supreme Court, contending that the words "under God" are divisive. During oral testimony, Chief Justice Rehnquist reminded Mr. Newdow that the congressional vote to add the words was unanimous, which did not sound very divisive. Mr. Newdow responded, to a round of applause, that the vote was unanimous because an atheist cannot get elected to office; suggesting, as had Ms. Jacoby, that atheism is a worldview worthy of legal protection.

On the surface, this appears to be another instance of the rights of the majority pitted against the rights of a minority, but the facts in the Elk Grove case distinguish it from the event at the National Cathedral in several significant ways. The school in Elk Grove is a public institution supported by government funding. Unless the child's parents are willing and able to send her to a private school at their own personal expense, she must attend public school somewhere in her home district, or run the risk of violating state compulsory education laws. In accord with previous federal case law concerning school prayer, every child in California, including Mr. Newdow's, has the right to refrain from reciting the Pledge. Mr. Newdow believes that it is unfair that any family has to make such a choice. He finds the need to reject a practice supported by a majority of families a form of social oppression. He insists that the words "under God" should be removed from the Pledge for it to pass constitutional muster.

Consideration of the case is complicated by the fact that the child's mother, Sandra Banning, retains exclusive legal custody of the child, including sole authority to make decisions about her education and welfare. She was never married to Mr. Newdow, and the child never lived with him. She is a practicing Christian, has chosen to bring her daughter up that way, and has no problem with her daughter reciting the Pledge like other schoolchildren in California. Furthermore, concerned about the welfare of the ten-year-old, she filed a motion in court to have the case dismissed in order to spare her daughter the ordeal of a public trial that could be disruptive in her own school district, the rest of the state, and possibly the rest of the country. She believes the challenge has been psychologically harmful to her daughter. The child herself never expressed any resistance to participating in the exercise with her classmates. A magistrate judge and a federal district judge both ruled that the Pledge is constitutional, and dismissed the case. Then a divided appeals court in the Ninth Circuit reversed the earlier decisions, finding that the school district's policy interferes with Mr. Newdow's rights to direct the religious education of his child. The state then appealed the case to the U.S. Supreme Court.

Mr. Newdow's dramatic oral testimony before the High Court attracted attention from the national media. In June 2004 the Court voted eight to nothing (Justice Scalia recused himself because of public remarks he had previously made on the issue) that Mr. Newdow had no legal standing to bring suit in the case because state authorities had granted Ms. Banning legal custody over her child.[60] While the ruling did not require the Court to address the substantive issues underlying the case, several justices availed themselves of the opportunity to do so by writing concurring opinions. Their thoughts on the subject shed light on the terms of the discussion that frames this book. One of the more remarkable developments to emerge around the high-profile case was the strong support that lined up behind the Pledge from groups and institutions that are characteristically identified with a separationist position on the First Amendment. They included both of the major teachers unions, organizations of school administrators, and the *New York Times*.

Writing for the court, Justice Stevens acknowledged that the Pledge was a "patriotic exercise designed to foster patriotic unity" and pride in common national principles, a role that the Court had long ascribed to the public schools. Among the core American principles mentioned in his opinion were freedom, equal opportunity, and religious tolerance. The Pledge itself had been conceived in 1892 as an exercise for school-children and part of a national campaign commemorating the four hundredth anniversary of Columbus's discovery of America. In 1954 Congress amended the text of the Pledge to add the words "under God." The change, inserted during the Cold War, was made to distinguish American democracy from the godless Communist regime of the Soviet Union. A House report accompanying the legislation, noted by the Court, observed, "Our Nation was founded on a fundamental belief in God." Signing the legislation, President Dwight Eisenhower added, "From this day forward, the millions of our children will daily proclaim . . . the dedication of our nation and our people to the Almighty."[61]

Writing on the merits of the case, and joined by Justices O'Connor and Thomas, Chief Justice Rehnquist opined that requiring teachers to lead willing students in reciting the Pledge does not violate the Establishment Clause of the First Amendment. Recalling the origin of the disputed words added during the Cold War, the chief justice remarked that today they probably mean different things to different people: for example, that God has guided the destiny of this country, or that that it exists under God's authority. He then turned to history, reminding us that throughout time American presidents have consistently acknowledged God's and religion's role in the nation's development. In addition to Washington and Lincoln, he mentioned Woodrow Wilson, Franklin Delano Roosevelt, and Dwight D. Eisenhower, all of whom invoked the Deity in public pronouncements.[62] He cited congressional actions that ordered "In God We Trust" inscribed on American currency, and the Supreme Court's own tradition of starting each session with "God save the United States and this Honorable Court."

Chief Justice Rehnquist concluded that the Pledge is "a patriotic exercise, not a religious one; participants promise fidelity to our flag and our nation, not to any particular God, faith or church." He declared that Mr. Newdow's objections do not give him veto power over a practice that allows others to willingly engage in a ceremony prescribed by Congress. Justices O'Connor and Thomas wrote their own concurring opinions on the substantive merits of the case. The reluctance of five members of the Court to engage in a more substantive dialogue left a strong impression, however, that the Court, as the country, is divided over religion. Mr. Newdow senses this too. In 2006, he represented a group of parents who agreed to initiate another lawsuit, whose standing in the case could not be challenged.

• • •

There are several broad observations we can make at this point that will help to structure the larger discussion to follow in the remaining chapters. The first is that religion, morality, and politics have always shared a common place in American public life, in some times more comfortably than in others. Generally, polls show that Americans remain persuaded that religion has a positive effect on individual character, and are receptive to faith playing a role in politics, but within boundaries that remain unsettled.

At either end of the political spectrum, there are secularists who believe that faith should play no role in public life, and devout observers who believe that religious teaching should provide a moral compass for policymakers. Most Americans fall somewhere between the two poles, and they appreciate the need to protect both freedom of religion and freedom from religion. Finding the correct balance has never been easy, but there are broad analytic considerations that can be useful in working our way through the problem.

For those individuals whose faith is central to their moral outlook, it is difficult to separate religion from politics, or at least from those political questions that have a clear moral dimension. However, the implications regarding how one acts on that faith, or is permitted to, differ for the individual in private life as compared to the individual in public life. Accordingly, protecting the right of a private individual to act falls under the legal domain of the Free Exercise Clause of the First Amendment; limiting the authority of the public official to do the same comes under the domain of the Establishment Clause. But of course, distinguishing the private person and the public person, even within the same individual, may be more difficult than it first appears. Private citizens, when they choose to, can assume the role of political activists without aspiring to public office; public officials have a private dimension to their lives that they may choose to exhibit publicly.

As a private citizen I might form my political viewpoints on the basis of my religious convictions; I might further argue my public position about an issue on the basis of these convictions; and I might further yet try to influence policy on the basis of these same convictions. At some point my outspokenness, and especially my efforts to influence policy, may become problematic for those on the other side who do not share my convictions; yet it is debatable whether my action as a private citizen represents a threat to the religious freedom of my adversary.

If I assume the role of a public official who has the capacity to more directly shape or make policy that affects others, the stakes are quite different. As a religious person, my position on moral questions discussed in the public arena most likely would have been shaped by my faith-based convictions. While some citizens might take exception to the fact that I articulate my public positions accordingly, I could be accused of being disingenuous if I chose to conceal the moral basis of my position. As a public official, I have a legal obligation to obey the law. It is arguable whether I have a moral obligation to follow a law that I believe is ethically wrong, especially if I am willing to accept the consequences of my actions.

Another aspect of the larger dilemma, which may actually be of greater consequence, concerns the manner in which I use my office to change the law or policy in a way that affects others. Here we might distinguish between policy preferences that are based purely on religious convictions, and those that may be justified on the basis of a more secular moral construct.[63] And again, there is a reasonable distinction between the roles played by legislators and executives who make public policy and that of judges whose responsibility it is interpret the law.

We do not need to attempt to resolve these questions at this point of the discussion, now that we have begun to lay them out. But before going on to the next chapter, there are a few points on the peculiar nature of education policy that are useful to consider. The public school is a unique institution in the way that it brings the public and private lives of citizens together. As a parent I have a legal obligation to educate my child. As a public institution the government-run school has the authority to determine how this should be done. In fact those public officials who make education policy do not only have authority to tell my child how she should behave when she is on the premises of the school itself; they actually have the authority to tell my child how she should think and act after she leaves the school, and in her private life. Whether I agree with what they tell her may or may not actually count as a matter of law and policy.

3

TENNESSEE TALES

It has been called the "Trial of the Century." John T. Scopes was a general science teacher and part-time football coach in Dayton, Tennessee, who in 1925 stood accused of violating a state law that prohibited teaching about evolution in the public schools. The courtroom drama was hyped by the presence of two star attorneys: Clarence Darrow, who had joined the defense team, was one of the most famous criminal lawyers in the country; William Jennings Bryan, who was with the prosecution, had been the Democratic Party's candidate for president three times, and served as secretary of state under President Woodrow Wilson. Darrow was a brilliant litigator, Bryan a charismatic orator; Darrow was a religious agnostic, Bryan a religious fundamentalist.[1]

The trial attracted hundreds of reporters, most of whom were sympathetic to Scopes, including the irascible H. L. Mencken, who referred to evolutionists as Neanderthals. The trial made national headlines through the month of July, which proved to be exceptionally hot even by Tennessee standards. On the seventh day of testimony, Judge John T. Raulston moved the trial outside onto the courthouse lawn, not just to escape the stifling heat of his close chamber, but for fear that the tremendous crowd of spectators would collapse the wood floor.

Scopes had been filling in for the regular biology teacher, who was out sick. Stretched a bit beyond his own expertise, he knew enough about the subject to disagree with the new law that the state legislature had passed earlier in the year. Scopes had decided to teach from the textbook *A Civic Biology* by George William Hunter, which embraced Charles Darwin's theory of natural selection. Darwin's *Origin of Species* had received a mixed response from the scientific community when it first appeared in 1859. Though it was not his purpose to challenge biblical teaching, Darwin was fully aware that his analysis contradicted the grand act of creation depicted in the Book of Genesis.

As with most revolutionary theories in science, Darwin's revelations were greeted with some initial skepticism.[2] They provoked technical quibbles over his methods of discovery. Many scientists proceeded to take from the theory whatever suited their own philosophical predilections. T. H. Huxley, an agnostic, interpreted evolution as an empirically based rejection of Christianity. Asa Gray of Harvard, a devout Christian who had arranged for the book's publication in the United States, tried to reconcile its findings with a theistic theory of evolution. Princeton theologian Charles Hodge rejected the *Origin of Species* as a work of atheism that could not be squared with the Scriptures.

By the end of the nineteenth century, evolutionary theory had worked its way into the American high school curriculum through an influential textbook by Gray that perpetuated the idea of a Supreme Creator overseeing the entire process.[3] Fundamentalists did not take up the fight against evolution until the 1920s, when compulsory education laws shot school enrollments upwards, and more families were feeling the effects of public schooling.[4] The new curricula designed around Hunter's book appeared when America was already convulsing from the culture wars stirred by the Jazz Age. That generation was at once trying to come to terms with a new music, a new sexuality, the women's vote, and more conspicuous divisions between whites and blacks—not to mention the city against the town, and the north against the south. Many traditionalists made an easy connection between the flapper morality portrayed by writers like F. Scott Fitzgerald and the decline of religious values. The rise of evolutionary theory was seen as part of the larger slide towards materialism in both learning and culture.

Nearly half the states, including most in the South, had seriously considered passing legislation similar to Tennessee's that banned the teaching of evolution. However, only Arkansas followed suit, when in 1928 it adopted a popular referendum into law. By the time Tennessee passed the Butler Law in 1925, curriculum disputes had already broken out over such topics as sex education and patriotism. Passage of the law brought cries of outrage from leading educators at Harvard, Princeton, Yale, and the local campus at Vanderbilt. Scientists at the state university in Tennessee stayed quiet to avoid irritating the legislature. Governor Austin Peay is said to have signed the legislation as a way to curry favor with religious groups to gain their support for increased funding of the public schools, assuming that the prohibitions would never be enforced.[5] The arrest of John Scopes proved his assumption wrong.

When the American Civil Liberties Union (ACLU) first ran an ad in a Tennessee newspaper offering to take a test case for a cooperative defendant—not yet identified as Scopes—it saw the dispute primarily as one of academic freedom. A member of the organization's executive committee taught at the same New York City high school as George Hunter, the author of the controversial textbook Scopes used in Dayton. As the ACLU attorneys saw it, the Butler Law compromised the freedom of teachers in Tennessee to teach science as they saw fit. Since First Amendment case law had not developed sufficiently to allow the Establishment Cause to be applied to override actions by the states, ACLU strategists did not think that it was wise to argue the case on religious grounds. Defense attorney Clarence Darrow saw things differently. When asked about his objective in the Scopes case, he replied, "We have the purpose of preventing bigots and ignoramuses from controlling the education of the United States."[6]

Clarence Darrow brought his own crusade to Dayton, which made Roger Baldwin, the founder of the ACLU, reluctant to include him on the defense team. Darrow was a notorious secularist.[7] Like his intellectual mentor, Robert G. Ingersoll, the "Great Agnostic," Darrow considered Christianity a "slave religion" and regarded science as the only source of truth. Apart from his reading of the law, Baldwin understood that Darrow's raw animosity towards religion could be a liability in a Tennessee courtroom in 1925 (just as voucher advocates appreciated that religion-based arguments could be problematic at the end of the same century). In the 1920s, Tennessee, as many other states, still required public school children to read the Bible daily. Judge Raulston began each day of the trial with a prayer delivered by a local clergyman. Recognizing the risks inherent in a First Amendment argument, Darrow chose to argue that the Butler Law violated religious freedoms protected in the Tennessee constitution, claiming that it imposed biblical teaching on public school children.

It is unfortunate that most people's familiarity with the Scopes trial is based on the movie dramatization that appeared in 1960 starring Spencer Tracy, Frederick March, and Gene Kelly. The movie, *Inherit the Wind*, was taken from the play by Jerome Lawrence and Robert E. Lee. When the play opened on Broadway in 1955, the writers issued disclaimers indicating that their presentation was only loosely based on the historical record. Their work was a response to McCarthyism and the narrow-mindedness, paranoia, and the diminution of civil rights it engendered. The play and the more popular movie that followed were also a distortion of what transpired in Dayton, Tennessee, in 1925.[8]

Among the more egregious distortions was the characterization of William Jennings Bryan, Darrow's chief adversary. Bryan is portrayed as an ignorant, bigoted, religious fundamentalist. He was certainly a fundamentalist, but the character of the man was more complex than the caricature painted by Hollywood.[9] It is not unusual to see religious fundamentalism lumped together with ignorance and bigotry, and Hollywood is at least partially responsible for that popular perception. *Inherit the Wind* is an illustration of how prejudice, when emboldened by artistic license, can discard the truth. The popular movie not only typecast Bryan, it typecast religion and its most devout observers in the mind of the American people. The image stuck.

William Jennings Bryan was elected to Congress at the age of thirty as a populist Democrat from Nebraska. Known as the "Boy Orator of the Platte," he grabbed national attention at the Democratic Party convention of 1896 when he took on the conservative incumbent president, Grover Cleveland, to support policies more sympathetic to farmers and laborers. His speech was tinged with the messages of democratic majoritarianism and Christian social justice, both of which came to define his political persona. It won him the nomination and almost the election, after which he picked up the two additional titles that accompanied him to the famous trial, "Great Commoner" and "Peerless Leader." As a speaker and a writer, Bryan championed the direct election of senators, the progressive income tax, a ban on corporate campaign contributions, and women's suffrage, but his egalitarianism did not cross the hard racial lines of nineteenth-century politics. Bryan was also a pacifist, which led him to resign as secretary of state when President Wilson entered World War I against Germany. It wasn't that Bryan was sympathetic to the Germans. In fact, Bryan's attitude towards the Germans was very much affected by his view of evolution, and vice versa.

First of all Bryan was not convinced that there was sufficient evidence available in 1925 to accept evolution as a scientific fact. In his opinion, it simply had not been proven. As he argued, "Evolution is not truth; it is merely a hypothesis—it is millions of guesses strung together."[10] He was also troubled by the social implications of the theory. Social Darwinism placed humanity in brutal competition, resulting in winners and losers. Progress occurred through a harsh process of elimination, based on the notion that some people were naturally superior to others, an idea the Germans embraced all too readily. There was an inherent racism to scientific and social Darwinism that neither Bryan nor Darrow wanted to deal with in the context of the Scopes trial. The full title of Darwin's influential book was *On the Origin of Species by Means of Natural Selection, or the Preservation of Favored Races in the Struggle for Life*.

This racism was reflected in the biology text that Scopes used to teach children at his Dayton public school. According to Hunter's book, "At the present time there exist upon the earth five races or varieties of man, each very different from the other." The "highest type" was "the Caucasians, represented by the civilized white inhabitants of Europe and America."[11] The passage explains why many black leaders at the time renounced evolutionary theory, including Rev. John W. Norris of the African Methodist Episcopal Church, who wrote a statement in support of Bryan's case before the Dayton court.[12]

The theory of natural selection also became a "scientific" justification for eugenics, a form of genetic engineering that encouraged reproduction among "better people" and discouraged procreation among those deemed inferior. By 1935, thirty-five states had passed laws requiring the segregation and sterilization of people considered unfit to procreate, a designation that included criminals, the mentally ill, and individuals with physical disabilities.[13] Hunter's *Civic Biology* was supportive of the practice, noting, "If such people were lower animals we would probably kill them off to prevent them from spreading. Humanity will not allow this, but we do have the remedy of separating the sexes."[14]

Bryan's principal legal argument in the trial flowed from his majoritarian political philosophy. It hinged on the prerogative of an elected state legislature to set education policy for the public schools. As an employee of the state, Bryan held, Scopes had an obligation to obey the law. As a private citizen, Scopes was free to believe whatever he wanted about evolution or the Bible, but he could not advocate it when on the job. Bryan thought, however, that assigning criminal penalties to Scope's infraction was excessive, and offered to pay his fine. It is also important to recognize that Bryan's primary motivation in pursuing the case was his religious conviction about the Bible, which he believed was the source of truth. His main problem with evolution was that it contradicted the Holy Scripture, which Darrow brought out in his biting cross-examination of Bryan.

The major problem with the law that Bryan defended was that it sought to remove evolutionary theory from the science curriculum because of its incompatibility with biblical teaching. The legislature had exercised public authority to protect and advance a religious doctrine. The law made it a crime for any employee of a state-operated college or public school "to teach any theory that denies the story of the divine creation of man as taught in the Bible."[15]

Scopes was convicted of a misdemeanor and fined one hundred dollars. Judge Raulston accepted Bryan's legal argument, and deferred to the power of the legislature to direct the education of public school children. The media portrayed the ruling as a victory of religion over science, as it was. The ruling was upheld by the Tennessee Supreme Court in a three-to-two decision leaving the Butler Law intact. Scopes's conviction was overturned on a technicality, quashing the possibility of further appeal.

Many school boards in the South subsequently took it upon themselves to impose various kinds of restrictions on the teaching of evolution. Texas and Louisiana refused to approve textbooks that mentioned evolution. In 1968 the United States Supreme Court finally struck down the antievolution law in Arkansas as a violation of church-state separation.[16] Anticipating the decision by the High Court, the Tennessee legislature repealed the Butler Law in 1967. Darrow's argument triumphed at last. In the aftermath, antievolutionists began to demand that "creationism" be taught in public schools as an alternative theory. Then in 1987 the Supreme Court ruled seven to two that creationism is a religious belief, and not scientific.[17] Seventy-two Nobel Prize–winning scientists had signed an *amicus* brief against the Louisiana law that had required the teaching of "creation science."

As the story goes, Bryan's sudden death four days after the famous trial was brought on by the humiliating cross-examination he suffered at hands of Darrow, a story that the litigator seemed to relish. If Bryan were alive for the subsequent rulings, he would have countered that the exclusive teaching of evolution compromised the religious freedom of parents who believed that human life really began with Adam and Eve rather than with an ape. His challenge to the validity of Darwin's proposition would have been less persuasive, in light of sixty-odd years of accumulated scientific evidence supporting the theory, and subsequent revisions that have sought to distance Darwinism from its inherent racism and its association with eugenics. But the question still stands regarding parental prerogatives. And there is also the dangling issue of academic freedom on the part of teachers, left unaddressed in the Scopes trial, which can now be raised by the other side.

What if a public school teacher in Tennessee today truly believed in creationism over Darwinism, and insisted on following his conscience while in the classroom? The problem here still is that he would be using his public school position to advance a religious doctrine, which in 1987 the Supreme Court found a violation of the Establishment Clause. The teacher might choose instead to challenge the theory on the basis of its scientific validity, as Mr. Bryan had done in 1925 and many contemporary opponents of evolution do under the rubric of intelligent design. This could raise other objections. Now the teacher would be challenging the prevailing consensus in the scientific community, and defying a state or local curriculum policy based on that consensus. As Clarence Darrow discovered in Tennessee, the courts have generally been deferential to legislatures and school boards on such curriculum questions.

The reasoning behind the judicial practice is to allow publicly elected bodies a wide degree of latitude in setting educational standards for states and school districts. It is a reasonable position; nevertheless, as we know from the Scopes trial, legislatures and school boards can make mistakes. These popularly elected bodies can also be reckless with the rights of minorities, especially minorities who run afar from prevailing thought. Unfortunately the only recourse for the dissenting teacher is to convince policymakers of the validity of his position. Ordinarily, he would not be allowed to use his position in the public school as a podium for advancing his own dissenting viewpoint, especially if that viewpoint were religiously based, for fear of violating the First Amendment rights of parents and students. (Academic freedom is a more potent concept in higher education, but we will not take that up here.)

What if, as Bryan alleged, a parent had a religious objection to the public school curriculum that teaches evolution? Certainly it makes reasonable sense to design the school curriculum around a body of knowledge that has the support of the scientific community. Should parents, however, be expected to accept the prevailing wisdom of professional scientists as if it were infallible? In 1925, Hunter's controversial textbook spoke with great certitude on the issues of race and eugenics, as if it were a refined elaboration of Darwin's earlier work. Science characteristically speaks with certitude, but the discoveries of one generation are often a rejection of those of an earlier generation.[18] With regard to evolution, the debate is typically understood as a disagreement between a set of scientific positions based on empirical evidence and a set of religious propositions based on faith. While it makes sense to shape public policy around the former kind of proposition, compelling an individual parent to accept the proposition as truth is another matter, especially when it contradicts the teaching of her faith.

The fact is that most adults accept evolutionary theory as a matter of faith in the sense that they do not fully understand the concept. Yes, they do comprehend the reasoning behind the theory and the narrative of how we have evolved from apes, the same way that they understand the narrative presented in the Book of Genesis about Adam and Eve in the Garden of Eden. But they do not understand the construction of scientific proofs that allows scientists to speak with authority on the way we have evolved. It is notable that Mr. Darrow did not want Scopes to take the witness stand in Dayton, for fear that, if asked, the general science teacher would not be able to fully explain why he believed evolutionary theory was valid.[19] Scopes was not a scientist, nor even a biology teacher. Nor are most parents. Should the state be allowed to compel them to accept something they do not understand when the lesson contradicts their religious beliefs?

Many religious doctrines are not susceptible to empirical proof. True believers would argue that to measure the validity of faith-based propositions by scientific standards is like using a ruler to measure the temperature of water. What does it mean to have religious freedom if the academic community, in the context of schooling, has the implicit authority to subject religious teaching to scientific scrutiny? Is it possible to accommodate the faith-based beliefs of religious fundamentalists without allowing them to impose their beliefs on others?

Just weeks before the 2004 election a school board in Dover County, Pennsylvania—a rural town that defied the Democratic state majority by giving President George Bush 65 percent of its votes—enacted a policy that required biology teachers to discuss "intelligent design" in conjunction with evolution.[20] The policy was immediately challenged in federal court by a group of parents who claimed that intelligent design is a religious doctrine. Weeks before the court reached a decision to nix the policy as unconstitutional, the voters of Dover County took matters into their own hands. In a contested school board election that occurred exactly one year after George Bush was returned to office, they voted to replace all eight school board members who had supported the controversial policy.

On the same day of the Dover County school board election, the state school board in Kansas adopted a set of new science standards requiring schools to teach alternatives to evolutionary theory. It gave rise to another suit, but the legal dispute became moot in the summer of 2006 when voters ousted the majority on the school board and subsequently reversed the controversial policy.

Also in 2004 a school board in Cobb County, Georgia, had affixed a sticker to its science textbooks that read, "This textbook contains material on evolution. Evolution is a theory, not a fact, regarding the origin of living things. This material should be approached by an open mind, studied carefully, and critically considered." In January 2005 Judge Clarence Cooper ruled that, given the religious nature of the challenges that have been historically launched against evolution, the stickers "convey a message of endorsement of religion."[21] In 2006, an appeals panel for the Eleventh Circuit returned the case to the trial court, indicting that it had insufficient evidence to determine whether or not the sticker policy was religiously motivated. This case also became moot when a new school board decided to remove the stickers.

Both the Pennsylvania and Georgia cases involved plaintiffs who objected to the incorporation of religious teaching in the public school curricula. Their immediate outcomes were not surprising in light of the 1987 Supreme Court decision outlawing the teaching of creationism. The Kansas case seemed to be heading towards a similar conclusion. In all three cases, the political press corrected the faulty policies. None of the cases, however, speaks to the kind of protection that might be afforded parents who challenge the content of a school curriculum that offends their religious sensibilities. That is the subject of our next case.

• • •

Fast-forward sixty-one years, from 1925 to 1986. We are still in eastern Tennessee, but this time in Hawkins County, rather than Dayton. Once again we find religious fundamentalists at the center of a dispute over the curriculum used in public schools. This time the fundamentalists were the aggrieved parties challenging the Holt, Rinehart & Winston reading series that had been adopted by the school district. A small group of parents took exception to the readings, claiming the material had offended their religious sensibilities. As in Dayton, the dispute led to a high-profile trial that attracted national media attention. As in Dayton, the media lined up almost uniformly against the fundamentalists, with reporters referring to the trial as "Scopes II." What began as a local imbroglio between parents and school administrators eventually exploded into a controversy that involved strategists from a number of large national organizations, all bringing their own political baggage to the cozy rural community.[22]

The little eruption in Hawkins County provided a prime opportunity for two national organizations to face off, each offering resources, political advice, and legal counsel to the opposing sides. Concerned Women for America (CWA) was founded in 1979 in opposition to the Equal Rights Amendment, which, its organizers alleged, undermined traditional female roles and family values. By the mid-1980s, CWA claimed a half a million members, and expanded its mission to take on sex, violence, and vulgarity in the media as well as abortion, gay rights, and secular humanism. The organization supported voluntary school prayer, the teaching of creationism, and school vouchers. A keynote address delivered by President Ronald Reagan at its 1987 annual convention affirmed CWA's growing significance as a political and social force to be reckoned with.

People for the American Way (PAW) was started in 1978 by television producer Norman Lear in response to the emerging influence of televangelists like Jerry Falwell and Pat Robertson, who had helped bring Ronald Reagan to power. Lear had been responsible for creating such television standards as *All in the Family*, *The Jeffersons*, *Good Times*, and *Maude*. His campaign to protect free thought from the new Moral Majority enlisted numerous Hollywood stars, including Barbra Streisand, Robin Williams, Jane Fonda, and Martin Sheen. Other groups that joined the fray, or at least took an interest in the case from near or far, were the American Civil Liberties Union, National Education Association, Americans United for the Separation of Church and State, American Jewish Congress, American Jewish Committee, National Council of Churches, Christian Legal Society, the Rutherford Institute, and the Moral Majority—plus a procession of experts who testified on behalf of one side or the other.

The second Tennessee tiff was set off one day when Vicki Frost's sixth-grade daughter came home from the Church Hill Middle School with a Holt reader called *Riders of the Earth*. The thirty-one-year-old mother became outraged when she found that the book presented a secular humanist perspective contrary to her fundamentalist Christian beliefs. She shared the materials with a number of other religious families, including Bob Mozert, who would help her lead the resistance against forcing children to read materials that contradicted the teachings of their faith. According to Vicki Frost, Mozert had two advantages that would allow him to be a more effective advocate for their cause in eastern Tennessee: He possessed a college education, and he was a man. With a master's degree from Appalachian State University, Mozert, an insurance adjuster, was better educated than the men who sat on the local school board, most of whom were fairly traditional and conservative themselves.

Like most of eastern Tennessee, Hawkins County was dominated by Republicans. With a population of 44,565 people, it had more than a hundred houses of worship.[23] Superintendent of schools Bill Snodgrass was known to be a "very religious" man. School prayer and Bible reading were not uncommon in the public schools, despite the fact that they were forbidden by the United States Supreme Court. But, according to this small group of disgruntled parents—seven families in all—life had begun to slip into moral degeneration. Some schools were no longer reciting the Pledge of Allegiance at the beginning of the school day; they were not observing a moment of silence for quiet prayer and meditation, as required by state law; there was no student dress code. The Holt reader was the last straw. Or so they thought.

There were a number of items that alarmed Vicki Frost as she paged through the stories contained in the Holt reader, most of which would not trouble the average parent even in traditionalist, churchgoing Hawkins County. She spotted signs of Hinduism and New Age religion, but no mention of Christianity. She found veneration of the zodiac, astrology, and Greek gods and references to evolution, mental telepathy, and witchcraft. In one passage from *The Diary of Anne Frank*, Anne had urged her friend to seek "some religion," as if to imply that all religions were the same. Frost also had problems with passages taken from *Macbeth* and *The Wizard of Oz*.

Frost, Mozert, and the other families joined forces to form Citizens Organized for Better Schools (COBS). Altogether they had eighteen children in several district schools. While some of the parents had considered demanding that the offensive materials be struck from the curriculum, in the end they instead requested that their own children be given the opportunity to use another reader. In the beginning, all but one of the principals in the district went along with this alternative. Then, after consulting with local pastors, the school board decided to require all children to use the Holt readers or risk suspension. When Vicki Frost entered her daughter's school to remove her from the reading class, she was arrested. At that point, the parents decided to take the case to federal court, claiming that the school board had violated their free exercise rights under the First Amendment.[24]

In two separate pretrial proceedings Judge Thomas Gray Hull initially dismissed the case on the ground that exposure to a broad range of thinking did not amount to a constitutional violation but, to the contrary, taught tolerance.[25] When the decision was appealed, the Sixth Circuit Court of Appeals declared that the constitutional issues at stake were sufficient to warrant a full trial before a judgment could be rendered. Judge Hull complied, and as he heard the evidence, he became more sympathetic to the pleas of the parents. Hull was a home-grown moderate Republican, the son of a blacksmith. A judicial prag-matist by reputation, he sought to achieve a resolution to the dispute that would not unfairly burden either the parents or the school district.

The parents did not want their children assigned readings that con-tradicted their religious views, or even materials suggesting that one form of religious teaching was as good as another. They sought an alter-native to the required text. They were willing to provide school officials with a list of acceptable readings so that their children could be taught in another room by another teacher, and not be exposed to the stories assigned to the other children. The school district was concerned about setting a precedent that would grant parents a line-item veto over the standard curriculum. Such a practice could become both costly and unmanageable. Nobody questioned the parents' sincerity about their religious views, but they were widely perceived in Hawkins County as a bunch of religious quacks.

While the legal arguments were being presented in Judge Hull's courtroom, a public relations campaign was being launched in the media by both sides. According to Stephen Bates, the author of *Battle-ground*, the parents came out on the short end in the press coverage.[26] Michael Farris, the attorney for the parents, predicted that if his side lost, Christians in America would have fewer rights than blacks in South Africa. Tony Podesta, the president of PAW, framed the dispute as a battle over censorship. PAW successfully shaped the news reports along those lines, even though the parents were not attempting to eliminate anything from the curriculum or dictate what other people's children should read. Dan Rather told viewers on the CBS *Evening News*, "Some parents want to ban textbooks that teach evolution and what they call 'anti-Christian' values.'"[27] Other reporters interpreted the objection to the Anne Frank statement as an expression of anti-Semitism, which was not evident in the Hawkins County dispute.

Judge Hull remained aloof from the distortions and hyperbole that shaped public perceptions of the case, and tried to reach a compromise between the two sides.[28] He surmised how unlikely it was that any reading series on the state list would be totally acceptable to the plain-tiffs. At the same time he understood that the "uniform, compulsory use of the Holt series . . . is by no means essential to furthering the state's goals." This was not like the choice between evolutionism and creationism, or science against religion. This was about the use of literature to teach reading. There were no basic truths at stake from an educational point of view. It was a conflict over values. The judge also did not want to saddle the state and the school district with a legal precedent that could be unaffordable or disruptive. Nor did he think it was wise to put public school teachers in the position of worrying about offending someone every time they went about their daily classroom activities.

Judge Hull decided to permit the aggrieved parents to opt out of the reading program, but to do so under the auspices of the state's home-schooling law. These parents would be able to apply the law with regard to a single subject area. Students would be excused from their reading lessons in school, and their parents would be expected to oversee an alternative program at home. Under the terms of the law, the students would still be required to take state-administered standardized tests to demonstrate proficiency. This was preferable to the take-it-or-leave-it policy adopted by the school board, which would force parents to either subject their children to lessons that violated their beliefs, or to forgo the benefit of a free education in the public schools. In the meantime, the state and the school district would not be burdened with the responsibility of producing an acceptable alternative to the standard reading curriculum.

In an attempt to limit the impact of his decision, Judge Hull ruled, "This opinion shall not be interpreted to require the school system to make this option available to any other person or to these plaintiffs for any other subject." Any lawyer reading the decision, however, knew that it set a legal precedent that opened the floodgates to further litigation. Judge Hull was vilified in the press for siding with religious fundamentalists. His decision was referred to in various newspapers as "peculiar," "preposterous," "absurd," and "outrageous."[29] In a letter targeted at potential contributors to raise funds for mounting a legal appeal, Tony Podesta of PAW wrote, "We all know the story behind the original 'Scopes Monkey Trial.' Scopes II will prove to be far more threatening because in 1987 the issue is no longer limited to evolution or one school teacher." He continued, "These attacks are being made by the

Religious Right in an attempt to force one intolerant version of 'God's law' on everyone."[30]

People for the American Way did appeal the case, and eventually won in a three-to-nothing ruling handed down by a very divided panel of the Sixth Circuit.[31] On July 9, 1987, each of three judges delivered a separate opinion based on a different line of reasoning.[32] Chief Judge Pierce Lively, a Reagan appointee, wrote for the court. He concluded that "mere exposure" to the materials in question did not impose an unconstitutional burden on the religious rights of the plaintiffs. Reading itself was a passive act that did not entail the affirmation or rejection of a particular set of beliefs. The assignment did not coerce children to behave in a way that was contrary to their faith. There was no real activity involved other than reading. But, of course it was the reading itself to which the parents objected.

Judge Cornelia Kennedy, a Carter appointee, saw the case differently. She focused on the school district's interest in "promoting cohesion among a heterogeneous democratic people." She did not deny that the required curriculum was a form of values inculcation. She relished it. That, for her, was the purpose of the public school. In a democracy students must be given an opportunity to form their own ideas, even if it means contradicting what is taught to them at home. Judge Kennedy was concerned that the opt-out program would be "disruptive" and lead to "religious divisiveness." Of course it was the imposition of the required curriculum on disgruntled families that caused the division.

Judge Kennedy seemed to be suggesting that it was the job of school officials to enlighten children beyond the narrow-minded views of their religious parents. What she defined as democratic cohesion was in essence a state-imposed system of philosophical conformity. While finding that children had the right to form their own opinions, she was not very receptive to the privately formed opinions of the parents. Should we conclude that such rights erode with age?

Though he voted with the majority, Judge Danny Boggs, another Reagan appointee, was more sympathetic to the pleas of the parents. Judge Boggs was persuaded that exposing children to ideas prohibited by their faith did represent a religious burden. The question is whether the burden was sufficiently heavy to constitute a violation of the First Amendment. It was not just a specific passage that the parents objected to, but the "overall effect" these readings had on the children. He noted that it was "a bit ludicrous" in an age when students were provided with individualized instruction for a host of reasons, ranging from language to interests, to view the accommodation sought by these parents as excessive. The state already had a home-schooling statute that allowed students to opt out of the public education provided in their communities. The plan that Judge Hull offered at the trial seemed reasonable. In the end, however, Judge Boggs came down on the side of the school district. Under state law, it was the prerogative of school district officials to determine the proper school curriculum—like it or not. As he put it, "The school board is entitled to say 'my way or the highway.'"

This was not a novel argument. William Jennings Bryan had made it before Judge Raulston's court in Dayton, but he was more thorough in explaining the political theory behind his point. The school board and the state legislature enjoyed such a prerogative, he reasoned, because they were chosen by a majority of the electorate. That is the way democracy is supposed to work. Bryan had made that point sixty-two years prior to the *Mozert* ruling. Through the present day the federal courts leave a wide berth of discretion for state and local decision-makers when it comes to education policy.

The parents in the *Mozert* case took their appeal to the United States Supreme Court, but the Court declined to hear it. As is the custom, there was no explanation given as to why the High Court would not take the case. That was the end of it.

• • •

State and local discretion over education policy is by no means absolute. Federal courts can and do intervene when fundamental constitutional rights are at stake. American political theory leaves it up to the courts to protect the rights of minorities when political majorities act irresponsibly. The Supreme Court did so in 1968 when it struck down the Arkansas law that prohibited teaching evolution in the public schools as a violation of the Establishment Clause, prompting the Tennessee legislature to void its own antievolution statute.

The federal appeals court was less sympathetic when it came to re-viewing the free exercise claim of fundamentalist parents in Hawkins County.[33] As legal scholar Nomi Maya Stolzenberg contends, the judges on the appellate panel apparently did not understand the nature of the complaint.[34] For these parents "mere exposure" of their children to the Holt readers violated their religious principles because their religion did not permit them to read anything that contradicted the Scriptures. This admittedly was a rather strict, one might say, unusual interpretation of religious obligation, even by standards that were commonly held in traditionalist Hawkins County. But it was theirs, and according to most observers, it was genuine.

For these fundamentalist parents, not all religions were the same. Nor was secularism a form of governmental neutrality. As they saw it, secularism was a particular worldview. This is not an altogether unreasonable interpretation of the secularist perspective. Susan Jacoby, the author of *Freethinkers,* and Michael Newdow, the father who did not want his daughter to recite the Pledge of Allegiance in school, argued the same point in demanding that the state accommodate their deeply felt rejection of religion. For them secularism is a point of view that should be accounted for in the context of governmental decision-making. A comparison with the positions adopted by Ms. Jacoby and Mr. Newdow—also unorthodox by most common standards—is useful in explicating the predicament of the parents in *Mozert.*

There was no satisfactory way to accommodate Ms. Jacoby in the context of the ecumenical service at the National Cathedral, other than to prohibit it, which would have compromised the free exercise rights of the participants. What excused the state from providing Ms. Jacoby with a specific accommodation in the case of the ecumenical service is the fact it was both private and voluntary. While the president was present, it was not a governmental function. Therefore, while Ms. Jacoby was unhappy with the event that took place, there was no need for the state to offer her specific relief.

Mr. Newdow's situation was notably different. Mr. Newdow's daughter was compelled to attend public school in California unless he or the child's mother was willing to assume the financial burden of sending her to a private school. If the parents in the Newdow case had agreed that they did not want their daughter reciting the Pledge, the state would have been required to accommodate them. According to the *Barnette* decision handed down by the Supreme Court in 1943, children whose parents so object must be given an opportunity to opt out of the Pledge exercise, in order to avoid any hint of a state-imposed ideology that offends individual sensibilities.[35]

Judge Lively, mindful of the requirements set down in the earlier *Barnette* case, dealt with the implications head-on, but not satisfactorily. In his judgment, the two cases differed substantively. The Pledge exercise requires action on the part of participants that affirms their belief in what they are reciting; reading does not. Judge Lively did not appreciate the sense of religious obligation that the *Mozert* parents communicated to the court. He, for the most part, ignored it. He judged the situation by secular standards.

Judge Kennedy's opinion takes the matter a step further. She understood the Holt reading program as an alternative to the religious viewpoint of the parents and embraced it as that. Her position relies on the presumption that the state has a responsibility to promote tolerance though its educational system, and that the viewpoint of the parents undermined tolerance. In fairness to the parents, it is important to remember that they were not trying to impose their beliefs on other people's children. They demanded that a worldview they had renounced for religious reasons not be imposed on their own children. Their claim suggests that state and local officials were exhibiting intolerance towards them. They were perfectly comfortable with the fact that the great majority of families in the district adhered to a different religious perspective and were content with the prescribed curriculum. That, according to most definitions of the word, is the very meaning of tolerance: You follow your conscience, I'll follow mine; and we can live in peaceful harmony.

Judge Kennedy's opinion implicitly introduces other considerations that could have been taken up in both the *Scopes* and the *Mozert* cases concerning the interests of the children. Up until this point we have analyzed the debate as a contest between state powers and parental or teacher rights. What about the students? A serious problem with the state prohibition against teaching evolution—in addition to the Establishment Clause violation—is that it denied students information that reflected the state-of-the-art consensus in the scientific community. It omitted a significant scientific truth.

As mentioned earlier, the stakes in the *Mozert* case were notably different. There was no scientific truth in dispute. The entire controversy was about a conflict between individual or group values and those endorsed by the state. Therefore we have the free exercise claim. One could argue, supposedly on behalf of the children, that it was in the best cultural and educational interests of the children to expose them to the literature that was being read by their peers in public school. It was the values inherent in this very culture, however, that the parents were rejecting as a matter of conscience, at least for their own children. Shouldn't the discussion of what is in the best educational interest of the child begin with the presumption that the parent is in a better position to judge than the state, or more specifically an administrator or elected official acting on behalf of the state? In the next two chapters, I will more fully discuss why the presumption should lie with the parental prerogative, but here I want to make a pertinent observation about the judicial process.

It is notable that a federal panel dominated by appointees of President Ronald Reagan could not bring itself to accept the compromise worked out by Judge Hull in his modest attempt to find a fair resolution. The appellate court's standard for review appropriated a generous amount of discretion to the government in the context of a free exercise claim, even recognizing that the parents' viewpoints were somewhat unusual. If governmental decision-makers can take it upon themselves to measure the reasonableness of a person's religious convictions when no other person is being harmed, or when the state is not being burdened, then what does it mean to have religious freedom?

Let me frame the question in a different way: Is the blanket of legal protections offered by the Establishment Clause to ensure an individual's freedom from religion more secure than the protections provided by the Free Exercise Clause to ensure the freedom of religion? I will argue that the answer to that question is yes, and explain why as we get further into the book. It is equally important to appreciate, however, that the factors undermining the religious freedom of unconventional religious minorities are not entirely legal in nature.

The political environments that surrounded the *Scopes* and *Mozert* trials were similar in a number of respects, which are instructive beyond the details of the two Tennessee cases. First of all, there was a tendency on the part of the press to treat deeply religious people with a certain degree of suspicion, bordering on disdain. Such suspicion rages more fiercely when religious groups are assertive about their legal rights or the exercise of political influence. One explanation for this sentiment is that the viewpoint of devout observers is understood to be a product of revelation rather than reason, a dichotomy that many, if not most, religious people do not accept.

This negative predisposition by the press not only shapes public perceptions, it also indulges prejudices that are already held by many citizens within the mainstream. This underlying suspicion foists a peculiar vulnerability on religious people, by making it easier for their adversaries to portray them as extreme or unreasonable—to the point of subjecting them to misrepresentation and distortion, which were evident in both the *Scopes* and *Mozert* cases.

The message sent to judicial decision-makers in such situations is also quite strong. It tells them that a sympathetic ruling handed down on behalf of such a group will be susceptible to similar scrutiny, distortion, and condemnation, as Judge Hull painfully learned. Despite his best efforts to act fairly, the judge was treated as if he were an irresponsible ignoramus. His was a lonely position. There was no public outcry in *Mozert* from respected scholars at Ivy League universities that perhaps the government should be more sensitive to the demands of conscience motivating the parents, as had happened on behalf of Mr. Scopes. To the contrary, one Harvard psychologist who testified in the Mozert case described Judge Hull's ruling as a form of "child abuse."[36]

The underlying principle operating here is that religious parents—because they are more irrational than the rest—should be expected to abide by secular standards in the upbringing of their children whether they want to or not. There is little room left to accommodate the demands of conscience once the majority speaks. I wonder what the reaction of the scientific community would have been in 1925 if William Jennings Bryan had gathered the courage to challenge the patent racism present in the textbook used by Scopes on the grounds that it violated his belief in human equality. I suspect that the response would have been similar to that of the rest of society in the mid-1920s, for its sensibilities were blinded by the same racial prejudices, albeit more enabled by the authority of its assumed empiricism.

Once we accept the notion of a common system of public schooling designed to promote a common set of values, as envisioned by Judge Kennedy, the "live and let live" presumption that necessarily precedes attitudes of political and religious tolerance becomes somewhat compromised. When a parent enrolls her child in a public school, she and the child enter the public arena and relinquish a certain measure of freedom. Unless special arrangements are made, they are expected to accept the prevailing instructional norms—including explicit and implicit educational values that underlie these norms—all in the name of democratic tolerance. At some point the practice is neither democratic nor tolerant, especially when the norms unnecessarily undermine the dictates of conscience.

Two days after the *Mozert* case was decided by the Sixth Circuit, the Eleventh Circuit heard an Alabama case in which a group of fundamentalist parents claimed that that forty-four textbooks in home economics, social studies, and history advanced secular humanism and inhibited their religion. Here, as in numerous other challenges around the country at the time, the parents asserted that secular humanism is a form of religion. Separationist groups, who filed a total of twenty-six *amicus* briefs in the *Smith*[37] case, saw this as another attempt by the religious Right to censor reading materials in the public schools. Once again the court sided with the school board, finding that school officials were seeking to instill such values as "independent thought, tolerance of diverse views, self-respect, maturity, self-reliance, and logical decision making."

The *Smith* court never addressed the question of whether secular humanism was an alternative belief system. It did determine, however, that the compulsory assignment of the books in question did not convey "a message of governmental approval of secular humanism or governmental disapproval of theism." If the court had concluded that secular humanism is a form of religion, it would have been required under existing constitutional standards to prohibit use of the books. Even so, since the books in question were assigned by public authorities and required of the students, their use in the public schools had all the markings of government approval. In that sense they offended the religious sensibilities of the aggrieved parents the same way that the Pledge of Allegiance offended Messrs. Barnette and Newdow, who were entitled to an exemption.

Of course the parents in Alabama, as in Hawkins County, did retain the option to leave the public schools, and pursue a private or religious education that was more in line with their beliefs. But exercising that option is itself a burden because it forces parents to surrender a free public education and bear the cost of tuition on their own. In a society that supposedly values religious liberty, it is unfair to force families to make a choice between accepting educational requirements that contradict the teachings of their faith or assuming financial burdens that are not imposed on others. To make matters worse, not all parents can afford to entertain such an option, including, I suspect, most of the parents who took it upon themselves to challenge the school boards in Alabama and Hawkins County. For such parents, there is no choice at all. This amounts to a very narrow definition of religious freedom. It conditions the opportunity to enjoy the full benefits of such freedom on one's economic capacity to pay for it.

4

WHY SCHOOLS MATTER

IN A SLIM VOLUME on New York City during the eighteenth century, historian Carl Kaestle presents a picture of education that reveals sharp differences from schooling as we know it today.[1] Public schools did not exist. Education, where it was found, seemed to proceed in a haphazard manner, with most arrangements between teachers and pupils being temporary. The great majority of children were taught to read and count at home, or under the supervision of the local minister, with great attention given to the Bible. It was generally understood that instruction taken outside the home would serve to reinforce the religious and moral teaching that occurred inside the home.

The Anglican, Dutch, and Jewish denominations ran charity schools for paupers in their own congregations, in fulfillment of an assumed social obligation. Prosperous families sent their children off to boarding schools, but there were also small independent private academies nearby for those who could afford to pay. Preparation for the trades was accomplished through an apprenticeship, which provided cheap instruction for the child and cheap labor for the master. Some of these relationships were cruel and exploitive; others were nurturing. Rather than a distinct profession, teaching was a part-time occupation undertaken by men who earned some of their living in another trade, perhaps as an engineer, clerk, accountant, or jeweler, if not the ministry. A teacher could make about as much money as a ship carpenter.

Up until 1800, New York's burgeoning population of nearly sixty thousand people was ethnically and racially homogeneous (religion was another matter). It was composed mostly of native-born Dutch and English Protestants. Half of the four thousand African-Americans living in the city then were still slaves.[2] A close examination of Kaestle's old black-and-white snapshot reveals two characteristics that most distinguish education in early New York from what we now have throughout America. Along with the casual nature of the entire enterprise, education was highly diverse, and it was without political conflict—characteristics, I propose, that go hand in hand.

This calm would disappear with the emergence of the common school. Once it was determined that we should all go to school together and learn from a standard curriculum, education became political. Because it was always assumed that the common curriculum would go beyond teaching the basics to incorporate certain fundamental values to which we should all subscribe, the common school created a crucible for fierce disagreement.

As American society became more pluralistic—the Irish began arriving in 1816—it was only a matter of time before some citizens began to question whose values would be taught. More often than not, throughout our history, the answer to that question has been the same. What is taught in public schools reflects the values, and the prejudices, of those who rule. I do not use the word *prejudice* here to be provocative. I am making a historical observation. All societies harbor prejudices—blind spots if you will—that can only be seen for what they are with the passage of time. Even the most enlightened leaders, immersed in their own social milieu, cannot appreciate the flaws in such sentiments, because the widely held beliefs upon which they are based remain largely unquestioned. Because they enjoy high currency, these prejudices are eventually reflected in the school curriculum. Either explicitly or implicitly they become a part of the lessons we pass on from one generation to the next through the public schools.

Thomas Jefferson's plan for public schooling, proposed to the Virginia Legislature in 1779, was a case in point.[3] Although it was not adopted, his proposal is generally considered one of the most well conceived arguments for public education extant—precise in its terms, forward looking, politically astute, democratic in spirit and in purpose. Jefferson's ward-based plan for education was integrally tied to his vision of direct democracy, which he thought was superior to the representative system of government created under the federal constitution.

Jefferson's scheme involved two levels of schooling over seven years. The first three years were made available to all free children, and paid for through public funding. During this time pupils would be taught the "three R's," in addition to Greek, Roman, English, and American history. The next four years of education, called grammar school, would initially be opened to boys who successfully completed the first three. During the fifth year, weaker students would be weeded out, and only a select group was deemed eligible to complete the last two years of study. Grammar schools would offer a more comprehensive curriculum financed through private funding, the greater burden falling on the families whose children were in attendance. Provision was to be made so that one poor student in each district—those with the "best and most promising disposition and genius," would also be admitted to the more selective grammar schools free of charge.

Jefferson understood that an educated citizenry is a prerequisite to a healthy democracy, so as to insure that popular participation in government is intelligent, informed, and public-spirited. The history that he wanted assigned had taught him that education was essential to protect individual freedom from the threat of a governmental tyranny. His bold plea to the state legislature to establish a universal system of free public schools was well ahead of its time. Nevertheless, when the details of Jefferson's plan are examined closely, they reflect the deep biases of the era in which they were written. It is notable that women were excluded from advancing to a higher level of education, and blacks were not to be educated at all. In Jeffersonian society, women were not expected to participate in government, and blacks lived under slavery. His plan, as enlightened as it may have been, not only reflected the social order of the time but also reinforced it.

Notwithstanding the obvious gender and racial discrimination inherent in Jefferson's grammar school scheme, there are signs of a meritocracy in it, even an honest attempt to overcome the disadvantages of poverty by creating extraordinary opportunities for otherwise gifted children. But there is also something revealing about his expectations, the fact that he believed only one poor boy in each district would prove to have the intellectual and moral material to merit inclusion among this select population of students. It appears that the principal author of the Declaration of Independence, who in a moment of literary exuberance declared that "all men are created equal" (we can take him at his word on the gender issue), might have had cause to qualify his statement if put to the test. His qualifications would have been well received by his contemporaries. Writing in the language of the twenty-first century, he might have been inclined to assert that class is a reliable predictor of both intelligence and virtue, which would have se-verely tarnished his liberal credentials. This, of course, is speculation on my part, but not unreasonable.

We do not need to speculate when it comes to Jefferson's attitudes on race. While at times he expressed discomfort with the institution of slavery (though not enough to free his own slaves), Jefferson's con-victions on the issue of race are well established. Jefferson accepted the popular "scientific" evidence that blacks belonged to a distinct race between apes and men, and were inferior in mind, body, and imagina-tion to whites. As he speculated, in his *Notes on Virginia*, "I advance it, therefore, as a suspicion only, that the blacks, whether originally a distinct race, or made distinct by time and circumstances, are inferior to whites in the endowments both of body and mind."[4] He had similar views towards Native Americans, and on both counts his thoughts were in accord with the thinking of his time.[5] Even when he contem-plated freeing the slaves and offering them the benefits of an education, Jefferson was convinced that blacks and whites, because of the scars left from slavery, could not live side by side. His long-term solution for freed slaves was to establish a self-contained colony for them, preferably in Africa. These regrettable views were reflected in the plan he put before the Virginia legislature in 1779.

If Jefferson's vision of education was impaired by his "blind spots" with regard to race and gender, Horace Mann's would be obstructed by his attitudes concerning religion and ethnicity. While not Jefferson's intellectual peer, Mann's thoughts on education would prove to be more influential. Mann, who served as secretary of education in Massa-chusetts from 1837 to 1848, is considered the father of the common school. His aspirations for public schooling, detailed in his annual re-ports to the state board of education and other writings, are among the most important documents in the chronicles of American education.[6]

Mann also appreciated the important role education plays as the lifeblood of a democracy, but his notion of democracy was different from Jefferson's. Jefferson's democracy, set in the lush Virginia country-side, was animated by face-to-face transactions among citizens living in small communities, of which the public school would be an integral part. The decentralized structure of the ward system, in which like-minded citizens would assemble in self-contained districts, was designed to accommodate political and social pluralism. More focused on the representative nature of American government, Mann's goal was to produce good republicans who could vote for wise and decent political leaders. He did not embrace pluralism.

Mann's agenda was the more socially ambitious of the two. His program was a response to the wave of immigration that had washed over the cities of the Northeast, bringing in many Catholics from Ireland. Between 1846 and 1855, 1.4 million immigrants arrived from Erin's shores; their proportion of the Boston population alone rose from 2 percent to 20 percent.[7] Mann's driving ambition was to make good Americans of them. His response to the growing diversification of the urban population, also spurred by the arrival of Germans who came speaking no English, was to use the "grand machinery" of education as a tool for making the "pliant" offspring of the new arrivals more like the people who were already here. He sought nothing less than to mold the "'raw material' of human nature" into something different from what it was.[8] As generous of heart as Mann was towards the new arrivals, his educational scheme was presumptuous and patronizing.

There were many aspects of Mann's agenda that would be considered progressive by contemporary standards. Schools would promote the physical well-being of the urban poor through health and physical education programs. They would literally cleanse the unwashed mass of newcomers by teaching them personal hygiene. A decent education would, hopefully, make the Irish and Germans—who were prone to drinking, fighting, and street crime—more law-abiding.

The classroom would prepare men and women for work, and in so doing lift them out of the poverty that infested the melancholy tenement villages where they lived. And if Mann had his way, education would not only equip these poor souls for labor on the docks and in the factories, but it eventually would pave the way for them to assume their place in the professions as scholars, scientists, inventors, and judges. Taken to its logical end, education could function as a great leveler, bringing about economic and social equality. Horace Mann's vision of the common school was the articulation of the American dream. The public school was a key ingredient of the hope that made the United States a beacon of opportunity for people from other lands. For that, we, the sons and daughters of immigrants, should be grateful.

Horace Mann's assimilation program, however, went too far. His head was so buried in the biases of the age in which he lived, that it blinded him to the identity, aspirations, and values of the very people he wanted to help. Carried to an extreme, Mann's grand avenue of American assimilation shrank down to a narrow alley of homogenization. Like the members of the founding generation, Horace Mann assumed that in order for men to be good citizens (women did not qualify), they needed to be good people. Similarly, he believed that the ultimate source of all moral teaching was the Bible. So Horace Mann's common school curriculum included a strong dose of moral training, as it was presented in the Bible; or I should say, his Bible—the King James edition of the Protestant Bible.

Along with a daily regimen of reading from the Scriptures, children would be expected to say Protestant prayers and sing Protestant hymns as part of their classroom exercises. During Mann's tenure as state secretary, five members of the eight-person state board of education were members of the Protestant clergy; most local school committees were also controlled by churchmen.[9]

As a gesture of magnanimity towards Catholics, Jews, Baptists, and others who did not adhere to the mainstream religion, Mann decreed that the Bible should be read without comment so that the daily routine would not be taken as a form of indoctrination.[10] Many Protestant leaders were dismayed by Mann's concessions to religious minorities, preferring a more direct form of instruction. Mann himself was incapable of comprehending how his "nonsectarian" Protestantism might be offensive to those who did not follow its teachings. The full realization of his educational vision required immigrant children to forsake the religious and cultural traditions of their own parents. A Unitarian who had been raised in a strict Calvinist home, Mann could not conceive of either morality or religion apart from his own Christianity. As he himself explained with certitude in his last report to the Massachusetts Board of Education, "No student of history, or observer of mankind, can be hostile to the precepts and the doctrines of the Christian religion, or opposed to any institutions which expound and exemplify them."[11]

No individual delivered so stern a rebuttal to Horace Mann's religious presumptions as John Dewey, who, by most measures, was the most prominent educational philosopher of the twentieth century.[12]

Dewey's intellectual perspective would introduce new biases to schooling. His blind devotion to secularism would help usher the mainstream of American educational thinking into the twenty-first century, reflecting a larger public philosophy that was shared in ruling circles, if not by the population as a whole.

Dewey saw himself as a true son of the Enlightenment. Raised in Vermont by devout Congregationalist parents, Dewey by the age of thirty was ready to denounce organized religion as "otherworldly."[13] Convinced that religious teaching had exerted too much influence on American society, he wrote that there is "nothing worth preserving in the notions of unseen powers, controlling human destiny to which obedience, reverence, and worship are due."[14] A more enlightened form of education would rid mankind of such "savage and degraded beliefs." Science would liberate us from the "servile acceptance of imposed dogma" suffered at the hands of the clergy.

John Dewey wanted to harness public education as an instrument for social change.[15] Like Jefferson and Mann, he understood how learning could nurture democracy. He wanted to equip children with the critical thinking skills needed to advance individual freedom and challenge institutional authority—not only government authority, as Jefferson had hoped, or the family, as Mann had encouraged, but also organized religion. For him the capacity of citizens to think critically was essential to a free society. Dewey's extraordinary faith in the power of education to liberate the masses from their own cherished traditions, however, grew into a form of proselytizing in itself. Enforced by governmental authority under the legal sanctions employed through public education, Dewey's thinking furnished a philosophical foundation for an institutional arrangement that compromised the very freedoms he wanted to realize.

For Dewey, education was an "art based on scientific knowledge,"[16] and the public school teacher was the "prophet of the true God."[17] As he preached in a widely read article that appeared in the *New Republic* in 1922, "If we have any ground to be religious about anything, we may take education seriously." But the only education that Dewey had any tolerance for was education informed by his own secular worldview. His bias against teaching from a religious perspective is perhaps most evident in his statement against released time for religious instruction.

In his mind, religious instruction was not only divisive, but it also undermined the unifying mission of the public schools. His thoughts are worth quoting at length, for they would later be reflected in the halls of government, including the United States Supreme Court:

> The alternative plan of parceling out pupils among religious teachers drawn from their respective churches and denominations brings us up against exactly the matter which has done most to discredit the churches, and to discredit the cause, not perhaps of religion, but of organized and institutional religion: the multiplication of rival and religious bodies, each with its private inspiration and outlook. Our schools in bringing together those of different nationalities, languages, traditions and creeds, in assimilating them together upon the basis of what is common and public in endeavor and achievement, are performing an infinitely religious work. They are promoting the social unity out of which in the end genuinely religious unity must grow. Shall we interfere with this work? Shall we run the risk of undoing it by introducing into education a subject which can be taught only by segregating pupils and turning them over at special hours to separate representatives of rival faiths? This would be deliberately to adopt a scheme which is predicated upon the maintenance of social divisions in just the matter, religion, which is empty and futile save as it expresses the basic unities of life.[18]

Perhaps only the passage of time will allow us to appreciate the overwhelming bias inherent in Dewey's vision of American education, for it remains steadfastly with us today as a pedagogical guidepost. Certainly, his perspective is not as pernicious as the racial attitudes that permeated Jefferson's educational vision, or even the religious particularism that shaped Horace Mann's. But, as the American democratic experiment moves into its third century, the obstinate secularism that public education has inherited from Dewey's influential worldview should give us reason for concern. Like Horace Mann's program for assimilating the immigrant population, it shows little tolerance for religious or philosophical pluralism, except to the extent that it can be undone by the curriculum adopted in the public schools. In Dewey's mind, the social and political pluralism brought about by religious diversity was in fact damaging to American democracy. That premise should give us pause in a country that supposedly draws strength from the differences that characterize its people.

When such a narrow view of the world is emboldened by the power to govern what and how other people's children are taught, it represents a particular threat to personal freedom. When it is supported by a more pervasive popular disposition, it is a symptom of a larger problem. Ellwood Cubberley, an influential education professor at Stanford University who idealized education as an instrument for social engineering, summed up the prevailing attitude in 1909 when he rejoiced, "Each year the child is coming to belong more to the state and less to the parent."[19]

AT THE CENTER

As far back as can be remembered, religion has been at the center of American education, as a source of both inspiration and agitation. Reluctant to rely on parents to act responsibly towards the proper upbringing of their children, in 1642 the Massachusetts Bay Colony empowered town officials to hold parents accountable, under penalty of fine, for their children's ability "to read and understand the principles of religion."[20] It was assumed that there was no better way to promote literacy and morality than by familiarization with the Bible. If the power to impose fines proved ineffective in getting parents to accept their ordained responsibility, then the local selectmen, after a judicial hearing, could declare the negligent parents unfit and assign their children to an apprentice.

In 1647 the legislature passed the Old Deluder Satan Act requiring all towns of fifty or more households to hire a teacher of reading and writing in order to thwart the "old deluder Satan" whose "chief project" was to "keep men from knowledge of the Scriptures."[21] Towns with more than a hundred families were required to establish a grammar school. The new law was significant not only for advancing the move towards formalized schooling, but because it set a precedent for having a higher government establish educational standards for local communities. This subtle assumption of government power was also a first step in a long process that would require parents to surrender responsibility for a function that was customarily performed in the home. The state of Massachusetts codified these colonial practices in 1789, when it passed a law requiring localities to set up their own schools. Only six of the original thirteen states had education provisions in their constitutions. As a rule, the southern states relied on more informal arrangements than their New England counterparts, at least into the early nineteenth century.[22]

The Puritans who settled in New England during the seventeenth century were well educated and religious. Of those who came from Britain between 1630 and 1646, 130 were graduates of either Oxford or Cambridge, and of those, 98 were ministers.[23] Their sacred quest, presumably commissioned by God, was to "create a community of 'visible saints' committed to Christian brotherhood and conduct."[24] Education was instrumental in attaining this lofty ideal. Since the clergy were among the best educated in society, it made good sense to have them take up the task. It is with a bit of irony that, a hundred years later, Congregationalist ministers were among the first to protest the pan-Protestantism in Horace Mann's common school curriculum, not for its being religious, of course, but because Unitarianism had diluted the true word of God. Eventually it was the Irish who would mount the most formidable challenge to the school curriculum. With the quickened pace of immigration, they were the only group that had the numbers to do so.

In the meantime the religious persuasion of the Protestant mainstream accounted for much of what was taught in the public schools. The lessons went beyond Bible reading and prayer to include English language instruction (for foreign speakers) and American political and moral principles. Government officials were convinced that many of the newcomers were not ready to enjoy the freedoms assumed by most Americans. Without a strong value-based curriculum in the schools, educators feared that the level of morality and intelligence might be lowered to resemble that of the foreigners. An odd mixture of religion and science was incorporated in the temperance campaign launched by the Woman's Christian Temperance Union (WCTU).[25] That powerful organization, founded in 1874, set standards for textbook approval, published its own quarterly journal, and distributed a list of thirty "scientific facts" that children were expected to learn.

Although some of the WCTU's objectives were not completely lacking in merit, the scientific assertions put forward in its educational materials were overstated to the point of absurdity.[26] It was alleged, for example, that even a single drink would lead to an uncontrollable craving for another. Alcohol would not only ruin a person's moral character and home life, it would eventually eat away at the flesh and pickle the inner organs. These claims were all adopted as a component of science instruction, and more than 22 million schoolchildren were exposed to the literature in all but three states. In fact it was not temperance, in the sense of moderation, that the WCTU promoted, but complete abstinence. Drinking was portrayed as the source of all that was evil. The organization also took on a host of worthy causes that included women's suffrage, pay equity, day care, occupational safety, and smoking.

A substantial part of the temperance campaign was directed at immigrants, especially the Irish and their church. One Temperance Society publication read: "When drunkenness shall have been done away, and, with it, that just relative proportion of all indolence, ignorance, crime, misery, and superstition . . . then truly a much smaller portion of mankind may be expected to follow the dark lantern of Roman religion."[27] As one survey of nineteenth-century textbooks found, anti-Catholicism was the most common theme in a steady diet of reading material foisted on schoolchildren.[28] These messages, reinforcing the claim that Catholicism was a false and dangerous creed, were interspersed with a strong dose of religiosity along the lines of mainstream Protestantism, in which God was seen as a guiding force over natural and human history. Even Darwinism was explained as the product of divine wisdom.

What was it that fueled the animosity towards Catholics? The explanation varies from place to place and from time to time. In one sense, the hostility reflected a common bigotry towards immigrants, and the awkwardness with which the newcomers assimilated into an unfamiliar American culture. In another, it was the expression of deep philosophical disagreements between people of different faiths. Because of the Vatican's open insistence on its own infallibility in matters of faith and the expectation that all Catholics would follow its moral teachings, there was a genuine concern that the "Romans" would be loyal to a foreign power.[29] More practically speaking, nativist, Whig, and Republican Party activists were threatened by the growing political power of the Irish, which would enhance the fortunes of the Democratic Party. It was not possible to separate these factors because they fed upon each other. Religious differences seemed to provoke natural feelings of distrust, and many partisans capitalized on these suspicions to advance personal and political objectives.

The net result of these tensions was to treat religious, cultural, and political differences as a threat to the overall well-being of the republic, and to ameliorate the problem through a program of unification in the public schools—much as Horace Mann and John Dewey, in their distinct ways, had prescribed. The conflict exploded when Catholics, disturbed by the content in the public school curriculum, demanded support for their own schools. By then Horace Mann's notion of the common school had spread beyond Massachusetts, as did the ensuing conflict. While Protestants saw the demand for financial support as a blunt attempt by Catholics to use public money to achieve private ends, Catholic leaders saw it as a way to use their own tax contributions to educate their children in schools that would not offend their rights of conscience.

Catholics were not the only, or even the first, minority group to seek public support for their schools. In 1820 the Bethel Baptist Church in New York City was granted a portion of the common school fund to set up a school for poor children of all faiths.[30] When it received permission from the legislature to apply for funds to expand, it drew opposition from the Free School Society (a predecessor to the Public School Society), which claimed that the money was being used for religious rather than civic purposes—assuming that the two were incompatible. In 1825, at the Society's urging, the Common Council passed an ordinance that disallowed funding for any religious society. A new controversy flared in 1832, when the Roman Catholic Orphan Asylum and the Methodist Episcopal Church School separately applied for a share of the common school funds. The Common Council agreed to aid the orphanage, but, citing the 1825 ordinance, rejected the request from the church school.

During the nineteenth century, between 75 percent and 80 percent of the schools in the country required Bible reading.[31] In all cases the official Bible in use was the Protestant Bible. By 1925, twenty-six lawsuits had been filed in nineteen states in attempts to remove the Bible.[32] Sixteen of these suits were brought by Catholics. All but five of the challenges were unsuccessful. Most state courts, reflecting the pervasive political consensus, viewed the custom as a nondenominational secular exercise that was permissible under law. One Maine Court went so far to decree, "If the majority of the school be Protestants, the committee can enforce such a system of instruction upon all."[33]

Children were subjected to corporal punishment for refusing to participate in Bible readings and other religious exercises. When Catholic leaders in Boston objected to the beatings in 1834, an angry mob set fire to the Ursuline Convent. Two years later, thugs destroyed the residence of Archbishop John Hughes in New York, and the state militia had to be called to protect St. Patrick's Cathedral.[34] In addition to protesting the religious content of the public school curriculum, Hughes had the audacity to demand public support for parochial schools. In 1844 violent rioting broke out in Philadelphia, leaving thirteen people dead and a Catholic neighborhood burned to the ground, after Bishop Francis Patrick Kenrick demanded that either all Bible reading should be taken from the schools, or that Catholics should be permitted to read their own.[35] Such rioting occurred in dozens of cities through the middle of the century.

The year 1854 was a watershed for the anti-immigrant Know-Nothing Party. It elected seventy-five members to the United States Congress, and captured the legislatures of Massachusetts and Delaware. Within two years it took control of the state governments in Connecticut, New Hampshire, Rhode Island, Maryland, and Kentucky, and made inroads in New York, Pennsylvania, Tennessee, Virginia, Georgia, Alabama, and Louisiana.[36]

In 1852 Massachusetts passed the nation's first compulsory education law, a measure that was at least in part designed to reel in the infidels who had resisted the religious orthodoxy of the governing party. Two years later, with the Know-Nothings in control of both the governorship and the legislature, Massachusetts enacted a constitutional amendment prohibiting aid to religious schools. The party also tried to pass measures that would curtail the rights of immigrants to vote and hold office. Abraham Lincoln sized up the Know-Nothings accurately in 1855: "As a nation we began by declaring that 'all men are created equal.' We now read it, 'all men are created equal except Negroes.' When the Know-Nothings get control, it will read, 'all men are created equal except Negroes and foreigners and Catholics.'"[37]

Eventually the Catholic population would cluster in proportions sizable enough to demand changes through political channels. Between 1869 and 1872 the school boards in Cincinnati, Chicago, Cleveland, New York, Buffalo, and Rochester, responding to protests by Catholics and Jews, voted to prohibit Bible reading and religious exercises in the public schools. By then, many other schools and school boards around the country already had adopted informal arrangements to accommodate religious minorities. Fights over aid to religious schools, however, were just coming into high gear. Well into the nineteenth century, religious schools in New York, New Jersey, Connecticut, Massachusetts, and Wisconsin received some support through public funding.[38] The more the issue of public support became identified as a Catholic cause, the stronger grew the resistance. These confrontations were not limited to the Northeast or to the state and local levels of government.

As early as 1802, the Ohio constitution guaranteed access to state-supported schools. Its bill of rights included protection for poor children who had been discriminated against in some counties and towns; but the protections did not cover black or Native American children, who were either not educated, or educated in separate schools.[39] The legislature did not appoint a state commissioner of education until 1837, the same year that Horace Mann assumed the role in Massachusetts. Mann's counterpart in Ohio, Samuel Lewis, shared similar goals: free universal education, confined within the usual racial bounds, purported to support republican ideals, laced with moral development as it was conveyed through the Protestant Bible.

It was not until 1850 that the Ohio legislature followed through on its commitment to public education by calling for a "thorough and efficient system of common schools." This, in the words of one delegate to the constitutional convention, was made possible by the removal of a single great impediment, "the rivalry of schools created by different sects."[40] The deal was cemented in a constitutional provision that banned any religious sect or sects from having control over school funds belonging to the state. Parents were still permitted to educate their children in religious schools if they could afford to do so on their own; but the prohibition of state support eliminated the option for all but a privileged few. Twenty-five years later, Ohio governor Rutherford B. Hayes, eyeing his party's nomination for the presidency, sent a letter to Congressman James Blaine of Maine, suggesting that the Ohio provision could serve as a model for a federal constitutional amendment, and a way for Republicans to mobilize anti-Catholic sentiment against the Democrats.[41]

Michigan inserted an antiaid provision into its constitution in 1835. Within a decade, the Catholic population in Detroit had grown to considerable size, and after a long dispute with Protestant leaders, the city school board passed a provision in 1845 that allowed Catholics to use their own Bible in the classroom. In 1850, the antiaid provisions in the Michigan constitution were expanded. When Catholic leaders subsequently tried to get a share of the school funds appropriated to parochial schools, one Detroit newspaper portrayed their effort as a conflict "between the Jesuit Priesthood and American Citizens." Catholics in Minnesota also attempted to get a parochial aid bill through the legislature in 1853, but it was roundly defeated.[42]

When the diocese of Chicago was established in 1843 and Bishop William Quarter set up Catholic schools, disgruntled Protestant activists warned that "a most troublesome, factious, and expensive religio-politico element"[43] was on the scene. When Catholic priests requested entry into the public schools to provide the children of their parishes with religious instruction, opponents saw it as another sign of the church's "antirepublican" tendencies. In 1855, members of the Illinois legislature elected by the Know-Nothing Party managed to pass a law rejecting all aid to religious schools.

Because the education of the Mexican and Native American populations in California originated with the mission schools, public support of religious institutions there was generally accepted through the early years of statehood.[44] Many public schools in fact began as church schools, including the first elementary school, which was started in the Baptist Church of San Francisco. This changed when the gold rush of 1849 brought Anglo-Saxon Protestants to the West who resented the Catholics and looked down on the Spanish. In 1852 the legislature disqualified denominational schools from receiving assistance. The provision was temporarily reversed the following year. Then in 1853, when the Know-Nothings captured the governorship and both houses of the legislature, the Ashley Act was passed, revoking all financial assistance to parochial schools.

By the last quarter of the century, the debate over funding for religious schools had grown into a national issue. Republicans and nativists had become increasingly alarmed by the power of the Irish political machines to swell the ranks of the Democratic Party, especially in urban centers, which the Irish would eventually control.[45] As much as the establishment was motivated by its desire to protect the prerogatives of the one true faith, religion was an effective tool for rallying the troops against the growing "Catholic menace" that would make a bid for political power.

Religion has always been an easy ploy for political opportunists. In 1875 President Ulysses S. Grant, responding to growing pressures within his own party, made a speech at the convention of the Society of the Army of Tennessee in which he pledged to "encourage free schools, and resolve that not one dollar, appropriated for their support, shall be appropriated to the support of any sectarian schools."[46] The speech was widely publicized. It placed the national Republican Party firmly in the camp of the common school cause promoted by Protestant leaders. It was also a convenient distraction from the corruption scandals that were plaguing Grant's own administration. An article that appeared in the *Universalist Quarterly* explicitly tied Grant's proposal to the anti-Catholic cause and the campaign to stop an alleged attempt by the church to make the country "bound in the spiritual obedience to his holiness, the Pope of Rome."[47] When Grant presented a centennial message to Congress that year, he proposed a constitutional amendment that would prohibit the direct or indirect appropriation of state and local school funds for the benefit of any institution run by a religious sect or denomination.

Grant's charge was taken up by Republican congressman James G. Blaine of Maine, who sought to run for the White House and was mounting a campaign against "Rum, Romanism and Rebellion." The political demagoguery behind the move was transparent for all to see. It was also effective. In the course of debate in the House of Representatives, one member referred to a "sinister sentiment of religious bigotry" behind the bill. The charges were repeated in the Senate. The proposal was approved by majorities in both congressional chambers, but it fell four votes shy of the supermajority needed in the Senate to amend the Constitution. All was not lost, however. The strong support that the measure garnered in the two popular branches of the federal government was indicative of a pervasive national mood. Blaine did not win his party's nomination, but it went to Rutherford B. Hayes, the Ohio governor who originally floated the idea of joining anti-Catholic bigotry with national politics. Hayes was subsequently elected president. Blaine's name had been put before the convention by none other than Robert Ingersoll, "the Great Agnostic."

In the aftermath of the constitutional battle, Congress incorporated "Blaine amendment" stipulations in the enabling legislation that authorized new territories to apply for statehood. As a result, territories located in the northwest and southwest regions of the country could not qualify for admission to the union unless their constitutions included provisions banning the use of tax revenues for religious institutions.[48] The drafters of the new state charters willingly complied.

Debate that occurred at state constitutional conventions reflected the same religious animosities evident in Congress. One delegate in the Washington territory denounced the Jesuits as the "enemy of the country," intent on "destroying the public schools." Colorado became eligible for statehood after President Grant personally campaigned for passage of the enabling legislation and arranged for his friend, Edward McCook, to become territorial governor. Apart from federal intervention, the movement to legally exclude religious funding was already afoot in many states and territories. By 1876, fifteen states had passed similar legislation; by 1890, twenty-nine had incorporated these prohibitions in their constitutions. These provisions remain effective today in more than two-thirds of the states as the singular legal impediment to aid for religious schools.[49]

Animosity towards foreigners and their religions continued to play a role in the formation of education policy into the twentieth century. By 1919 thirty-seven states had passed laws that made it illegal to teach in a language other than English.[50] In order to smooth their arrival to America, immigrant communities often set up schools that taught in their native languages. Many of these schools also had a religious orientation that allowed families to preserve customs and traditions they had brought from the old country.

Following World War I, German immigrants fell especially susceptible to discriminatory language restrictions. Iowa banned the use of German outright. Kansas did not allow German to be used in public meetings. South Dakota outlawed the speaking of German at public meetings, church services, public schools, and private schools. The presence of German in the schools was especially bothersome to those who had embraced a narrow view of patriotism. Most understood that it was futile to eliminate foreign languages among adult immigrants. The schools, however, were supposed to make good Americans of their children, not perpetuate old ways or divided loyalties. There was no such creature as a hyphenated American for the nativists.

By 1910 the Lutherans had been operating more than thirty-three hundred schools, mostly in the West and Midwest.[51] In 1920, Robert T. Meyer, a fifth-grade teacher in Hampton County, Nebraska, was arrested for teaching in German at the Zion Lutheran School. Settlers in the southeastern part of the state had opened the church school almost immediately upon their arrival in 1873. By 1915, the parish had grown so large that a second school building was opened, requiring the hiring of a second teacher. After the war broke out, the windows of the Zion school were blown out with shotgun blasts, and all the books, except for the Bibles, were torn to shreds.

When Meyer was convicted, he launched an appeal that took his case all the way up to the highest court in the state, where he lost. He then brought his case to the United States Supreme Court. While the High Court acknowledged the state's legitimate interest in fostering a common civic identity among its citizens, it found that the language law had interfered "with the calling of modern language teachers, with the opportunities of children to acquire knowledge, and with the power of parents to control the education of their own."[52] The *Meyer* decision established a precedent for a subsequent ruling in which the Court struck down a Hawaiian statute restricting attendance at Japanese-language schools.[53]

In 1922, Oregon enacted a law approved in a statewide voter initiative requiring all children between the ages of eight and sixteen to attend public schools, making it illegal to enroll at a private or religious school. The idea for the initiative was concocted by the Ku Klux Klan and the Scottish Rite Masons, who wanted to insure the growth of public schools that they thought the Catholic Church was trying to destroy. The Klan, also persuaded that blacks, Jews, Catholics, and im-migrants were naturally inferior, wanted these groups to attend school as a way to erase their differences. This law took Horace Mann's notion of assimilation through education to a new extreme. Oregon seemed like an odd place for this to happen, since only 8 percent of the popula-tion was Catholic, 13 percent foreign-born, and 0.3 percent black.[54] But this is the kind of a situation in which impassioned majorities, fueled by bigotry, work their way to the detriment of fundamental con-stitutional rights.

The Oregon law was challenged in federal court by the Sisters of the Holy Names of Jesus and Mary, who ran a number of parochial schools, and by the directors of the Hill Military Academy, which was nondenominational. The Protestant Episcopal Church, North Pacific Union Conference of Seventh-day Adventists, and American Jewish Committee filed *amicus* briefs in support of the suit. Lutheran, Presby-terian, and Congregationalist ministers spoke out against the law, as did editorials in the *New York Times*, *Chicago Tribune*, *Boston Tran-script*, and *Philadelphia Public Ledger*. The case worked its way up to the U.S. Supreme Court, which unanimously struck down the law in 1925. While sympathetic to the state's desire to forge a common education for resident children, the Court found that the law violated the basic rights of parents. It ruled:

> The fundamental theory upon which all governments in this Union repose excludes any general power of the State to standard-ize its children by forcing them to accept instruction from public teachers only. The child is not the mere creature of the State; those who nurture him and direct his destiny have the right, cou-pled with the high duty, to recognize and prepare him for addi-tional obligations.[55]

A *prima facie* reading of the *Meyer* and *Pierce* decisions could leave a reasonable person with the impression that the rights of parents to oversee the education of their children are inviolable. The *Mozert* case that arose in Hawkins County, Tennessee, in 1986 (discussed in chapter 3), indicates otherwise. Vicki Frost's plea to allow her daughter to read literature that did not offend her religious sensibilities was not even given a full hearing by the United States Supreme Court. Her experience is more indicative of the current legal landscape. The American judiciary at the federal and state levels customarily defers to state and local authorities when it comes to matters of education policy. This is problematic for a number of reasons.

It was always assumed that American schools would go beyond basic instruction and convey the core values of the larger society. Unfortunately, the lessons taught not only reflect the biases and misconceptions of the same society; at times, they have been patently wrong. An appreciation of such fallibility is perhaps the most compelling argument for granting parents a generous share of discretion when it comes to determining what is best for their own children. The social contract that parents enter into when they enroll their children in a public school—whether willingly, or for lack of choice—involves palpable risks to individual freedom. Consciously or not, the institutional arrangement, sanctioned by state power, implicitly carries the assumption that those who are in charge have a real grip on what society needs in order to advance.

For the great majority of parents whose view of the world is aligned with that of the ruling majority, the arrangement may not seem like much of a compromise, which explains the overall governing consensus. For those who see the world differently, the consequences of the arrangement can be substantial. The greatest risk to freedom occurs when there is a broad political consensus on values that cannot be verified, one way or the other, by objective measures.

Jefferson had it right about the importance of studying history: it educates us to know the difference between democracy and tyranny. But Jefferson did not fully appreciate that even idealistic social engineers like himself could get it wrong and thereby delay the progress that education is supposed to propel. An important lesson we can draw from studying educational history is that one of the great enemies of educational freedom is intellectual certitude. It is an especially formidable adversary when teamed with its sometime accomplice—false science, which has been responsible for perpetuating ignorance about a host of subjects big and small, ranging from race to alcohol.

An even graver problem in the twenty-first century is that those who govern the education of other people's children do not need the authority of science behind them in order to make their decisions stick. They just need to be convinced that they are right, as Vicki Frost and her neighbors in Hawkins County would discover. Episodes like that, and others we will examine, should alert us to be more vigilant about the prerogatives we grant to political bodies that make education policy.

From time to time, the judiciary has been interventionist when constitutional rights are at stake, but not necessarily to the benefit of religious observers. Most First Amendment case law involving education has focused on the Establishment Clause. It is more frequently invoked to protect nonobservers, or people who are seeking freedom from religion, rather than freedom of religion. Michael Newdow's attempt to strike the words "under God" from the Pledge of Allegiance is an example of a failed attempt along these lines. A federal judge's rejection of an attempt by the Dover County, Pennsylvania, school board to incorporate intelligent design in the curriculum, and a similar judicial reaction to an attempt in Cobb County, Georgia, to post a religiously motivated message on the cover of a textbook, are more representative of the current case law. Voters' removal of Christian conservatives from the school boards in Dover County, Cobb County, and Kansas is more indicative of the present political landscape. A familiarity with the Bible wars of the nineteenth century is an ample reminder of the kind of abuses possible when religion is allowed to have an overbearing influence over the school curriculum. But that was then.

If Horace Mann was the father of the common school movement that defined educational thought in the nineteenth century, John Dewey is the foster parent that guided its development through maturity in the twentieth. Secularism has replaced Protestantism as the prevalent philosophy. Because this perspective is shared so widely in governmental and social institutions that shape public policy, it more closely reflects our current social bias and the attendant risks.

5

POLITICS, EDUCATION, AND RELIGION

BY THE END of the twentieth century the subject of religion had virtually disappeared from the American public school curriculum. When in the late 1970s the Pulitzer Prize–winning historian Frances Fitzgerald completed her study of American history textbooks, she concluded that their authors were "silent on religious matters."[1] Reading this literature, a student was left with the impression that religion played no role in the formation of the country or its aspirations. A decade later, when psychologist Paul Vitz conducted a survey of elementary school texts in history, social studies, and reading, he found a similar reluctance to deal with the subject of religion.[2]

Textbook companies were squeamish about the possibility of offending someone, so they set up their own rigid criteria for self-censorship that excluded religion and any other controversial topic. Reviewing the industry guidelines, Diane Ravitch discovered that religion and political issues were avoided at all costs.[3] Even the traditional American holiday of Thanksgiving was problematic because not all families celebrate it. The lovely story about the Pilgrims feasting with the Indians, familiar to most American schoolchildren, had already been scrubbed of its religious content, for it masks the historical fact that President Washington and the Congress originally celebrated Thanksgiving as an occasion for prayer, an acknowledgment of the "many and signal favors of Almighty God."[4] Thanksgiving did not become the national holiday we know it to be today until the presidency of Abraham Lincoln.

The publishers of textbooks were responding to a variety of pressures. On the one hand they were taking their cues from government officials who had set out to secularize the curriculum. On the other hand, they were responding to activist groups on both the left and the right, who would kick up a storm when offended by books adopted in public schools. Ravitch describes the industry guidelines as a strange brew of "left wing political correctness with right wing fundamentalism."[5] Controversy, whatever the source, was deemed bad for business. It is notable that after the federal appeals court in the *Mozert* case approved the contested Holt reading series used in Hawkins County, Tennessee, the publisher decided to excise most of the controversial passages to avoid more negative publicity. After children whose parents did not want them to read the materials were forced to do so, those whose parents liked the materials were no longer able to acquire them. Then again, the publisher's facile deletion of the disputed sections confirms assertions that they were never so indispensable from the start.

In 1995, a study conducted by the American Textbook Council (ATC) concluded that religion was beginning to work its way back into the American classroom.[6] The reversal was brought on by criticisms from scholars who had pointed out that it is impossible to explain the advance of civilization without taking into account the influence of world religions.[7] The omission might have been accommodating to certain groups, but it was also erroneous and misleading. Publishers responded by expanding their coverage of Judeo-Christian and non-Western religions.

The council, however, was not happy with the way religion was portrayed. The ATC report found that treatment of the subject in social studies and civics texts was sorely one-sided. The prevailing thematic foundation of the curriculum, according to the report, was to caution students about preserving the wall of separation between church and state. The curriculum did not give sufficient attention to the role that religion played in the nation's founding. Many books portrayed religion as being "backwards" or "repressive." Very often the only religious episodes students encounter in their history courses concern the Puritans and the Scopes Trial, which reinforce the notion that religion is dark, irrational, and superstitious. One might add, that while there is much factual material available in these two episodes to construct a damning image of organized religion, many popular depictions of them, including those presented in the schools, are exaggerated to the point of distortion.

The secularization of the public school curriculum that transpired during the twentieth century was part of a larger social phenomenon evident not only in higher education, but also in the arts, literature, and politics.[8] If the lessons taught in the schools about religious rights focused on separation at the expense of accommodation, they only reflected what was going on in the courts. As was true in the nineteenth century, the values promulgated in the schools reflected the values of the larger society, or at least the values of those who dominated political and social institutions. The twentieth century—and, one might add, what little we have seen of the twenty-first—was different in one large respect. In the nineteenth century, the ruling ideology seemed to reflect a majority consensus, one that was particularly harsh on religious minorities. By the end of the twentieth century it was unclear whether the ruling consensus around secularism, still harsh on religious minorities, thoroughly reflected the will of the American people.

Notwithstanding the fact that real popular divisions exist on the topic of religion, American public attitudes also betray a deep ambivalence on the question. This ambivalence was evident in the polls we discussed in the second chapter. Americans want to protect the rights of conscience for those who are sincerely devout, and they welcome religious influences as a bromide for the evils of politics, yet they want to keep religion in its proper place—although they are not quite sure exactly where that place is. This popular ambivalence has permitted the secular tendencies of governmental decision-makers to prevail because the resulting policies affect only a small minority of people who want to live their lives according to their faith. The reelection of President George W. Bush in 2004 put the country at a significant crossroad, and posed a crucial political question about the future course: Would having a fundamentalist Christian in the White House who is assertive about his faith push the public agenda over the legitimate boundaries of church-state separation? Or would it prompt a secularist backlash that could jeopardize the legitimate rights of religious minorities?

It is notable that as the nation was gingerly stepping into the twenty-first century, new political battles were raging over the teaching of evolution. The more recent debate has some new elements that distinguish it from the controversy John Scopes precipitated in Dayton, Tennessee, in 1925. As we saw in the Dover County dispute, opponents of evolution now claim that a body of evidence exists to support a theory of divine creation that is more consistent with biblical teaching. They assert that their position rests on scientific evidence rather than religion or revelation. The mainstream scientific community, including the prestigious National Academy of Science, has rejected this theory—commonly referred to as intelligent design. None of this is surprising in this day and age. Most advocate groups have become adept at assembling copious material to support their causes. Since 1925, however, mainstream science has amassed a more sophisticated regimen of proofs to validate Darwin's central thesis.

A more interesting development concerns polling data, which shows that a majority of the American people subscribe to some version of creationism.[9] In a national poll taken in 2000 by People for the American Way, 68 percent of the respondents said they believed evolution is compatible with the idea that God created humans and guided their development. Many mainstream religious leaders take a similar position. Another survey conducted by CBS News in November 2004 showed that 60 percent of the population favored teaching both evolution and creationism in the public schools (37 percent favored creationism over evolution). In a 2005 survey conducted by the Pew Research Center, 64 percent of the respondents said they were open to teaching both evolution and creationism (38 percent preferred to replace evolutionism with creationism).[10] In the same poll, 41 percent favored letting parents have the main say over how evolution should be taught, while 28 percent favored teachers and scientists, and 21 percent favored school boards.

Other studies have found disagreement among public school science teachers. In Oklahoma, as many as 48 percent of such teachers surveyed believed that strong scientific evidence existed to support creationism. If the American Civil Liberties Union now adopted the position that it originally took in the *Scopes* trial, it might argue that those teachers who believe in creationism have a right to teach it under the rules of academic freedom. For now, we will assume that the courts have settled the question, and that within the bounds of federal and state legal standards school districts have the authority to determine what gets taught in their classrooms.

In February 2005, the *New York Times* published a story in its science section that cited surveys indicating that many public school teachers skip over evolutionary theory in order to avoid riling parents and activists who oppose it.[11] The article was soon followed by an editorial deriding the practice, which violated the curriculum requirements set down in most states.[12] The editors were right to be concerned that teachers might be "afraid" to teach what they thought they should teach, but a closer look at teachers' responses suggests that the reasoning behind their behavior was more complex and varied. The *Times* article also noted a number of surveys taken in various states indicating that about one-third of the biology teachers who were asked said that they support the teaching of intelligent design. In another study conducted at the University of Georgia several years earlier, about 30 percent of the scientists polled admitted that they not only believed in God, but also believed that God communicates with people through prayer.

A front-page article that appeared in *Education Week*—a widely read and well-regarded newspaper in education—sheds more light on the subject.[13] Aside from those teachers who agree with evolutionary theory or intelligent design and those who are afraid to teach it, some teachers apparently believe that a more balanced approach to the subject is pedagogically sound. As one science teacher from Washington state explained it, "I kind of drew a line early on that there is science, and the Bible didn't have an aspect in it." He expressed concern, however, that in many schools "any criticism of Darwin is seen as almost blasphemous." He elaborated, "To say there's no part of science that can be questioned—that's not good science." Another teacher from Kansas, who is opposed to introducing religion in the public school, explains that he tries to make the discussion less divisive. He tells the students that he is there to teach science, not religion, but he acknowledges that there are many mysteries in the natural world for which the scientific community has no answers. This, he asserts, "sure does leave a lot of room for religious revelation."

Other teachers interviewed in the *Times* and *Education Week* articles admitted, "I don't force things." Or, "I have to live with these people." Another simply tells his students that, notwithstanding a broad consensus within the scientific community supporting evolution as an empirically based theory, it remains controversial. Such responses do not necessarily convey fear so much as a desire to address a controversial topic in a less combative way. Unlike policymakers and editorial writers who deal with such issues from afar, teachers need to face the convictions of evolution's opponents on a more human level. This is no reason to betray the scientific truths that they are supposed to teach; but direct contact with parents and others who are concerned probably makes them more inclined to teach in a more sensitive way. Some might, like Mr. Scopes, be reluctant to concede they do not fully understand the scientific protocols that allow researchers to uphold evolutionary theory with such conviction. The *Education Week* article cites a study of state science standards conducted at California State University, which found that nineteen states were doing a "weak to reprehensible" job explaining evolution.

Whatever their level of scientific understanding, classroom teachers—perhaps more than anyone else—know that it is impossible to force someone to believe what they don't believe, or vice versa, despite the evidence that supports evolution. There is nothing wrong with treating the infidels with due respect. There is nothing wrong with acknowledging controversy, or distinguishing between science and religion. The job of the public school teacher is to teach science, rather than to refute religion. He or she should be required to do the former, but not expected to do the latter. Since the founding of the common school, educational policymakers have taken it upon themselves to disabuse children of the religious traditions that they bring to school from home. In Horace Mann's century the presumption was made in the name of nondenominational Protestantism; in John Dewey's, it was done in the name of secularism. In both cases the purveyors of the curriculum claimed to be speaking the enlightened truth to the ignorant masses. By the end of the twentieth century, the play script had been written. The public school and organized religion were cast as principal protagonists.

RELIGIOUS INSTRUCTION

The 1950s marked a transitional period in American life.[14] The country had survived the depression, and capitalism was beginning to pay dividends. The civil rights movement was about to emerge from the nation's conscience. The war in Europe was over, but the Cold War had just begun. America was leading the free world against godless Communism. This was the time when the voices of popular preachers like Rev. Billy Graham, Bishop Fulton J. Sheehan, and Norman Vincent Peale filled the airwaves with sermons that wedded God and country. Hollywood turned out blockbuster movies like *The Robe*, *The Ten Commandments*, and *Ben Hur*. Rock and roll was an odd curiosity for young and old that competed with other musical genres, including religious songs like "I Believe."

The fifties were also the time when Senator Joseph McCarthy wielded congressional power to persecute Hollywood luminaries suspected of Communist ties. Patriotism ran high, and religion fueled its energy. In 1952 president-elect Dwight D. Eisenhower opined in the *New York Times*, "Our government makes no sense unless it is found in a deeply felt religious faith—and I don't care what it is."[15] Eisenhower subsequently began his 1953 inaugural address and every cabinet meeting thereafter with a prayer. The lead float in the inaugural parade was "God's Float," adorned with pictures of churches and the words, "In God We Trust." In 1954, the words "under God" were added to the Pledge of Allegiance. By the middle of the decade, sales of the Bible reached a record high, and it was not unusual for books with religious themes to appear on best-seller lists. It was a period of record church attendance.[16]

Underlying the outward piety of the 1950s was a popular ambivalence about the place of God in everyday life. Beneath the surface of the new civic creed was a shallow religiosity. As Will Herberg explained in his insightful exploration, *Catholic—Protestant—Jew*, American faith had become both homogenized and secularized.[17] While there was a palpable movement afoot among some religious and political leaders to turn the United States into a "Christian nation," Herberg fixed his attention on a spirit of toleration that obscured religious differences. As Americans were attesting to their own devotion, polls consistently revealed that they were ignorant about matters of faith, the Bible, and religious teaching. Most could not explain what their beliefs were, differentiate between Protestantism and Catholicism, or tell the Old Testament from the New Testament.[18] Despite the high levels of church attendance, this was not a population of people who were living their lives according to the teaching of their faith. Then, as now, the truly devout were only a small segment of the American populace. Nevertheless, by the end of World War II, religion had made its way into the public schools—not as part of the standard curriculum, but in the form of released time.

Released-time classes were an accommodation that did not impose religion on students who had no interest in receiving it. It was purely voluntary. Those who desired religious instruction were given the opportunity to take classes with Protestant, Catholic, or Jewish clergy who were invited into the school buildings on a weekly basis. Released time was treated as an elective, and for a considerable amount of time it was popular with children of the three major faiths. Between 1935 and the end of the war, enrollment grew from 250,000 to 1.5 million students.[19] By 1947, the number of students participating exceeded 2 million.

Catholics were especially enthusiastic about the idea. As Bishop John Hughes of New York had hoped a century earlier, released time allowed public school children to get religion in school without violating their rights of conscience. Protestants were more divided. Baptists tended to stand by their historic demands for church-state separation. Many ministers were also concerned that the program would hurt attendance at Sunday school. A certain amount of competition ensued among the different sects to determine whose message would dominate the training, but most Protestants supported the practice.[20]

The response in the Jewish community was most interesting. It lent credence to Herberg's thesis about the homogenization and secularization of American religion; but Jews too were divided.[21] Many Jewish leaders felt that a program that allowed children to break out of class and go their separate ways would accentuate the differences between Christians and Jews. The American Jewish Congress, the American Jewish Committee, and the Anti-Defamation League officially opposed released time. The membership of the same organizations was more conflicted. Some feared that opposition to the popular program would make Jews appear "selfish" or "secular," alienating people of other faiths who wanted to participate. By 1946, twenty-five hundred students were enrolled in released-time classes in New York, twenty-three hundred in Boston. Many Jewish educators embraced released time as a way to show Christians that Jews valued religion, and to promote tolerance among children of different creeds. As one Jewish supporter put it, "It is a more positive kind of labeling."

The issue came to a head when a committee composed of Protestant, Catholic, and Jewish clergy in Champaign, Illinois, got permission from the local school board to offer religious instruction on a released-time basis during the school day. One person who vehemently opposed the program was Vashti Cromwell McCollum. A self-described "humanist," McCollum claimed that as a result of her refusal to enroll him, her son was taunted and beaten by the other students. The mean treatment forced her to transfer her son to a private school in another town. She and her husband, a professor at the nearby college, were allegedly subjected to threats and hate mail after it became clear that they would challenge the program in state court. The title of her personal memoir—*One Woman's Fight*—bore a striking resemblance to the subtitle of Steven Bates's book about Vicki Frost in the *Mozert* case.[22] Thirty years earlier, Vashti McCollum was on the other side of the church-state debate from Vicki Frost. She also had different objectives. Vicki Frost wanted permission to remove her daughter from the reading program that offended her. Vashti McCollum wanted to make sure that nobody's child could participate in a program that offended her. McCollum ultimately had her way in court.

McCollum sought an injunction from the circuit court in Champaign County, Illinois, that would order the school board to adopt rules "prohibiting all instruction in and teaching of religious education in all public schools." Her petition was initially denied. The court found that the school board had general supervisory power over the use of public school buildings, and that the program did not violate either the federal or state constitution. The ruling was affirmed by the State Supreme Court of Illinois. When McCollum appealed to the United States Supreme Court, the state ruling was overturned by an eight-to-one vote. Writing for the majority in 1948, Justice Hugo Black ruled that the program in question violated the Establishment Clause of the First Amendment because tax-supported public school buildings were being used to disseminate religious doctrines.[23]

While the Court recognized that a private interdenominational organization was implementing the instruction at its own expense, it found that the state had provided these sectarian groups with an "invaluable aid" by delivering students for religious classes through the enforcement machinery of compulsory education laws. This was a remarkable line of reasoning. Not only did the Court effectively ignore the voluntary nature of the program, its allusion to compulsory education was counterintuitive. One could reasonably argue that because students are required to attend school, the state has an obligation to accommodate their desires to receive religious instruction with minimum inconvenience. Instead, eight members of the Court parlayed the state's authority to mandate compulsory education into an excuse for burdening the religious practices of the students who complied with the law, with little regard for the families who wanted religious training.

Justice Felix Frankfurter filed a separate concurring opinion that would go further than any prior governmental pronouncement in formalizing the antagonism between public education and organized religion. Frankfurter, a self-proclaimed philosophical secularist, found that the released-time program was divisive in that it (1) undermined the function of the public school in instilling a uniform set of public values, and (2) accentuated feelings of separatism between the majority of students who participated in the program and the minority who did not, contributing toward a sense of religious persecution among the latter. Echoing philosopher John Dewey, he reasoned that "the public school is a symbol of our democracy and the most pervasive means for promoting our common destiny. In no activity of the state is it more vital to keep out divisive forces than in its schools." He suggested that by "sharpening the consciousness of religious differences," the program created a psychological climate for religious segregation and persecution.

There you have it. Justice Frankfurter was claiming, in no uncertain terms, that a state-imposed uniformity in thinking had to take precedence over the religious preferences of parents. Even a generous interpretation of state power to develop a common civic culture does not carry an unlimited prerogative to mold the minds of children, but no such limitation was acknowledged in this opinion. Frankfurter's contention was at odds with the definition of parental rights outlined in the *Meyer* and *Pierce* decisions from the 1920s, which had defeated attempts in Nebraska and Oregon to eradicate educational diversity among ethnic and religious minorities attending nonpublic schools.

Frankfurter portrayed religion as a divisive force that could undermine the unifying role of the public school.[24] He saw it as the Court's job to quell potential disagreement. The underlying premise of Frankfurter's opinion is that disagreement—especially religious disagreement—is bad for American democracy. While Frankfurter expressed concern with the subjective impressions that released time would make on the minority of students who chose to refrain from religious exercises, he showed little regard for the preferences or rights of the majority who wanted to receive it. His opinion marked the beginning of a line of reasoning on the High Court that applied the Establishment Clause to protect the purported interests of the state in general, and nonbelievers in particular, against the free exercise claims of religious believers.

Vashti McCollum's son may have been the target of ridicule and abuse as a result of his nonparticipation and his family's subsequent efforts to end the program; but such treatment was not a necessary result of the program's implementation. Not everyone on the Court was in agreement with Frankfurter. Justice Jackson, one of three justices who cosigned the concurring opinion, cautioned against the Court's interfering with local school authority, and specifically addressed the effects of the program on those students who declined it. Recognizing that dissent can set one apart from others, and that the right of dissent is protected by the Constitution, he reminded his colleagues that the law does not "protect one from embarrassment that always attends nonconformity, whether in religion, politics, behavior or dress."

The "embarrassment" and "isolation" arguments still resonate in constitutional litigation. We saw them arise in the Pledge of Allegiance case recently brought in California. As in McCollum, Mr. Newdow's child also had the legal option to refrain from a school activity that offended her father. Both cases, however, raise a more practical question about the source of a child's discomfort in such situations. Surely, as Justice Jackson opined, there is discomfort associated with being different, but the feeling of isolation is deepened with resentment from others when a disgruntled parent who enjoys the freedom to opt out launches a campaign to prevent a majority from having any options.

In Mr. Newdow's case, neither the child nor her mother, who was legally responsible for her daughter's upbringing, opposed the Pledge. The child's mother, in fact, pleaded with Mr. Newdow to spare their daughter the ordeal of a controversial lawsuit that drew national attention. Parents do bear some responsibility for the psychological burden that dissent brings upon their children, and it should not be taken lightly when they make a decision to protest popular policies. The same holds true for parents who oppose prevailing policy for religious reasons, like those who object to evolution in the science curriculum, or particular readings in literature.

Justice Frankfurter's opinion in *McCollum* included a brief history of religious freedom in America. He not only made references to the writings of Thomas Jefferson and James Madison, as would become customary in First Amendment jurisprudence; he also quoted President Ulysses Grant and Rep. James Blaine, whose controversial proposal to amend the Constitution in 1875 was so offensive to Catholics. Frankfurter also introduced the legacy of Horace Mann to the discussion, but erroneously suggested that the founder of the common school had successfully ridded public education of religious content. The *McCollum* decision proved to be both controversial and unsettling. Many Protestant leaders who had opposed aid to religious schools saw released time as a reasonable compromise that burdened neither the wallets of taxpayers nor the consciences of parents. Now, all of a sudden, it was gone. In hindsight, 1948 was a year in which positions hardened as the country became polarized over the religion question.

One of the organizations that had filed an *amicus* brief on behalf of McCollum was the Baptist Joint Conference Committee, led by Joseph Dawson. Mr. Dawson, a Mason who had been involved in conflicts over religion with the Catholic Church, was instrumental in the formation of Protestants and Other Americans United for the Separation of Church and State. Its founding manifesto, drafted in 1948, referred to a "powerful church, unaccustomed in its own history and tradition to the American ideal of separation of church and state."[25] It called upon all Americans to join the campaign for separation. This campaign would take shape on several levels—politics, public relations, and law—and it would prove to be effective. The organization remains active today, but it has dropped the word *Protestants* from its name, along with the anti-Catholic rhetoric.

In 1949, Paul Blanchard published an incendiary book called *American Freedom and Catholic Power*, which read like a nativist tract from the nineteenth century. In it, he claimed that it was necessary to build a "resistance movement" in order to "prevent the church hierarchy from imposing its social policies on the schools, hospitals and government."[26] He blamed Catholics for producing the majority of white criminals, and called parochial schools "the most important divisive instrument in the life of American children." Blanchard's book was a best seller. It drew praise from educator John Dewey, who applauded it for its "exemplary scholarship, good judgment, and tact."[27] The *New York Times* refused to advertise the book. Publisher Arthur Hayes Sulzberger explained in a letter to the *Christian Herald*, a Protestant publication, that the book was "an attack upon faith—not upon church."[28] Blanchard followed with another popular book in 1951, in which he declared that Catholicism and Soviet Communism were parallel threats to American democracy.[29] He later wrote the postlude to Vashti McCollum's memoir about her campaign to abolish released-time instruction in the public schools.

In 1952 the Supreme Court handed down a decision that, in a manner of speaking, was a partial retreat from *McCollum*. With Justices Black, Frankfurter, and Jackson dissenting, it approved a released-time program in New York in which religious instruction was offered to students outside the public schools at private expense. In writing for the majority, Justice Douglas specifically acknowledged the important and positive role that religion plays in American life, noting:

> We are a religious people, whose institutions presuppose a Supreme Being. . . . When the State encourages religious instruction or cooperates with religious authorities by adjusting the schedule of public events to sectarian needs, it follows the best of our traditions.[30]

Opponents of the program argued that it imposed administrative burdens on the school system. The Court found that for the public school to make it difficult to practice religion would "show a callous indifference to religious groups," and favor those who do not believe in religion over those who do. The majority concluded that the Bill of Rights does not require "hostility to religion," nor does it command the government "to throw its weight against efforts to widen the effective scope of religion."

While opponents brought up the psychological considerations Justice Frankfurter had raised on behalf of the nonparticipants in *McCollum*, the issues of embarrassment, isolation, and identity failed to sway the Court in the *Zorach* case. Ironically, although the Court spoke of the need to cooperate with religious institutions and their members, the one major difference between the Illinois and New York programs was that the latter made religious instruction more inconvenient, forcing children to leave their school buildings. *Zorach's* legal effect was to keep religious instruction off the grounds of the public school. Its practical consequences were less clear, in part because of uncertainty over the prior impact of the *McCollum* ruling. Public reaction to *McCollum* had been so hostile that many communities chose to ignore it. Estimates suggest that released-time enrollments at public schools continued at about 80–90 percent of their pre-*McCollum* levels in the aftermath of the decision.[31]

There were also permutations on the original model: classes offered after school, during the school lunch hour, at other public facilities, or at a rented community center, to mention a few. By 1953, participation rose to its pre-*McCollum* level—about 2.5 to 3 million nationally. At the end of the decade, administrators of these programs were estimating that released-time enrollment exceeded 3 million in more than three thousand communities in forty-five states—by then, mostly outside public schools. In a national survey of public school administrators published in 1962, 72 percent said they believed that released time for religious instruction was either of some value (60 percent) or of great value (12 percent).[32]

PRAYER AND RELIGIOUS OBSERVANCES

States and school districts increasingly turned to prayer and other forms of observance as a way to keep religion in the public school. In many jurisdictions prayer and Bible reading had been popular practices all along. In 1963, thirty-seven states and the District of Columbia allowed religious exercises in their public schools, thirteen actually required Bible reading as a matter of law, and thirteen permitted Bible reading on the basis of state law or judicial interpretation. Reports indicated that there were variations by region with regard to Bible reading, but the incidence among schools was nevertheless high: 76 percent in the South, 67 percent in the East, 18 percent in the Midwest, and 11 percent in the West.[33] The low percentage of schools in the West and Midwest is generally attributed to "Blaine amendment" prohibitions that were incorporated into state constitutions as a condition for admission to the union.

Prayer and Bible reading were religion of a different order from the released-time programs reviewed by the Supreme Court earlier. Even when the latter were carried out in public schools, they were voluntary and privately run. Prayer and Bible reading were administered by public school officials, and implemented as a matter of public policy. They were a throwback to the days of Horace Mann, or in many instances, a continuation of local customs that originated in the nineteenth century. As early as 1943, the United States Supreme Court had upheld the right of a Jehovah's Witness to refrain from saluting the flag in a public school as a matter of conscience, with six justices accepting the argument that the Pledge could be seen as a form of idolatry.[34] That was before the words "under God" were added. Although many jurisdictions permitted students to opt out of prayer and Bible reading, it was only a matter of time before the practices would come under federal judicial scrutiny. A considerable body of case law had already developed in the states dating back more than a hundred years. Of the twenty-three state appellate courts that had heard such cases, seventeen had ruled that the practice was permissible under federal and state constitutional law.[35]

In 1951 the New York State Board of Regents distributed a "Statement on Moral and Spiritual Training in the Schools."[36] The document was supposedly a response to a "dire need" prompted by "concentrated attacks by an atheistic way of life upon our world," yet it was packed with advisories to teachers about the need to be mindful of the "fundamental American value of separation of church and state," and warnings to avoid sectarianism or religious instruction. Based on its stated purpose, the publication could not be seen as neutral by parents who identified themselves as secular. It was interdenominational in spirit, but nonetheless religious.

The document included a "Regents Prayer" that state officials had asked a committee of Protestant, Catholic, and Jewish clergy to compose. It was recommended but not required for daily use in the public schools. The short prayer read, "Almighty God, we acknowledge our dependence upon Thee, and we beg Thy blessings upon us, our parents, our teachers, and our Country." I can recite the words from memory. When I first heard them some fifty years ago, I assumed they were written in the diocesan office of the parochial school I attended. They sounded like the prayer we dutifully recited before lunch. Now they seem reminiscent of the statements that American presidents customarily offer on Thanksgiving Day, most of which are heard by a relatively small segment of the population. The Regents Prayer was being recited in public schools on a daily basis. It was more than the acknowledgment of a Supreme Being that Congress added to the Pledge three years later; it was an attempt to communicate with God. It was drafted by members of the clergy. It went beyond the bounds of "ceremonial deism."

Shortly after the program began, the parents of ten students in the New Hyde Park school district on Long Island, with the advice of the New York Civil Liberties Union, brought an action in state court claiming that the Regents Prayer violated the First Amendment. The upshot of the litigation, which went all the way to the state's highest court, was for the prayer to be approved with a proviso that districts must give parents a chance to opt out. In 1961, a six-to-one majority of the Supreme Court (Justices Frankfurter and White did not participate) ruled that the Regents Prayer was "wholly inconsistent with the Establishment Clause." Declaring the prayer a "religious activity," it continued, "When the power, prestige and financial support of the government is placed behind a particular religious belief " it has the effect of "indirect coercive pressure upon religious minorities."[37] Justice Potter Stewart, the lone dissenter, countered that letting children who wanted to pray do so did not violate the First Amendment. To the contrary, he stated, prohibiting it is to "deny them the opportunity of sharing in the spiritual heritage of our nation." *Engel v. Vitale* was the first of three landmark decisions that would rid the public schools of organized religious observances, at least in theory.

Madalyn Murray O'Hair would became a national icon in the 1960s after she demanded that her son William, a seventh grader in the Baltimore public schools, be excused from daily prayers and Bible reading.[38] Not only was Murray an avowed atheist, she was alleged to have sympathies with the godless regime of the Soviet Union, to which, it was rumored, she sought to defect while surrendering her American citizenship. These suspicions grew larger when she hired a lawyer who had identified himself with the Communist Party. Like previous dissenters, her son William was tormented by his classmates, who branded him "a

Commie." As an adult, William grew resentful towards his mother and more understanding of his former classmates, many of whom had escaped totalitarian regimes in Eastern Europe and feared Communism desperately. William Murray eventually became an ordained minister, and in 1995 published a memoir under the title *Let Us Pray*, in which he advocated prayer in the public schools.[39]

Under Maryland state law public schoolchildren were required to read a chapter of the Bible without comment and recite the Lord's Prayer on a daily basis. Catholic children were permitted to use their own Bible rather than the King James version. Murray's initial request to have her son excused was refused by the principal and the school board. Then, under the advice from the state attorney general, Baltimore instituted an opt-out provision. By that time Murray had already decided to launch a suit, regardless of the option. As might be expected, her plea was not well received in the state courts. Like the state courts responding to the pleas of Catholics in the nineteenth century, the Maryland judiciary did not see Bible reading without comment as a sectarian activity. Moreover, a favorable response to Murray's demands was interpreted politically as giving preference to nonreligion over religion. Murray decided to take her case to the United States Supreme Court just prior to its ruling in the *Engel* case from New York.

In the meantime another case was brewing in Pennsylvania involving a state law requiring that at least ten verses of the Bible be read daily, without comment, in schools. Students were permitted to use either the Protestant, Catholic, or Jewish version of the Scriptures, but only the King James Version was distributed. A student could be excused from the exercise upon the written request of a parent or guardian. School officials in the Abington Township also mandated that the Lord's Prayer be recited, and did not permit students to opt out. The Schempp family had three children in the Abington public schools. Unlike Madlyn Murray O'Hair, they were not atheists, but claimed that the prayers and the Bible reading were contrary to their religious beliefs. With the help of the American Civil Liberties Union, they challenged both practices in federal court. When their case reached the Supreme Court, it was joined with the Murray case, and both the Maryland and Pennsylvania statutes were struck down.[40] Given the coercive nature of the requirements, this is all well and good. The principles that the Court laid down in the course of the *Schempp* ruling, however, raise other concerns that affect First Amendment jurisprudence until today.

The Court noted that on eight occasions in the previous twenty years, with only one justice dissenting, it had consistently applied the Establishment Clause to withdraw "all legislative power respecting religious belief or the expression thereof." Adopting a principle of "neutrality," it endorsed the right of every person to choose religious training, teaching, and observance "free of any compulsion from the state." The eight-to-one majority then enunciated the "purpose and effect" doctrine, which would become a standard for measuring the constitutionality of public programs that approach the legal boundary of church-state interaction. According to the test, "There must be a secular legislative purpose and a primary effect that neither advances nor inhibits religion" in order for a governmental action to "withstand the strictures of the Establishment Clause." Here a near unanimous Supreme Court was adopting secularism as a neutral legal concept. Modern-day secularists themselves hold that secularism is a worldview that in principle conflicts with religious belief. The problems inherent in this legal proposition would become more apparent as time wore on.

Writing for the majority, Justice Clark conceded that among the secular purposes sanctioned by the Court are the following: "promotion of moral values, the contradiction to the materialistic trends of our times, the perpetuation of our institutions, and the teaching of literature." If anything, Justice Clark's brief allusion to specifics would only serve to highlight impending legal questions and disagreements. How does one separate the teaching of moral values from religious considerations? Is secularism merely a concept that suggests the absence of religion in a given social context, or is it a worldview that deliberately opposes religion? Should secular institutions be given priority over religious institutions? And what about the teaching of literature? It was a widely popular selection of literature that offended the religious sensibilities of Vicki Frost and her cohorts in Hawkins County, Tennessee.

If the Supreme Court had set out on a course to secularize the public schools (in either sense of the term), it was doing so without the support of the American people. Reaction to the prayer decisions was largely negative.[41] A Gallup Poll released in August 1963 indicted that 70 percent of those asked opposed the decisions, only 24 percent approved, and 6 percent registered no opinion.

At a meeting of the National Governors Conference held in July, the state executives adopted a resolution urging Congress to pass a constitutional amendment that would permit "free and voluntary participation in prayer in our public schools." Congress was barraged with constituent mail urging it to do the same. Following the *Schempp* decision, 113 bills written to reverse it were introduced in the House of Representatives, and 27 were introduced in the Senate. In September, the House of Representatives voted unanimously to post the words "In God We Trust" behind the Speaker's desk. President Kennedy, who characteristically treaded carefully on religious questions, did the same with the prayer issue. During a regularly scheduled news conference held after the *Engel* ruling, Kennedy commented:

> The Supreme Court has spoken . . . we will have to abide by what the Supreme Court says. We have a very easy remedy here and that is to pray ourselves. We can pray a good deal more at home and attend our churches with fidelity and emphasize the true meaning of prayer in the lives of our children. I hope that . . . all Americans will give prayer greater emphasis.

Not all responses to the decisions were negative. A study of 185 editorials taken from newspapers in thirty-five states and the District of Columbia in the aftermath of *Schempp* found 61 percent in support.[42] Reaction to the prayer decisions, to some extent, got caught up in ongoing civil rights controversies and southern resentment over the aggressive stance the Court had taken on school desegregation. This is not to say that the southern response to the prayer decisions was insincere. But when segregationist governors like George Wallace of Alabama and Ross Barnett of Mississippi rose to champion prayer in the schools, they gave prayer a bad name in circles where it might otherwise have had support. For example, African-American leaders, including prominent ministers like Martin Luther King Jr., who were reluctant to alienate the membership of the Supreme Court in the prime years of the civil rights movement, publicly backed the prayer decisions. The same held true for black-owned newspapers, such as the *Amsterdam News* in Harlem and the *Chicago Defender*. Many northern Democrats who had signed on to the civil rights cause found themselves in an uncomfortable position when constituents communicated dismay over the prayer rulings. Prayer itself was an especially divisive issue in urban districts, which tended to be more religiously and ethnically diverse.

When Rep. Frank Becker (R-N.Y.) proposed a constitutional amendment that would allow voluntary prayer in public schools, it was not taken very seriously by prayer opponents. Rep. Emanuel Celler, the Brooklyn Democrat who chaired the Judiciary Committee, swore that it would never get out of his committee for full consideration in the House. When Becker produced 167 of the 218 signatures needed for a discharge petition, Celler decided to schedule hearings.[43] Celler used the hearings as a stalling devise so that the antiprayer forces could shift the political momentum that had mounted in support of a constitutional amendment. Among the key organizations testifying against the Becker amendment were Protestants and Other Americans United for the Separation of Church and State, the Baptist Joint Committee, the National Council of Churches of Christ, the American Jewish Congress, and the American Civil Liberties Union.

During the course of the hearings, Becker and his allies accused their opponents of being antireligious. Celler made a concerted effort to link the prayer lobby to segregationists in the South. As a result of such open antagonism, the significant substantive issues at stake were never fully debated on their merits. Nor could there be much hope that the legitimate claims of competing parties would be resolved in a fair and reasonable manner. On one side was the need to accommodate religious families whose faith demanded that their children participate in daily prayer; on the other was the need to protect parents who did not want their children subjected to any form of pressure to participate in a religious observance implemented by the state.

Chairman Celler ordered the staff of the Judiciary Committee to prepare a report that highlighted difficulties inherent in implementing a prayer amendment. Toward the end of the proceedings a group composed of 223 law school deans and legal scholars filed a statement urging Congress to refrain from making modifications to the Bill of Rights.[44] Their statement and the staff report dominated the press coverage. In June, the flow of mail to the House Judiciary Committee still favored a prayer amendment by a margin of 6,135 to 3,870.[45] The hearings, however, allowed Chairman Celler to amass sufficient organizational and media support to achieve his objective. Despite the fact that more than one hundred congressmen sponsored prayer resolutions, the issue died in committee, never to be considered on the floor of the House.

Those who prevailed on the Becker amendment basked in the self-assurance that they had rescued the constitutional principles that Thomas Jefferson and James Madison had bequeathed to the nation, but their perspective on the issue was not shared by many, perhaps most, of the American people. Surely the law professors, editorial writers, and opinion leaders who had come forth to deliver Becker's defeat did not speak for the majority of citizens who had expressed their viewpoints through opinion polls and letters to Congress. One lesson learned from the prayer battles in Congress, which separated politics of religion in the twentieth century from that of the nineteenth, is that the ruling majority did not necessarily speak for the popular majority. Another lesson learned from the episode is that the government cannot easily undo behavior that is entrenched in the culture and values of a significant portion of the citizenry.

To a large extent, state and local jurisdictions throughout the country responded to the prayer decisions in the same way that they responded to the released-time rulings, by simply ignoring them. A survey conducted by the Anti-Defamation League in September 1963 found that prayer or Bible reading continued in ten states, and were required in three others, while seven additional states took an official hands-off policy that let local school boards do what they pleased.[46] A separate survey taken in Connecticut found that less than 20 of the state's 169 towns acted to implement the court decision. A more detailed study of four midwestern communities conducted five years after the decisions were handed down found that "schools have continued to say prayers, read from the Bible, and conduct many other forms of supposedly unconstitutional religious observances."[47]

WINDS OF CHANGE

The High Court was not oblivious to the religious traditions valued by the mainstream of American society. Sometimes it was downright deferential to such sentiment. In 1961, it handed down four decisions

upholding state Sunday-closing laws. While recognizing that the original purpose behind such legislation was to encourage church attendance, Chief Justice Earl Warren, writing for the Court, construed the
contemporary objective—which he interpreted as "to set aside a day
of rest and recreation"[48]—as being more secular. In response to con-
tentions by appellants in one case, that not all religious groups observe
the Sunday Sabbath, the chief justice explained that designating one
particular day of the week for rest was necessary to achieve the secular
purpose of the laws.

The chief justice's viewpoint seemed to be shared by most Americans at the time. That same year, however, the Court struck down a
Maryland law requiring public officeholders to declare a belief in God.[49]
Then in 1963, the Court responded to minority religious concerns,
when it protected the right of a Seventh-day Adventist in South Carolina. The plaintiff in that case, *Sherbert v. Verner*, had been denied
unemployment compensation because her religion required her to observe the Sabbath on Saturday when her employer demanded that she
work.[50] The Court ordered the state to provide her with the benefit.

The prayer amendment gained momentum again in 1966 after the
Supreme Court refused to review an appellate ruling that allowed officials in New York City to prohibit voluntary prayers that were initiated
by a group of families whose children attended public school. This time
the sponsor of the prayer amendment was Senator Everett M. Dirksen
(Ill.), the Republican minority leader who had been a key ally of the
civil rights coalition assembled by President Lyndon B. Johnson during
the 1960s.[51] Dirksen presented his voluntary prayer proposal as an attempt to clarify the meaning of the prayer decisions by the Supreme
Court, rather than override them. Having received more than fifty-two
thousand letters backing the prayer amendment, Dirksen was convinced that he was representing the sentiments of the American people
when he brought his bill directly to the Senate floor without committee
sponsorship. The final vote was forty-nine "yea," thirty-seven "nay"—
a sizable majority, but not the two-thirds majority needed to enact a
constitutional amendment. Dirksen unsuccessfully tried again in 1967.
In 1971, Rep. Chalmers Wylie of Ohio introduced a similar proposal
in the House of Representatives. He managed to assemble the 217

votes needed to extract the bill from Emanuel Celler's Judiciary Committee, but the measure failed when it reached the floor of the House.

The prayer issue worked its way back to the High Court in 1985 in a case that would have serious implications beyond the immediate effects of the decision itself. This dispute began in Mobile, Alabama, when Ishmael Jaffree, an agnostic with two children in public school, challenged a state law that allowed teachers to provide for "a moment of silence" and "voluntary prayer."[52] The prayer stipulation had been added to the 1978 statute in 1981 at the urging of Governor Fob James Jr. One group of defendant-interveners was supported by Reverend Pat Robertson's National Legal Foundation, who joined the battle against the wishes of the school officials. They testified that textbooks used in Alabama promoted a philosophy of secular humanism, which would also need to be rectified if the statute in question were struck down. The controversy was joined by People for the American Way, whose lawyers enthusiastically took on the challenge, much as they had in the *Mozert* case.

The law was upheld at the trial level by Judge Brevard Hand, who ruled that the United States Supreme Court had "erred" in its reading of history, and that the Establishment Clause does not apply to state actions, but only to federal laws and regulations. Judge Hand's ruling was rejected by both the appellate court and the Supreme Court, which struck down the Alabama law. The final ruling contained important dicta that would guide First Amendment jurisprudence in a new direction.[53]

Writing for the Court, Justice Stevens made a distinction between the "moment of silence" and the "voluntary prayer" aspects of the statute under review, declaring, "The legislative intent to return prayer to the public schools is, of course, quite different from merely protecting every student's right to engage in voluntary prayer during an appropriate moment of silence during the school day." He further explained that under the original law, prayer was only one of many voluntary activities in which students could engage during the minute of silence, but that the addition of the prayer stipulation indicted that the "state intended to characterize prayer as a favored practice."

Speculation that the Court would approve a voluntary moment of silence was further fed by an elaborate concurring opinion written by Justice O'Connor and supported by Justice Powell. She stated, "Silence, unlike prayer and Bible reading, need not be associated with a religious exercise." She continued, "Even if a statute specifies that a student may choose to pray silently during a quiet moment, the State has thereby not encouraged prayer over other specified alternatives." For O'Connor, the crucial question was whether the state had acted to "endorse" religion, or give the impression that it had. Justice O'Connor had elaborated on the "endorsement test" in a 1984 decision, where the Court approved a holiday display in a public square that included Christian, Jewish, and secular decorations.[54]

More indicative of a new posture that was beginning to take shape on the Court was a pair of vigorous dissents in the *Jaffree* case, signed by three members of an emboldened minority. Chief Justice Burger and Justice White opined that the outcome of the case should have simply turned on whether a student had a choice either to pray or not to pray during the designated moment of silence. Justice Rehnquist launched into a more pointed criticism of the First Amendment jurisprudence that had dominated the thinking of the Court until that time, objecting to the emphasis placed on "Jefferson's misleading metaphor" denoting a "wall of separation between church and state." The future chief justice added that there is "simply no historical foundation for the proposition that the Framers intended to build the 'wall of separation' that was constitutionalized" by the Court. He went on to assert that the Establishment Clause was designed to merely "prohibit the designation of any church as a 'national one'" and "to stop the government from asserting a preference for one religious denomination or sect over others."

The national political dynamic had changed by this time with regard to the prayer issue specifically, and religion in general. Through the 1970s the principal advocate for the prayer lobby in Congress was Senator Jesse Helms (R-N.C.). Helms identified the issue as part of a larger campaign to neutralize federal judges who had taken it upon themselves to legislate from the bench, and enforce rules that betrayed the will of the American people. In 1980, President Ronald Reagan was elected, advocating a three-part agenda on education reform. In addition to the elimination of the United States Department of Education, the agenda included prayer in the public schools, and vouchers to provide tax-supported funding for children to attend private and religious schools.

At the end of his first term, Reagan, with the support of religious conservatives, was able to get his own school prayer amendment proposed in the Senate. It was sponsored by Senator Strom Thurmond (R-S.C.). Chairman Orrin Hatch (R-Utah) presided over Judiciary Committee hearings that sounded very much like a replay of the battles that took place over the Becker and Dirksen amendments: same players, same arguments, and a similar outcome. A Senate vote taken in 1984 gained a simple majority (fifty-six to forty-four), but insufficient support for the constitutional amendment sought by the White House.

After the *Jaffree* decision was handed down by the Supreme Court in 1985, a number of cases came before the lower federal courts challenging state provisions instituting a "moment of silence" in the public schools. Some of the statutes were sustained, others were not, depending on the details of the case. Today, about half the states in the country have some form of provision along these lines.[55] The prayer issue did not reach the High Court again until 1992, when a Providence family challenged the inclusion of a "nondenominational" prayer at the graduation ceremony in a public school. Such invocations and benedictions were not unusual at school events that took place outside the classroom. In 1983 the Supreme Court had approved a practice in Nebraska, where the legislature hired a chaplain whose job it had been to lead off each session with a prayer.[56] The Court, however, did not look so favorably on the graduation prayer.

Defenders of the practice, including Solicitor General Kenneth Starr, representing the administration of President George H. W. Bush, drew a distinction between the kind of pressure imposed upon students to conform in a classroom setting and that existing at a graduation ceremony, which students were not compelled to attend. Starr also emphasized the nondenominational character of the prayer in question. Writing for a five-person majority, Justice Anthony Kennedy ruled, "The Constitution forbids the State to exact religious conformity from a student as the price of attending her own high school graduation."[57] Recognizing the special significance of the graduation ceremony for Deborah Weisman and her family, Justice Kennedy deemed the prayer a form of state coercion. The other members of the majority found it sufficient to establish that the state had violated Justice O'Connor's endorsement test. Four other members of the court dissented on the ground that such nonsectarian exercises were a "longstanding American tradition."

The narrow ruling in *Weisman* laid out a set of principles that would lend clarity to the broad concepts articulated in the *Jaffree* case. The activity in question violated the Establishment Clause because it, like the Regents Prayer in New York, was a religious exercise created and directed by public officials. Unlike voluntary moments of silence, which students might use to pray or not to pray, students in Providence were forced to actively or passively subject themselves to prayer unless they were prepared to forgo attending their own graduations. The Providence case was another example of a "take it or leave it" policy foisted by a popularly elected school board on a minority of dissident parents—similar to what we saw in the *Mozert* case, only on a smaller scale, and garnering greater sympathy from the judicial branch. Commenting on the legislative chaplain case from Nebraska, the Court also suggested that the constitutional standards applied to protect children in a school setting were somewhat different from those that hold in adult situations. Justice Kennedy reasoned, "The atmosphere at the opening of the state legislature where adults are free to enter and leave . . . cannot compare with the constraining potential of the one school event most important for the student to attend."

The Supreme Court placed additional legal constraints on school prayer in 2000, when it nullified student-led and student-initiated prayer at high school football games in Santa Fe, Texas.[58] Although the prayers were organized and implemented by a formal process of student election, the six-person majority would not allow the school district to disengage itself from responsibility for what occurred at the pregame ceremony, since school officials had established the arrangements for student participation and ultimately granted permission for the prayers to be said. Moreover, the process did not provide sufficient protection for those students who were part of a religious or nonreligious minority. While a sporting event may not have been as significant to some students as a graduation exercise, it was still part of the extracurricular activity program supervised by the school. Although participation in the exercise was to some extent voluntary, the nature of the activity, conducted over a public address system, was not private.

The *Santa Fe* case highlights some of the practical considerations that arise when public schools attempt to create an environment that is accommodating to students who want to organize some form of prayer or religious observance as part of normal school activities. It is difficult to calculate the point at which the administrative hand of school officials has reached beyond the bounds of the Constitution. Nevertheless, it is the responsibility of the same officials to measure, protect, and enforce these boundaries. The idea of a nonreligious prayer is an oxymoron. Utterances that may seem nonsectarian to some families may offend others. The original suit in the *Santa Fe* case was brought by Catholic and Mormon parents in opposition to a "nondenominational" Protestant prayer that was clearly illegal. But deeply religious people have also questioned the value of having children recite words that are completely devoid of spiritual meaning. Finding words that are both acceptable and meaningful to all families becomes more difficult as school communities grow more culturally and religiously diverse.

6

FREE EXERCISE, VACATED
AND DENIED

GEORGE REYNOLDS was a man of faith and a good family provider. Because of his faith and his family, Reynolds was convicted of committing a federal crime in 1874. As a Mormon, Reynolds was compelled by his religion to have more than one wife; of which he had two. That put him in violation of the Morrill Act, which Congress had passed in 1862 to outlaw polygamy in the federal territories.

A thirty-two-year-old, Reynolds, who was secretary to Mormon leader Brigham Young, oversaw a rather modest household by the standards of the Mormon Church in Utah. Elders were known to have counted their wives by the dozen. They simply ignored the federal law, both before Reynolds's conviction and afterwards. With only two wives, Reynolds was an excellent candidate for launching a test case in a Christian country stricken with moral outrage over what was going on in Utah.

"Celestial Marriage" was not part of the original teaching of the Church of Jesus Christ of the Latter Day Saints. Joseph Smith, the founder of the church, started the practice in the 1840s—around the same time that Irish Catholics began to pour into northeastern cities—when he heard the voice of God and decided to marry a young woman who had been living with his family.[1] Smith's first wife, Emma, and the nine children she bore had not heard the same voice, so they never fully accepted the plural arrangement, though many more wives subsequently joined the clan.[2]

Nonbelievers allege that the voice Smith heard came from his pants pocket. He initially kept his polygamy a secret, sharing it with a few select members of the church hierarchy, who also partook in his unusual form of devotion. But Smith's revelation, following the example of the Hebrew patriarchs, became a central precept of the church he led. According to Mormon tradition, men and women had a moral

obligation to increase and multiply. The fathering of numerous children would help assure men a favored place in the afterlife. A wife's
place would be determined by her husband's. Smith became a martyr
to the cause in 1844, when, having been arrested, he was murdered by
an angry mob while sitting in jail.

Since men supposedly had greater reproductive power than women,
there was a natural-law argument attached to polygamy.[3] Men were not
only blessed with more years of fertility; the effective performance of
their reproductive role did not take nine long months, several of which
were taken up with physical incapacity. Since the sole purpose of sex
was to procreate, women were not supposed to have intercourse when
they were pregnant or lactating, leaving them unproductive for a time.
Moreover, males were more psychologically predisposed to the prospect
of having multiple partners. And husbands with a bevy of wives were
less likely to bother unmarried women and the spouses of other men.
It all worked according to God's natural design, as revealed in the
Scriptures. Who could have a problem with that? In the context of
plural marriage, poorer women were given a chance to improve their
station in life by hitching themselves to men of economic means, who
tended to dominate the marriage market and the church hierarchy.

It is said that Mormon women had to grant approval for their husbands to take on additional wives, and that most supported polygamy.
Women in Utah were among the first given the right to vote, enfran-
chised in 1870 by a unanimous vote of the territorial legislature.
Susan B. Anthony and Elizabeth Cady Stanton campaigned on their
behalf, and also opposed congressional action to outlaw polygamy in
the territory; which they understood to be a matter of personal
choice.[4] That was not altogether the case, however. According to
church teaching, women who denied their husbands additional wives
were considered selfish and unholy. Female suffrage in Utah was not
all that it was cracked up to be either. In reality, it enhanced the
power of polygamous men. A husband who arrived at the polling place
with a wagon full of like-minded voters was a political force to behold
in the frontier community.

Republicans in Congress had embraced the Morrill Act of 1862 as
a legal precedent for the eventual prohibition of slavery. Five years
earlier the Supreme Court's *Dred Scott* decision denied federal author-

ity to restrict slavery in the northern territories. Like slavery, marriage was a domestic institution that was customarily governed by state and local regulations. George Reynolds argued that because he was religiously obliged to have more than one wife, the Morrill Act violated his free exercise rights protected by the First Amendment. When his conviction was upheld on appeal, he took the case to the United States Supreme Court. In the first major religious liberty case to reach the High Court, the majority ruled in 1879 that the Constitution does not furnish individuals with an absolute right to practice religion.[5] Making a distinction between the protection of beliefs and of actions, the Court determined that Reynolds could not use the First Amendment as grounds to disobey a federal law.

The opinion written by Chief Justice Waite traced the history of religious freedom in America to the Virginia Act of 1785 and the writings of Thomas Jefferson and James Madison—all of which, from that point forward, would be treated with as much reverence by the Supreme Court as the words contained in the First Amendment itself. The *Reynolds* case was the first in which the Court invoked Jefferson's metaphor denoting a "wall of separation between Church and State." But, in fact, the *Reynolds* case was the culmination of a long political battle against the Mormons that mixed religion, common law, and federal rule-making. Marriage, according to the Court, is a "sacred obligation" upon which society is built in most civilized nations. Polygamy was an affront to the Christian notion of marriage, which was supposed to involve one man and one woman.[6] If a man could be permitted to marry more than one woman, then what in hell could the misfits of Christian civilization concoct next?

Chief Justice Waite rooted the regulation of marriage in the ecclesiastical courts of England prior to the reign of James I. He noted that plural marriage had "always been odious among Northern and Western Nations" and "almost exclusively a feature of the life of Asiatic and African people." In the last quarter of the nineteenth century, the Mormon Church in the Western territories, much like the Catholic Church in East Coast cities, posed a fundamental threat to the values of mainstream American Protestantism. The ruling majority was not about to tolerate either of these twin evils. In 1874, Republicans in Congress passed legislation to strengthen the ban on polygamy. Two years later a majority in both houses of Congress, urged on by President Grant and Congressman James Blaine, voted to maintain Protestantism in the public schools and prohibit tax support for schools run by religious institutions.

In 1887, seven years after a majority of local voters approved a state constitution outlawing plural marriage, Congress took another broad swipe at the Mormons in Utah when it invalidated the incorporation of the church and revoked the female franchise.[7] The bill was cosponsored by Senator George Edmunds, who earlier had been a vocal supporter of the Blaine amendment. In 1890, the Supreme Court again opined that Mormonism is "a return to Barbarism . . . contrary to the spirit of Christianity and the civilization which Christianity has produced in the Western world."[8]

Reynolds's lawyer had argued that the Utah Territory, authorized by Congress in 1850, had the same rights to self-government as those enjoyed by the states. Although state churches had been disestablished by then, it was generally understood that the First Amendment did not regulate religion in the states. When the Court was first confronted with the prospect of applying the religion clauses to actions taken by the states in 1845, it ruled that "the Constitution makes no provision for protecting the citizens of the respective states in their religious liberties; this is left to the state constitutions and laws."[9]

In a Pennsylvania case argued by Daniel Webster in 1844, Justice Story endorsed the contention that Christianity was part of the local common-law tradition, thereby abrogating any possible Establishment Clause claim against the state.[10] It was also widely accepted at the time for the states to enforce laws against blasphemy and Sabbath breaking. As we have already seen, for some time thereafter, Bible reading and prayer were ordinary features of the public school day. When the Supreme Court told the State of Oregon in 1925 that it could not outlaw religious schools, or the right of parents to send their children to such schools, it did so on the basis of the Due Process Clause of the Fourteenth Amendment, not the religion clauses of the First Amendment.[11] Two years earlier it had applied the same Due Process Clause against the State of Nebraska to protect the right of Robert Meyer to use the German language when teaching at a Lutheran school.[12]

For the first hundred years in the life of the republic, the Supreme Court did not adopt a separationist posture regarding the use of federal power. Nor did it do so for seventy-five years following the *Reynolds* decision. Disestablishment meant just that: no official national church. In 1892, the Court went so far as to assert that the United States is a "Christian nation," recalling the country's original settlement by people who were religious believers.[13] In 1899, the Court approved federal financing for the construction of a Catholic hospital in the District of Columbia, basing its reasoning on the secular nature of the hospital's mission.[14] In 1908, the Court allowed government money to be used to support religious schools for Native Americans, finding that the tribe was free to spend the funds as it saw fit.[15]

In 1930, the Supreme Court upheld a Louisiana law that set aside public funds to supply textbooks for children in public, private, and parochial schools. Here, in the landmark *Cochran* case,[16] the majority drew an important legal distinction between the direct benefits derived by the students involved, and the indirect benefits derived by the schools they attended—neither of which offended the Constitution. The "child benefit theory" would become an important legal doctrine in cases that involved aid to religious schools and their students.

In 1940, the first time a Jehovah's Witness went to the Supreme Court to determine whether a local school board could expel his children for refusing to salute the flag, eight justices said it could.[17] Both the trial judge in Pennsylvania and a unanimous federal appeals panel in the *Minorsville* case had ruled in favor of Walter Gobitis, accepting the argument that no harm had been done to other students when his two children objected to the Pledge on the basis of their faith. Gobitis claimed that the expulsion forced him to send his children to private school and incur personal expenses for the tuition, thereby burdening his practice of religion.

The High Court saw the matter differently. In an opinion written by Justice Frankfurter, it declared, "We live by symbols." It described the flag as "the binding tie of cohesive sentiment." Repeating the finding of the *Reynolds* case, the Court ruled that religious conviction "does not relieve the citizen from the discharge of political responsibilities." Anticipating his pronouncement on civic education in the *McCollum* released-time case, Justice Frankfurter exclaimed, "National unity is the basis of national security." He speculated that exempting the Gobitus children from their civic duty might "cast doubts in the minds of other children" and weaken their loyalty to the country. Three years later, Frankfurter wrote an angry dissent in the *Barnette* case that required such an exemption for conscientious objectors.

Throughout the 1940s and 1950s Jehovah's Witnesses initiated a series of cases concerning the authority of states and localities to regulate their door-to-door solicitations and distribution of literature, which were their primary means for proselytizing and a major source of irritation in the communities where they worked.[18] It was in one such successfully argued case from 1940, *Cantwell v. Connecticut*,[19] that the Court incorporated the Free Exercise Clause of the First Amendment as a protection against actions taken by the states. That in itself was a momentous precedent. Several of the rulings favoring the Witnesses, however, were made on the basis of free speech claims. These cases also provided significant legal precedent that would allow the Court, when it was so inclined, to overlook claims made on the basis of religious rights, thereby diminishing the Free Exercise Clause.

Barnette was a case in point. While the Witnesses viewed the flag salute primarily as a religious offense, the Court dealt with it as an offense against free speech, which was worthy of protection regardless of the religious claims posted by the plaintiffs. As Justice Jackson explained, "While religion supplies [the children's] motive for enduring the discomforts of making the issue in this case, many citizens who do not share these religious views hold such a compulsory rite to infringe the constitutional liberty of the individual."[20]

When the Bill of Rights was first adopted in 1791, it was generally understood that the original amendments did not apply to the states and were written to limit the powers of the national government only. This understanding was confirmed by the Supreme Court in a decision written by Chief Justice Marshall in 1833.[21] The legal pendulum began to swing in the direction of national power after the Civil War with the adoption of the Thirteenth, Fourteenth, and Fifteenth amendments. The amendments respectively ended slavery, granted citizenship to former slaves, and prohibited racial discrimination in the provision of voting rights.

It was the Court's interpretation of the Fourteenth Amendment that eventually carried the nationalization of individual rights into the twentieth century, but the process was long and gradual.[22] Its effects were felt most dramatically in the area of civil rights, especially in the promotion of racial equality. Beginning with the landmark *Brown v. Board of Education* ruling of 1954, which outlawed racial segregation in schools, the Warren Court applied the Equal Protection Clause to outlaw racial discrimination in a wide range of areas outside of education, including public transportation, public recreation facilities, and voting.[23]

In subsequent years the Supreme Court would use Fourteenth Amendment guarantees as an instrument for extending the rights of other protected groups, including women, the disabled, and gays. The fate of religious minorities, especially those who were devout observers, would be another matter. Their time would come much later, and in a circumscribed way. If anything, the application of the Establishment Clause to the states through Due Process would serve as a vehicle for guaranteeing freedom from religion rather than freedom of religion.

Seven years passed from the time the Court incorporated the Free Exercise Clause in *Cantwell* to when it incorporated the Establishment Clause in the landmark *Everson* decision of 1947.[24] From then on, it would treat the two First Amendment clauses as though they were in legal tension, the former designed to protect the rights of religious believers, the latter to protect nonbelievers. In far many more cases the latter would be applied to trump the former. Thus on a practical level, incorporation of the Establishment Clause did not expand the rights of religious believers; instead it worked to contract them.

Even the substantive due process rights that were formerly celebrated as fundamental liberties in *Meyer* and *Pierce* seemed to have escaped the consciousness of the federal judiciary when it came to religion. Establishment Clause considerations overshadowed all others with the emergence of a Supreme Court jurisprudence that would embrace secularism as a prevailing philosophy. As seen earlier, a large part of the secularization project focused on ridding the public schools of religion. In a broader sense, it sought to enforce a strict separation between government and religious institutions.

"A WALL OF SEPARATION"

At issue in *Everson* was a New Jersey law that provided transportation services for children in public, private, and religious schools. Following the child benefit concept articulated in the *Cantwell* textbook case, the Court suggested that to exclude parochial school children from a general public benefit program solely on the basis of their attendance at religious schools would constitute an infringement of their free exercise rights protected by the First Amendment.[25] In that sense, *Everson* was an accommodationist decision. But the convoluted opinion written by Justice Black also included language that would lay the foundation for a generation of separationist rulings.

Tracing the history of the First Amendment as if it were the history of Virginia, Justice Black drew heavily from the writings of James Madison and Thomas Jefferson, and for the second time in the Court's history invoked the latter's metaphor calling for "a wall of separation between church and state."[26] Both the majority and the minority erroneously treated the Establishment Clause as if it were the legal equivalent of the Virginia Statute of Religious Freedom drafted by Jefferson in 1777, inaugurating another powerful precedent.

The separationist posture was more in line with the overall thinking of Justice Black. Court observers were surprised by his approval of the transportation statute in question. Within a year, Black would write for the majority in the *McCollum* released-time case and define secularism as the preferred way to deal with religious pluralism in America. Legal historians have speculated that Justice Black veered from his usual course in the *Everson* finding in order to defuse charges of anti-Catholicism, which dated back to his prior association with the Ku Klux Klan in Alabama.[27] Black had been a member, participated in its hooded ceremonies, and received the endorsement of the Klan when he ran for the United States Senate. Revelations of his connection had sparked a political uproar when Black was nominated for the bench by President Franklin D. Roosevelt, who supposedly was unaware of his nominee's former ties.[28] In every subsequent First Amendment case on which he ruled, Black would cite his and Jefferson's separation edict as though it were the most significant precedent derived from *Everson*. Others who shared his philosophy would do the same.

Over a half century—from 1947 to 1997—the Supreme Court heard fifty-two Establishment Clause cases.[29] The majority of them dealt with education, exceeding the number concerning all other sectors of society combined. During this time, the first order of business, taken up in thirteen separate cases, was to limit aid to parochial schools and the children who attended them. On this there was a strong consensus throughout the country. While Protestant leaders and the American public were divided over the Court's secularization of the public schools, the only group that consistently supported government aid to religious schools was the Catholics, whose parochial schools accounted for 90 percent of all nonpublic school enrollment through the mid-1960s.[30]

The Joint Baptist Committee, National Association of Evangelicals, and National Council of Churches all joined forces to build a wall of separation between church and state "especially as the state might interrelate with the Roman Catholic Church."[31] Protestants and Other Americans United for the Separation was founded in the same year that *Everson* was decided. Soon thereafter the organization sent an open letter to the *New York Times* accusing Catholic leaders of trying to subvert the Constitution.[32] *Everson* permitted the new alliance to hoist its sentiments on a legal banner, taking it beyond the usual anti-Catholic vitriol.

The Court employed the child benefit concept again in 1968, when it approved a New York state law that authorized local school districts to lend textbooks covering secular subjects to religious schools. Based on the "*Schempp* test" adopted in the Bible-reading case, petitioners had argued that the "purpose and effect" of the law in question was to advance religion, even though the benefit was available to children at nonreligious private schools. The *Allen* Court held that because the books in question were limited to secular subjects, they did not support the religious mission of parochial schools.[33]

Citing *Everson*, Justice Black issued a fuming dissent in which he derided "religious propagandists" behind the law who sought to achieve "complete domination and superiority of their particular brand of religion." In an attempt to differentiate the facts in this case from *Everson*, he contended that textbooks are not the equivalent of bus transportation, because books are "at the heart of every school," which, as "essential tools of education," cannot be divorced from the instructional mission of the school. Notwithstanding his inflammatory language, and the fact that the child benefit concept originated in a textbook case, Black had a point.

Religious schools exist for the purpose of propagating religion. If such institutions are to take their missions seriously, their religious values should pervade most aspects of the curriculum. There may not, as some would argue, be a biblical approach to the teaching of arithmetic; but religion can certainly work its way into social studies and history lessons, not to mention life skills courses that deal with moral and behavioral issues like alcohol and sex. As we have already seen, religion can also influence the selection of literature. The *Allen* decision would set judges and lawyers on a fool's journey to decipher which aspects of religious school activity were not religious, as if they were trying to figure out which end of a horse barn smelled less like a horse. Under the standard adopted in *Allen*, the best strategy for a religious school to follow if it wanted to be eligible for government funding would be to detach itself from the purpose for which it was created.

The *Allen* opinion also gave birth to the "divertibility" concept, in which separationist lawyers would argue that money saved on the cost of teaching secular subjects at parochial schools could be diverted into religious activity. That is also true. Theoretically, even money parents save on transportation services, once disposable for discretionary use, could be funneled into the general coffers of a parochial school or church. The only way to avert the risks posed by divertibility is to prohibit any funding whatsoever for religious schools and the children who attend them. That, of course, is what strict separationists wanted. As Justice Black postulated in his angry dissent, "State aid to religion and religious institutions generates discord, disharmony, hatred and strife among our people." His own intemperate language in the same opinion was an exquisite example of the dangers Justice Black feared. Whether such dangers, to the extent that they exist, provide ample reason to justify discriminating against parochial school children in the award of general public benefits is another question.

Everson was only the first leg of a three-legged stool upon which secularists would build their legal wall of separation. *Lemon v. Kurzman*,[34] decided in 1971, was the second. It nullified a state statute that subsidized the salaries of parochial school teachers who taught secular subjects. In *Lemon* the Court purported to set down definitive standards that would guide First Amendment jurisprudence into the future. Under the "*Lemon* test," three criteria must be met in order for public funding to be permitted under the Establishment Clause: The program in question must (1) have a secular public purpose, (2) may not have the primary effect of advancing or inhibiting religion, and (3) may not foster excessive entanglement between church and state. Despite the promise they held out, the criteria that the Court outlined in *Lemon* raised as many questions as they answered.

Did the secular criterion require the Court to treat religious institutions with neutrality in the distribution of general public benefits, or was it meant to disqualify religious institutions and their members from all public benefits? Were some public benefits more problematic than others? How could one distinguish between a primary effect and a secondary effect of advancing religion? Was the Court serious about checking school authorities whose actions inhibited religious beliefs or practices? What about the divertibility of funds? In this particular case the Court was concerned that the level of state scrutiny needed to protect against diversion would lead to an excessive amount of government entanglement in the affairs of religious institutions, as if to suggest that the burden regulation imposed on lawful beneficiaries was reason enough to deny them their rightful benefits—something akin to banning automobiles to free up drivers from the burdens of traffic regulation.

Writing for the Court in *Lemon*, Chief Justice Burger remarked, "Our prior rulings do not call for total separation between church and state. . . . Some relationship between government and religious organizations is inevitable." Adding to the confusion, *Lemon* came on the heals of the *Walz* ruling, decided a year earlier, which approved granting tax exemptions to religious institutions.[35] In his *Lemon* opinion, Chief Justice Burger cited *Walz* extensively, including its admonition against "sponsorship, financial support, and active involvement of the sovereign in religious activity." But isn't tax relief a form of indirect support?

Writing for the Court in *Walz*, Chief Justice Burger had rejected the idea of strict separation in favor of "benevolent neutrality." Urging the Court to treat religious institutions as it does other nonprofit institutions, Justice Harlan prescribed "an equal protection mode of analysis on the tax question." In yet another opinion Justice Brennan noted, "Government grants exemptions to religious organizations because they uniquely contribute to the pluralism of American society by their religious activities." *Walz* made the legal contortions rendered in response to divertibility concerns seem trite, but they continued. Education funding seemed to warrant special monitoring.

Nyquist was the third major Establishment Clause ruling handed down to enforce separation. Decided in 1973, it invalidated a New York law that offered an assortment of benefits to nonpublic schools and their students. The law granted funds for the maintenance and repair of school buildings, tuition allotments for low-income families, and tuition tax relief for more fortunate parents. It was passed at the behest of the Catholic lobby, which sought to rescue its parochial schools from a worsening financial predicament. Because the benefits provided by the law were made available only to students at nonpublic schools, the Court found that it violated the neutrality principle governing general benefit programs.[36] In a companion case, striking down a partial tuition reimbursement for private school students in Pennsylvania, the Court ruled that the program had the "impermissible effect of advancing religion" because it furnished "an incentive to parents to send their children to sectarian schools."[37] Both cases set important legal precedents; both were based on reasoning that was ridiculously flawed.

The benefits derived from the New York law were made available to religious and secular private schools (and their students). While it is true that the same benefits were not given to public schools and their students under the law in question, there would have been no reason to include them. New York State was already providing funding for the maintenance and repair of public schools under existing programs, and public school children receive their education free of tuition because of funding furnished by state and local governments. The reasoning in the Pennsylvania case is also ludicrous. The law in question relieved a small part of the financial burden parents assumed when they chose to send their children to a private or parochial school. Even if the law had paid the full tuition, it only would have equalized the financial burden that exists between the public and nonpublic school populations. That alone is not an incentive.

There are numerous reasons why parents who send their children to public school might prefer to transfer them to private or religious schools. Many parents don't because the existing funding arrangement, which limits financial support to children in public schools, gives them an incentive to stay where they are. To put it differently, the present funding arrangement is a disincentive against enrolling one's children in private and parochial schools. The arrangement is a practical obstacle for families who do not have the means to pay tuition on their own. As we have already seen, it can be a particular burden to people of faith.

In 1940, when Walter Gobitis of Minersville, Pennsylvania, refused to let his children salute the flag, they were expelled from public school. In 1986, when Vicki Frost of Hawkins County, Tennessee, refused to let her daughter read materials assigned in her public school, the school board told her to take it or leave it. The Supreme Court was not sympathetic to Gobitis's complaint that the expulsion created a financial burden to his practice of religion. His cause, however, was vindicated in 1943, when a Jehovah's Witness named Barnette persuaded the Supreme Court that conscientious objectors must be given the opportunity to opt out of an exercise that could offend their religious sensibilities.

Frost never even got a full hearing by the Supreme Court when she wanted to opt out. Barnette's attorney strengthened his legal argument against forced recital of the Pledge by aligning it with a free speech claim, on which the case was decided. Thereafter, other successful plaintiffs—like Steven Engle, Madalyn Murray O'Hair, the Schempps, Ismael Jaffree, the Weismans, and the anonymous Mr. Doe of Santa Fe—were able to wrap their cases against various forms of religious observances in public schools in the more potent Establishment Clause. Frost—like the students who sought released time for religious instruction in the *McCollum* case—was at a distinct disadvantage relying entirely on the Free Exercise Clause as a basis for her argument, which time and again proved to be a less powerful ally in Supreme Court litigation.

One should not be left with the impression that the Supreme Court was entirely consistent in its thinking on the First Amendment. While the "wall of separation" was raised to new heights through the 1970s and early 1980s, there were numerous inconsistencies in decisions that came down, especially on the school funding issue. In one case the Court disallowed a program that reimbursed parochial schools for administrative costs incurred for teacher-prepared achievement tests in compulsory subjects; in another it approved the reimbursement of similar costs for standardized tests. It prohibited state funding for staff and materials in auxiliary services such as counseling, guidance, and speech; but it permitted aid for diagnostic speech, hearing, and psychological testing. It ruled that while textbook loans are a legitimate benefit to children, loaning instructional equipment had "the unconstitutional primary effect of advancing religion."

Although states could offer students transportation to parochial schools, the states were not allowed to give the same students a ride to a park or museum. The Court also ruled that public school teachers could not furnish government-supported remedial services to disadvantaged students on the premises of parochial schools. A majority of justices affirmed without comment a lower-court finding that it is permissible to exclude religious school students from transportation services made available to their public school peers. While recognizing that these services were permitted under the Establishment Clause, the lower court had determined that the denial of the same services did not violate the free exercise rights of students in religious schools. It further concluded that the strict requirements of church-state separation contained in the Missouri constitution served as a "compelling state interest" mitigating "any possible infringement of the Free Exercise Clause."[38]

Walz remained the huge tax-exempt elephant in the courtroom that justices had difficulty seeing when it came to reviewing funding programs under the Establishment Clause. But the exceptional case of the decade was *Wisconsin v. Yoder*,[39] perhaps the most red-blooded free exercise decision in history. In a trial held in the Green County Court House in southern Wisconsin, Jonas Yoder, Wallace Miller, and Adin Yutzy had been found guilty of acting "against the peace and dignity of the State." Failing to send their children to high school, they had violated the state compulsory education law.

The three fathers in the *Yoder* case were members of the Old Order of Amish. The Amish are deeply religious people who live a simple life close to the soil. They do not use electricity and prefer horse-drawn carriages to automobiles. They live in self-contained communities and are easily identifiable today by their unusual dress. Resembling eighteenth-century farmers, men wear broad trousers, thick suspenders, and wide-brimmed hats. Women are seen donning long aprons, plain capes, and simple bonnets. Their wardrobe is worn as an expression of their humility and their faith.

Amish children receive their elementary education in one-room schoolhouses, which prepares them to read the Bible, work the farm, and be good citizens. The Amish do not have high schools, and believe that sending their children to public schools would corrupt their religious values, which require their isolation from the modern world. Prior to their trial, the defendants proposed adopting a vocational educational plan similar to those that had been negotiated by their brethren in other states to comply with compulsory education laws, but Wisconsin officials would not go along. The Amish are not by nature a contentious people, and certainly not litigious. But they felt strongly that the strict enforcement of Wisconsin's compulsory education law violated their free exercise rights protected by the United States Constitution. Six members of the Supreme Court agreed, with only one member dissenting.

Although the Court recognized the state's legitimate interest in promoting universal education, it found that the state's interest was not of sufficient magnitude to override the free exercise claim. Writing for the Court, Chief Justice Burger insisted that "only those interests of the highest order and those not otherwise served can overbalance legitimate claims of free exercise." The justices were impressed with the sincerity of the plaintiffs' beliefs, which they described as being "of deep religious conviction, shared by an organized group and intimately related to daily living." They reached back nine years to cite as precedent the *Sherbert* case, which had protected the unemployment rights of a Seventh-day Adventist who would not work on Saturday. Despite the Amish's unusual lifestyle, their commitment to hard work, family, God, and community were consistent with mainstream American values. These characteristics distinguished the Amish from the Mormons of the nineteenth century, who had defied American mores, not to mention fundamental precepts of Christianity.

As defined by *Yoder*, the Free Exercise Clause could have served as a powerful tool in the legal arsenal of religious minorities against the Establishment Clause claims of others. It could have been an equal partner, so to speak, in the contest for the Constitution. But it was never able to measure up to its more muscular First Amendment sibling in determining the scope of religious rights.

EQUALITY, NEUTRALITY, AND FREEDOM

President Ronald Reagan's selection of William Rehnquist as chief justice in 1986 signaled a change of thinking on the Court, if not the nation. Rehnquist never enjoyed so comfortable a majority among his colleagues that he was able to mold the First Amendment to his own liking, but he was successful at assembling a majority enough times to revisit questions that were once thought to be settled. These questions concerned the place of religion in public schools, funding to religious schools and students, and a host of other issues outside of education.

Rehnquist had telegraphed his overall perspective on religion, or at least the Establishment Clause, a year earlier in the dissent he wrote as an associate justice in the *Jaffree* case. There he challenged the validity of using the Jeffersonian metaphor "consititutionalized in *Everson*" as a standard for judicial review. To round out his position, he added that the *Lemon* test "has no basis in the history of the amendment it seeks to interpret, is difficult to apply, and yields unprincipled results." Notwithstanding his protestations concerning past precedents, throughout Rehnquist's nineteen-year tenure as chief justice First Amendment jurisprudence would continue to revolve around the Establishment Clause. Free exercise would appear as an occasional sidebar to the main story that began to unfold in the early 1980s.

While *McCollum* had determined once and for all that clergy members would not be permitted to offer religious instruction in public schools on a released-time basis, Congress was buzzing with proposed constitutional amendments that would undo the effects of the controversial prayer decisions. In 1983 two additional bills were under consideration that had to do with access rather than prayer.[40] The Religious Speech Protection Act, sponsored by Senator Mark Hatfield (R-Ore.) and Representative Don Bonker (D-Wash.) would make it unlawful for any public secondary school receiving federal funds to discriminate against students meeting during noninstructional periods solely on the basis of the religious content of their subject matter. The Equal Access Act sponsored by Senator Jeremiah Denton (R-Ala.) and Representative Trent Lott (R-Miss.) would have applied a similar restriction on all public elementary, secondary, and postsecondary schools, regardless of whether they received federal funds. It also entitled both faculty and students to engage in prayer, religious discussion, and silent meditation.

Two years earlier the Supreme Court ruled that when a state university opened its facilities to student organizations, it must grant the same access to religiously affiliated groups. The "limited open forum doctrine" enunciated in Widmar v. Vincent[41] defined an equal treatment standard with regard to religious groups, but notably did so on the basis of the Free Speech rather than the Free Exercise Clause. The equal access concept is designed to prohibit discrimination against students with a wide range of philosophical beliefs, but Widmar was a religion case. The aggrieved students belonged to the Christian Legal Society, and they wanted to be treated the same way as the Students for a Democratic Society, or the Young Socialist Alliance, or the Women's Union. In upholding their freedom-of-speech claim, the Court rejected the University of Missouri's assertion that the Establishment Clause barred it from treating religious groups equally in awarding benefits. In 1982, the Court demonstrated reluctance to take up the prayer question again, when it refused to hear two cases involving voluntary prayer in public schools.

Widmar did not address whether the limited public forum doctrine applied to elementary and secondary schools, whose students were generally assumed to be more impressionable and therefore in need of greater protection from religion. Before the equal access legislation was passed, four federal appeals courts ruled against student religious groups seeking similar protection in public schools. The bill brought opposition from all the usual places, including the American Civil Liberties Union, American Jewish Congress, American Jewish Committee, Americans United for the Separation of Church and State, and People for the American Way. The National Education Association and the National School Boards Association also raised concerns.

The equal access legislation also had significant support. The Baptist Joint Committee, which had opposed school prayer and aid to parochial schools, was a key proponent. It was joined by a wide array of religious groups that included fundamentalists (Moral Majority and Concerned Women for America), evangelicals (National Association of Evangelicals, Christian Legal Society, General Conference of Seventh-day Adventists), liberal Protestants (National Conference of Churches, as well as Presbyterians, Episcopalians, and Quakers), and the Catholic Conference. A compromise measure was sponsored by Representative Carl Perkins (D-Ky.), the powerful chair of the House Education and Labor Committee.

Perkins was a New Deal Democrat with a liberal legislative record who was a conservative Baptist religiously. At the suggestion of Harvard law professor Laurence Tribe, who testified before Congress, Perkins wrote the law so that it only covered public secondary schools receiving federal aid, and added language to include "political and philosophical" as well as religious content, thereby making it more neutral. As passage became imminent, a broad coalition of advocates and opponents was brought together to draft guidelines for the implementation of the law. They included the ACLU, teachers unions, school administrators, and Protestant groups. The American Jewish Congress, which opposed the measure until the very end, published its own guidelines. President Reagan signed the Equal Access Act (EAA) into law in the summer of 1984.[42] The next order of business was to get school boards to comply.

Bridget Mergens attended Westside Community High School in Omaha, Nebraska, and she wanted to start a Bible club. The principal, superintendent, and school board in Westside denied Bridget and her friends permission. While the officials were willing to permit the students to meet on an informal basis, they refused to recognize the group as an official school club, claiming that there were no other noncurricular clubs at the school. There were other student clubs at the school, but school officials insisted that they were connected to the instructional curriculum. For example, they claimed, the chess club promoted logic and strategic thinking, the scuba diving club was part of physical education, and the photography, business, and honors society clubs were connected to various aspects of instruction. The school district won at the federal trial level; then the ruling was reversed by the circuit court of appeals. In 1990, the Supreme Court upheld the appeals ruling by eight to one, with Justice Stevens being the lone dissenter.

As with most cases that come before the High Court, *Mergens* was not simply a dispute between a local group and a government agency. It was the latest scene for a larger national debate about the proper place of religion in public schools. *Amicus* briefs were filed by the usual lineup of advocates that had been fighting the culture wars, the same that had participated in congressional debate over the EAA legislation. On one side were the Anti-Defamation League, the ACLU, the National School Boards Association, and People for the American Way; on the other side stood the Baptist Joint Committee, Christian Legal Society, National Association of Evangelicals, and U.S. Catholic Conference. Representing the administration of President George H. W. Bush was Solicitor General Kenneth Starr.

The *Mergens*[43] decision addressed the meaning of the Equal Access Act, its constitutionality, and its applicability to the facts in Westside High School. The Court agreed that the legislative intent of the act was to incorporate the logic of *Widmar* into law, and to address a perceived problem of widespread discrimination against religious speech in public schools. Conceding that Congress intended a low threshold for triggering the protections of the law, the Court defined the term "curriculum related" to mean an activity that is specifically taught in required coursework or results in academic credit. Relying heavily on the free speech claims of the students, the Court determined that the school's offer to allow them to meet informally had not satisfied the requirements of the statutory mandate.

Writing for a plurality, Justice O'Connor responded to the Establishment Clause concerns of school officials by declaring that the law in question had a "secular purpose," and did not have the primary effect of "advancing religion." Nor, she continued, would the actions required "convey the message that religion or a particular religious belief is favored or preferred." The plurality also rejected the district's reliance on the fact that school is compulsory and students are impressionable, stating that the high school students are "mature enough . . . to understand that a school does not endorse or support student speech that it merely permits on a nondiscriminatory basis."

Justice Kennedy, joined by Justice Scalia, filed his own concurring opinion, differing with Justice O'Connor's "endorsement standard" in favor of a more permissive test. As he saw it, the First Amendment precludes any government action that either gives direct benefits to religion to such a degree that it establishes "a state religion," or coerces a student to engage in a religious activity. Measuring Free Speech and Establishment Clause protections side by side, Justice Marshall filed a concurring opinion, signed by Justice Brennan, in which he issued a warning about the general application of the legislation in question, and the need to carefully review the specific nature of the limited open forum at a particular school before enforcing it.

In 1993 the Supreme Court ever so slightly extended the protections afforded religious expression under the Free Speech Clause, deciding that a public school district in New York must permit the pastor of the Lamb's Chapel Evangelical Church to use its facilities after school hours to show a religious film series. The district had customarily opened its doors for a wide range of "social, civic and recreational" events, but it had a policy against using its premises for religious purposes. Dr. James Dobson, the pastor, was also president of Focus on the Family, the politically active conservative organization that was instrumental in the passage of the EAA. (Dr. Dobson would gain national notoriety years later when he got involved in a raucous controversy over a cartoon character called SpongeBob SquarePants, which he accused of being used to promote homosexuality.) Since Dobson was not a student at the school, the EAA protections did not apply to his legal challenge on Long Island.

The Lamb's Chapel[44] case brought amicus briefs from the usual cast of secularist organizations, and a smaller number of religious organizations. A unanimous Court found that Dobson's exclusion was a form of "viewpoint discrimination" in violation of the Free Speech Clause. The film series in question, while Christian in orientation, conveyed the "profamily" message of Dobson's national organization. It was offered to the general public free of charge once per week over a period of five weeks. The Court was persuaded that Dobson's series—Turn Your Heart Toward Home—was comparable to other value-based programs the district had permitted, demonstrating that the district policy lacked neutrality. Among the other programs was a lecture series sponsored by the "Mind Center," which purportedly was a New Age religious group.

In 2001, the Court held six-to-three that another New York district had violated the free speech rights of the Good News Club when it would not allow the group to meet in its school facilities after school.[45] The club, a Christian organization, brought together children aged six to twelve for "a fun time of singing songs, hearing a Bible lesson, and memorizing scripture." Milford Central School officials had determined that the activities were a form of worship disallowed by the Establishment Clause, but the High Court disagreed. From *Widmar* through the present, the only thing more remarkable than the way the Supreme Court embraced the Free Speech Clause to hold off Establishment Clause claims is that it did so with little consideration of the Free Exercise Clause.

EQUALITY, NEUTRALITY, AND FREEDOM (CONTINUED)

The wall of separation began to show signs of perforation on the funding issue with the *Mueller*[46] decision of 1983, which approved a Minnesota law that granted tax deductions for education expenses incurred for tuition, textbooks, or transportation. Writing for the Court, Associate Justice Rehnquist distinguished this case from the facts in *Nyquist* by noting that the tax relief was made available to all families, including those with children in public schools. He addressed the "primary effect" challenge by observing that because "aid to parochial schools is only as a result of decisions of individual parents, no 'imprimatur of state approval' can be deemed to have been conferred on any particular religion or on religion generally." In this way Rehnquist also revitalized the child benefit concept that distinguishes between direct aid to schools and indirect aid.

There was a certain consistency between the Court's position on funding and the emerging public forum doctrine: So long as citizen interaction with religion is a voluntary matter of personal choice, and the state acts in a neutral fashion so as to not favor any one religion or religion in general, a program does not present an Establishment

Clause problem. The *Mueller* Court approved the Minnesota program while recognizing that 96 percent of the private school beneficiaries attended Catholic schools, further distancing itself from concerns raised in *Nyquist*. Justice Rehnquist once again took the opportunity to diminish the significance of the *Lemon* test, referring to it as "no more than a helpful signpost" in reviewing Establishment Clause challenges. During the same term, the Court upheld Nebraska's longtime practice of paying a chaplain (the same Presbyterian minister for sixteen years) to open its legislative sessions with a prayer. Putting aside concerns for secular or religious minorities who might be offended by the custom, the majority described the practice as a "tolerable acknowledgement of beliefs widely held among the people of this country."[47]

While the beneficiaries of the Minnesota program were predominantly Catholic, there was a significant realignment of political forces occurring on the aid issue nationally. President Ronald Reagan's championing of school vouchers had much to do with evangelical Christians who once opposed aid to religious schools and were now supporting it emphatically. The secularization of the public schools had prompted some religious people to flee public education and establish their own Christian academies.

Between 1961 and 1983, the number of Christian academies in the United States grew from 300 to 10,740. Enrollment at these schools increased between 1965 and 1982 from 110,000 students to more than 900,000. During the same period Catholic school enrollments dropped almost by half, declining from 5.6 million to 3 million. By 1985, 20 percent of the nonpublic school population—one million students in all—attended Christian academies. Their size being very small, the total number of Christian academies exceeded Catholic schools by 1,300 in 1984.[48] Public schools still accounted for 90 percent of the student enrollment, as they do today.

As registration at Christian schools grew through the 1970s, the American Association of Christian Schools (1972) and the Association of Christian Schools International (1978) were founded to lobby on their behalf. A 1980 survey of parents whose children attended these schools showed that they were as much attracted to these institutions for their basic curriculum, firm discipline, and moral values as they were for specific religious teaching.[49] Through the 1980s, as fundamentalists captured control of the Southern Baptist Convention, they split off from the Baptist Joint Committee, with whom they formerly stood on church-state separation. They, along with the National Association of Evangelicals, became a key part of the Christian Coalition assembled by Pat Robertson and Ralph Reed to capture the heart of the Republican Party, if not the country.[50]

In 1986 the Supreme Court unanimously approved a Washington program that permitted a blind student to use a public scholarship at a Bible college.[51] In a concurring opinion Justice Powell, the author of *Nyquist*, used the occasion to outline an emerging set of standards that was moving the Court in a more accommodationist direction. According to the guidelines, a program passes constitutional muster if (1) it is facially neutral regarding religion, (2) funds are made equally available to students in public and nonpublic schools, (3) any aid flowing to religious schools results from the private decisions of individuals. The opinion was cosigned by Chief Justice Burger and Justice Rehnquist.

The *Witters* decision is also notable because in it the Court left the door open for a separate state-level review on the basis of state constitutional law. Previously, the Washington supreme court had struck down the statute on the basis of the Establishment Clause of the First Amendment and its own state constitutional requirements for the separation of church and state, which were deemed to be more restrictive than the standards being applied by the United States Supreme Court. In *Witters*, the High Court only ruled on the First Amendment question, and left it to the state court to enforce its own standards. This was a concession in the federal balance of jurisdiction. Since the vast majority of states, like Washington, have prohibitive "Blaine amendment" provisions that were added to their constitutions in the nineteenth century, *Witters* meant that legal battles won by aid proponents in the federal courts could be fought again in the states.[52]

Two years later, the Court applied the three-part "*Lemon* test" to approve the Adolescent Family Act of 1982.[53] The law made grants available to public and nonprofit organizations for premarital counseling on sexual relations and pregnancy. There was no exclusion of religiously affiliated organizations from participation in the law; in fact, the congressional expectation was to the contrary. The majority in *Bowen* remanded the case back to the federal district court that originally found the act unconstitutional in order to determine whether specific grantees were using the funds to advance religion. As in the school cases, however, the Court was unwilling to categorically disqualify religious institutions from participation. Chief Justice Rehnquist explained for the majority, "This Court has never held that religious institutions are disabled by the First Amendment from participating in publicly sponsored social welfare programs." Unless otherwise proven in particular incidences, any aid derived by religious institutions would be treated as secondary and incidental.

The ruling provoked a spirited dissent by Justice Blackmun, signed by three other justices. While agreeing that religious institutions should not be routinely excluded from general benefit programs, he held that the program presented unusual risks because the message conveyed by some providers would be religious. As he put it, "There is a very real and important difference between running a soup kitchen or a hospital, and counseling pregnant teenagers on how to make difficult decisions facing them." Both the majority and dissenting opinions in *Bowen* are of special relevance to the more recent initiative by President George W. Bush to funnel federal funding to faith-based institutions for the delivery of social services. We will return to these considerations in a later chapter.

Through the end of the decade the Court continued to hand down decisions that seemed to push back the boundaries of separation on school funding. Interpreting the Establishment Clause in *Zobrest*,[54] the Court approved the assignment of a publicly funded sign language instructor for a student in a religious school. In the *Rosenberger* case[55] the Court juxtaposed the Free Speech and Establishment clauses, telling the University of Virginia that to withhold student activity fees from a student newspaper with a religious message was a form of "viewpoint discrimination." Quoting *Mergens*, Justice Kennedy renewed the distinction "between *government* speech endorsing religion, which the Establishment Clause forbids, and *private* speech endorsing religion, which the Free Speech and Free Exercise Clause protect."

Justice Thomas issued a concurring opinion in *Rosenberger* assessing the general state of First Amendment jurisprudence, which he characterized as being in "hopeless disarray." Citing *Walz*, he pointed to the absurdity of a situation in which the Court agonizes over aid to religious schools when it offers tax exemptions to the same institutions. He explained, "A tax exemption in many cases is economically and functionally indistinguishable from a direct government subsidy. . . . Whether the benefit is provided at the front or back end of the taxation process, the financial aid to religious groups is undeniable."

The Court also directly overturned two long-standing precedents. In *Agostini* [56] it removed a barrier that prevented poor children at parochial schools from receiving remedial instruction from public school teachers paid with federal funds. In the *Mitchell* case[57] it permitted religious schools to share direct federal assistance in the form of library, media, and computer materials. Writing for the Court in the earlier case, Justice O'Connor placed a great deal of emphasis on the supplementary nature of the aid in question, again ignoring the *Walz* dilemma. Writing for a four-person plurality in *Mitchell*, Justice Thomas sought to finally reconcile the doctrinal conflicts he identified in *Rosenberger* by introducing neutrality as the primary standard for reviewing aid. This proposition drew a sharp response from Justice O'Connor, whose concurring opinion in *Mitchell* raised considerations concerning divertibility, choice, the supplementary nature of the aid, and the indirect flow of funds to religious institutions—none of which dealt with *Walz* satisfactorily.

The most heralded aid case of the generation was *Zelman v. Simmons-Harris*,[58] which in 2002 approved a school voucher program in Cleveland, Ohio. Like the voucher programs that had been enacted in Wisconsin, Florida, Colorado, and the District of Columbia, the Ohio program had been designed to create opportunities for low-income children to escape failing public schools. Because the great majority of the schools the children with vouchers attended were religious schools, the program triggered a suit by the local teachers union, joined by the usual alignment of separationist and secular organizations. As the dueling sides gave oral testimony on a sunny day in February, a crowd of mostly black parents and children stood across the street from the Supreme Court building in Washington, holding signs and chanting freedom songs. One sign carried by a small boy said, "My Parents Should Choose My School." Another carried by a young mother read, "Choice is Widespread Unless You Are Poor."

The episode portrayed a new political reality. The constituency for aid to private and religious schools had expanded to include the children of the poor, most of whom were African-American or Hispanic. This would infuse the child benefit concept with the juice of social justice. National polls were showing strong support for school choice in minority communities, where attachments to local churches snuffed out demands for church-state separation. In neighborhoods where public schools had failed generations of students, the church was the center of political, social, and family life. Suddenly the anxieties of white liberal separationists seemed misplaced.[59] A bad education would do more harm to children than religion could. Voucher proponents had begun to take the high moral ground; theirs could no longer be portrayed as a right-wing cause promulgated by malcontents who were obsessed with a narrow religious agenda.

In each locality where a voucher program was enacted, it resulted from a political marriage of convenience between minority advocates, business leaders, and Republican politicians.[60] In Wisconsin, Ohio, and the District of Columbia strong voices were heard from the African-American community. In Florida and Colorado demands for choice were communicated in Spanish. In Wisconsin, an African-American mother named Polly Williams, who had been on welfare and became a Democratic member of the state legislature, aligned herself with Republican governor Tommy Thompson. In Ohio, a black grandmother and city council member from Cleveland named Fannie Lewis lined up her support with Republican governor George Voinovich. Fannie was in the courtroom the day that *Zelman* was argued and, encouraged by the interaction that transpired between the justices and attorneys, emerged from the building announcing to her allies, "We won!" In the District of Columbia, Mayor Anthony Williams, joined by the president of the city school board and the chair of the city council education committee—all black Democrats—broke ranks with Senator Ted Kennedy and other leading Democrats who tried to thwart the D.C voucher bill in Congress. Their leading Republican ally, who eventually signed the bill into law, was President George W. Bush.

Chief Justice Rehnquist wrote the five-to-four opinion in *Zelman*. According to the Court's reasoning, the Cleveland voucher program was upheld because it (1) has a valid secular purpose of providing educational assistance to poor children; (2) is neutral with respect to religion and provides assistance to a broad class of citizens; and (3) provides aid to religious institutions only as a result of independent decisions made by the parents of schoolchildren participating in program.[61] The chief justice further explained that the ruling was consistent with a line of judicial reasoning dating back to 1983, when *Mueller* approved tuition tax deductions in Minnesota. Citing *Walz* extensively, Justice O'Connor took a broader view of First Amendment jurisprudence, offering explicit examples of how the majority ruling was consistent with case law that allowed tax exemptions and other forms of government aid for religious institutions.

In a dissenting opinion, Justice Souter declared that the Cleveland program violated the long-standing constitutional requirement of church-state separation set forth in *Everson*. Citing Jefferson and Madison, he then proceeded with an incisive analysis of how the Court had gradually abandoned principles that had governed its thinking since 1947. Also citing the two Virginia sages, and echoing the claims registered by Justice Black in his *Allen* dissent, Justices Stevens and Breyer wrote separate opinions warning that any policy that compromised the wall of separation erected in *Everson* increased the risk of religious strife and conflict, which could shred the social fabric of American democracy. Justice Breyer insisted that as the country becomes more socially and religiously diverse, the risks of not enforcing strict separation are even greater than they were at the founding. Justices Stevens and Breyer have more recently drawn a connection between enforcing the religion clauses and avoidance of civil strife in the Ten Commandments cases of 2005, but with different effect for Justice Breyer, who took a more accommodationist position in *Van Orden*.

Despite the sea change in constitutional thinking since *Everson*, the Court's inattention to the Free Exercise Clause as a basis for enforcing First Amendment rights had serious implications for religious minorities. The judicial shift that had taken place since *Everson* merely set down what was permissible under the Establishment Clause. It did not broaden the range of protections afforded religious observers in the way that the Fourteenth Amendment had done with regard to other protected minorities. There were only two significant Free Exercise cases decided in the last decade of the twentieth century. Neither approached the sweep of freedoms afforded to the Amish in the *Yoder* case or those enunciated in *Sherbert*, which protected a Seventh-day Adventist's unemployment rights because she demonstrated to the Court that her religion did not allow her to work on Saturday.

The *Smith*[62] ruling of 1990 was actually a retreat from the robust reading of the Free Exercise Clause that was evident in *Yoder* and *Sherbert*. In *Smith* two employees of the State of Oregon were disciplined for using peyote, a controlled substance. The two workers, who were members of the Native American Church, claimed that the use of the drug was part of a religious ritual protected by the First Amendment. The Supreme Court found that the religious significance of the drug use was inconsequential so long as the law in question was not "an attempt to regulate religious beliefs, the communication of religious beliefs, or the raising of one's children in those beliefs." Given the facts of the case, this was arguably a sound decision. However, the governing principles laid down by Justice Scalia for the Court could have far-reaching consequences beyond *Smith*.

Under *Smith*, the government is not required to demonstrate that a "generally applicable" law promotes a compelling public interest, even if it makes the practice of religion impossible. *Smith* confers broad discretion to the will of political majorities in the face of free exercise claims by religious minorities, which Justice Scalia referred to as "an unavoidable consequence of democratic government." This interpretation diminishes the role that the Founders set for the judicial branch, which was to apply the Constitution to protect rights of minorities that are undermined by majorities.

The Court further clarified *Smith* three years later, when it supported the claim of the Church of Lakumi Babalu Aye.[63] Its members had violated ordinances by the City of Hialeah, Florida, which restricted the slaughter of animals. As part of the Santeria religion, the church ritualistically engaged in animal sacrifice. The ordinances were adopted by the city council in response to citizen complaints about the behavior of the Santerians. In writing for the Court, Justice Kennedy acknowledged that the city did not have to demonstrate a compelling public interest to enforce a neutral law of general applicability, but found that the law lacked neutrality because it specifically targeted the religious practices of one particular group. Given the cruelty of the actions in question, the merits of the decision are persuasive from a policy perspective. The point here is that it did not restore the Free Exercise Clause as an equal partner in the range of protections Americans take for granted under the Bill of Rights.

Congress responded to the *Smith* ruling with the passage of the Religious Freedom Restoration Act (RFRA), which President Bill Clinton signed into law in 1993. Stating that the Framers of the Constitution had recognized the free exercise of religion as "an inalienable right," the law prohibited government from "substantially burdening" a person's free exercise rights, even under the provisions of a generally applicable law, unless the government could demonstrate that the burden furthers a compelling governmental interest. Legislators and the president sought to restore a level of legal protection for religious rights statutorily that the judiciary had removed constitutionally in *Smith*. The Supreme Court would have none of this. In 1997 a six-to-three majority declared that the RFRA exceeded congressional power under the Fourteenth Amendment to enact legislation enforcing the Free Exercise Clause.[64] It ruled that while Congress can enforce federal rights incorporated by the Fourteenth Amendment, it does not have the power to create or expand constitutional rights.

The limits of the *Zelman* school voucher ruling became crystal clear in 2004, after Joshua Davey was told by authorities in Washington that his state scholarship was withdrawn because he wanted to use it to study for the ministry. Northwest College is an accredited Christian school, where Davey planned to pursue a joint major in pastoral studies and business administration. The Washington Higher Education Coordinating Board (HECB) and the Washington State supreme court agreed that if Davey used the public scholarship to study for the ministry, he would violate the Blaine amendment in the state constitution and a number of laws and regulations enacted to enforce its provisions. Washington's Blaine amendment can be traced directly to the bigoted anti-Catholic campaign launched in the nineteenth century by Congressman Blaine himself.[65] It was one of the states required by Congress to incorporate a similar provision in its constitution as a condition for statehood. Davey claimed that the prohibition violated his rights protected under the Free Exercise, Free Speech, and Equal Protection clauses of the Constitution. In a seven-to-two opinion written by Chief Justice Rehnquist, the Supreme Court disagreed.[66]

As Justice Rehnquist explained it, "This case involves a 'play in the joints'" that exists between the Establishment Clause and the Free Exercise Clause. (The free speech claim was dismissed.) Therefore, while the Constitution would allow the state to grant Davey his request, it did not require it. To put it differently, the state of Washington was allowed to define religious freedom more narrowly than it is defined in the American Constitution. The *Davey* case presented the Court with an opportunity to correct the jurisdictional imbalance fostered by *Witters*, but it took a pass. As the Court saw it, "Here the State's disfavor of religion (if it can be called that) is of a milder kind than in *Lakumi*." Davey was not prevented from attending an accredited Bible school or taking Bible courses with his scholarship; he was just not able to use the state scholarship to prepare for a career in the ministry. In a footnote, Chief Justice Rehnquist made reference to Thomas Jefferson's "Bill for Religious Liberty," and noted the particular relevance of James Madison's famous "Memorial and Remonstrance" against a proposed Virginia law that would have paid for the training of Christian ministers.

Once again we are faced with the prospect of applying eighteenth-century state standards (specifically Virginia's) to the American Constitution of the twenty-first century, but there are larger issues. With regard to Davey's case, we might begin by noting that according to the Supremacy Clause of the United States Constitution, federal law prevails over state law when the two are in conflict. While states have the authority to interpret their own constitutions under this arrangement, a central goal of the American civil rights movement and its incorporation of the individual protections through the Due Process Clause was to insure that fundamental rights could not be compromised by the states. Federal courts also have been fairly aggressive in using the Fourteenth Amendment to guarantee the rights of a diverse population of protected minorities—defined by race, gender, sexual orientation, disability, and even language.[67] Aside from the case of gays, these protections were statutorily fortified by acts of Congress that guarded against discrimination except in instances where a compelling governmental interest is at stake. They have been effective.

The *Davey* case was a stark reminder of the unique place religion holds in the lexicon of American civil rights. It is the only right for which a counterclaim exists in the very article of the Constitution that is supposed to protect it, a freedom from, as well as a freedom of, that over the past half century has been given priority by the courts in legal clashes that involve the two religion clauses.[68] There is no comparable freedom from the press, or freedom from speech, or freedom from a fair trial articulated in the document itself, pitched to weaken the foundation of the basic liberties enumerated.

This constitutional anomaly raises basic questions regarding the nature of religious freedom in America. Is the room "between the joints" of the two First Amendment clauses a place that furnishes government, at any level, with grounds for discrimination on the basis of religion? Could this have been what the Founders had in mind when they set out to define religious freedom in the new republic?

7

AGELESS WISDOM

It seems implausible: that soon after Congress voted to enact the First Amendment, it asked President George Washington to set aside a national day of "thanksgiving and prayer"; or that the same Congress initiated the practice of starting each legislative session with a prayer, and passed legislation to hire chaplains for the House and the Senate. The same Congress also reenacted the Northwest Ordinance, declaring that "religion, morality, and knowledge being necessary for good government . . . schools and the means of education shall forever be encouraged."

The language for the ordinance had been taken from the Massachusetts Constitution of 1780, drafted by John Adams, our second president, and it was copied into the New Hampshire Constitution of 1784. Of the original thirteen states, eleven restricted office holding to Christians, or more precisely Protestants. Delaware, South Carolina, and Georgia abandoned the restriction by 1789, and Pennsylvania modified its policy to exclude only atheists.

How did the founding generation actually view religion? Why should we care?

Let's take the easier question first. There are many reasons why we should care about what the Founders thought. Beyond historical curiosity—and a thriving fascination that Americans have with the founding generation[1]—there is the constitutional question of original intent. Legal scholars disagree over the extent to which the original thinking behind the document should serve as a guide for contemporary interpretation. On the one hand, constitutions are supposed to embody fundamental principles that shape the government and its relationship to the governed in perpetuity. On the other hand, it is not always practical to apply the thinking of the eighteenth century to the circumstances of the twentieth or the twenty-first.

For the past sixty years, many of our First Amendment squabbles have been over education; but, except for using it as a tool to "civilize" the native population, education at the time of the founding was not widely perceived as a governmental function. So religion's place in education was not a central constitutional concern. Nevertheless, if there is one thought that contemporary separationists and accommodationists share, it is that the Founders are on their side.

It is hard to avoid the contention of one's fidelity to "original intent" when considering matters that arise in a book of this sort, and those who have gotten this far in the reading might already surmise where I stand on it. That being said, I should confess that I am drawn to the Founders less as a source for resolving the precedent or intent debates than for their sheer wisdom on the subject at hand. This is not to suggest that there was universal agreement among the members of that august generation on matters of church and state, or that the thinking of any one individual was consistent over time. Nevertheless, their reflections can be enormously helpful in framing the questions that bog us down.

As we have seen, the writings of Thomas Jefferson and James Madison figure largely in the present constitutional battles, so a fuller understanding of the period in which they lived and the role religion played in it can be helpful. We also need to understand that American history is not synonymous with the history of Virginia. Each state, each region, had its own political and religious orientation that colored its approach to religious freedom.[2]

The New England colonies were dominated by the Puritans. Their landing in Boston harbor in 1630 following the earlier settling of Plymouth marks the original irony in American church-state relations. The Puritans had fled England to escape religious persecution by the Anglican establishment. After they arrived, they proceeded to set up the most faith-based government ever to appear on American soil, with little tolerance for dissent.

The leaders of the Massachusetts Bay Company believed they were the chosen people who had entered into a holy covenant with God to form a Christian state in the New World—more pure and true than the one they left behind. Their charter granted them wide latitude to act beyond the reach of royal authority. When Governor John Winthrop imagined his "City Upon a Hill," he thought he was on a divinely inspired mission. The Congregational Church became the official religion. Only its members could hold office. Catholics, Baptists, Quakers, and old church Anglicans were not warmly received. Religious dissenters were often jailed, beaten, or hanged.

The revised charter granted to Massachusetts in 1692 guaranteed religious freedom to all Protestants. As a result, the General Court required each town within the Bay Colony to choose its own church supported by local taxes. Town voters would select their own ministers, allowing for a decentralized, highly democratic government of sorts. In theory, any Protestant denomination could establish a locally governed church. Practically speaking, Congregationalists continued to control political and religious affairs, and nonmembers were required to contribute to the church in the towns where they lived. Even the religious revival kindled in the 1740s by dissidents like Jonathan Edwards did not shake Congregationalist dominance in Massachusetts, or the rest of New England for that matter.

Connecticut and New Hampshire followed the general pattern that prevailed in Massachusetts. While Protestant dissenters managed to control a few towns in the Bay Colony, Connecticut was even more uniformly Congregational. It was the only state in the union to maintain a preferred church after independence. New Hampshire from the outset exempted Anglicans, Baptists, Presbyterians, and Quakers from paying to support the locally established Congregationalist churches. Rhode Island was the great exception in New England, founded in 1636 by Roger Williams after he was driven from Massachusetts for his inflammatory remarks about religious freedom.[3]

Williams welcomed people of all faiths to his new settlement. Rhode Island became a safe haven for Baptists and Quakers, who had been regularly persecuted elsewhere. Its charter of 1663 was the first to use the term *liberty of conscience*. Long before Jefferson, Roger Williams promised to erect a "wall of separation between the garden of the church and the wilderness of the world."[4] Like Jefferson, he understood that joining the religious and governmental spheres was unhealthy for both, but Williams's emphasis was different. While Jefferson was more concerned with protecting the state from interference by the church, Williams was focused on protecting the church from the power of the state. Williams may have preceded Jefferson in time, but in the American constitutional order the emphasis eventually shifted, though somewhat artificially, with the enshrinement of Jefferson's frequently quoted words.

Unlike the Puritans, the members of the London Company of Virginia who settled Chesapeake Bay in 1607 were not dissenters from the Church of England. The charge they accepted from King James was to transplant Anglicanism to the New World. Their charter required ministers to teach the gospel as it was professed in the mother country, for whose support everyone was tithed. Governor Thomas Gates used the established church as an arm of the state, conspicuously participating in services and issuing orders about the proper observance of religion, which was treated as a civic duty. Like their neighbors to the north, the original settlers in Jamestown showed little tolerance for religious dissent. In England, religious differences had led to civil war and bloodshed. There was no place for that in the New World. Baptists, Catholics, and Quakers were especially singled out for their propensity towards disloyalty, and were dealt with harshly.

When the London Company surrendered its charter in 1624, Virginia became a royal colony with an appointed governor who had the power to review the credentials of any clergyman who wished to serve. Religious teaching was expected to follow the Thirty-Nine Articles of the Church of England. In 1662 the legislature determined that the governance of each parish would be put in the hands of a local vestry— twelve laymen empowered to hire the parish minister and run the business affairs of the church. These same men were also active in politics and loyal to the Crown, assuring close ties between church and state.

Distracted by the tobacco crop and hopes of prosperity, however, the Virginians were never so devout as the Congregationalists of New England. An elite class of gentlemen planters started to emerge. As the reach of the colony outpaced that of the established church and its active clergy, Presbyterians, Baptists, and Methodists began to fill the void, clustering in the mountains of the western backcountry. By the middle of the eighteenth century, religious diversification was coming about in Virginia as a matter of practice if not policy. The evangelical revival that had sprouted up in New England and worked its way through the Middle Colonies had finally reached the South, where its influence was more profound. Its passion and innate egalitarianism had a more natural appeal for commoners than the stiff hierarchy of the Anglican establishment.

Virginia served as a rough model of Anglican establishment for the rest of the South. Maryland had originally been founded by Catholic dissenters as a refuge from religious persecution, but after 1689 the Protestant majority anointed the Church of England the official church. The Carolinas had originally been founded with the assistance of English philosopher John Locke and the intention of fostering a more tolerant society. By the early eighteenth century, it fell into the pattern of Anglican establishment practiced by its southern neighbors. Georgia, settled in 1732, was the last of the original thirteen British colonies to come into being. By then the Anglican hold on the souls of American colonists was loosening. In order to attract immigrants to the far reaches of its boarders and stave off Spanish Catholics who occupied Florida, Georgia's trustees guaranteed religious freedom to all Protestants. They also welcomed Jews, who congregated in Savannah; but discrimination against Catholics continued openly.

While historians consistently gravitate to New England and Virginia to reconstruct the origins of American religion, it is perhaps the experience of the Middle Colonies that offers the most telling lessons for understanding the idea of religious freedom at the time of the founding. When the English conquered New Amsterdam in 1664, the Dutch Reformed Church had already been given official recognition by the government, so British authorities had a stake in disestablishment. Given Holland's more lax attitude towards religious conformity, and the diverse population already inhabiting New York, the idea of an established church never took hold.

Under the "Duke's Laws," every town in New York was required to support a Protestant church of its choice. But unlike New England, where one particular group prevailed, the mixed social structure of New York produced a system of multiple establishments, which allowed Presbyterians, Methodists, Lutherans, Quakers, and Baptists to gain a foothold. Even Catholics and Jews were making an early appearance on Manhattan Island.

From time to time, through the end of the seventeenth century, various royal governors in New York attempted to impose an establishment under the cope of the Episcopal Church. But demographic realities and more permissive attitudes towards religion did not permit it. Some towns actually had more than one established church, each supported by the taxes of its own members. New Jersey, which came under the influence of Scotch Presbyterians, also attracted a wide array of people of various faiths, leading to a more liberal system of toleration than that found in New York. The rule there was to have no establishment of religion on any level.

Taken in its entirety, but with particular reference to the middle regions, the history of the American colonies suggested that if intolerance would slow the way to religious pluralism, then the practical reality of religious pluralism eventually would force a greater tolerance—at least to a point. Religious inclusion rarely exceeded the boundaries of Protestant Christianity in its multiple pedigrees. William Penn's "Holy Experiment" was a notable exception. Although Penn founded Pennsylvania, and later Delaware, as a political sanctuary for Quakers, he hoped that people of all religious persuasions would be able to live peacefully together in the "City of Brotherly Love," free from government interference. But diversification also led to conflict. Even the peaceful members of the Friends Society, in firm command of the Pennsylvania legislature, were not above internecine fighting on matters of faith and politics. They eventually were able to agree on a law that excluded Catholics, Jews, and nonbelievers from political life.

Herein lies the paradox that faced the Founders as they went about the task of forming a government. The same pluralism that forced a wider accommodation to new groups also begot conflict. How could the flame of religious freedom be contained so that it did not ignite the fuel of religious animosity? Whatever the American Constitution meant at the federal level, it was not designed to interfere with the church-state arrangements that had been operable in the states, which, in the early years of the young republic, more clearly defined the temper of public life. God and religion remained ever present, but there was also a widening scope of religious freedom that accompanied the revolution. The overthrow of British rule had a particularly devastating effect on Anglicanism, which was closely identified with the Crown.

Immediately after the signing of the Declaration of Independence, North Carolina, South Carolina, Georgia, and New York adopted constitutions that eliminated the Anglican establishment and any preferential treatment given to the Church of England. Virginia passed a bill of rights that exempted some dissenters from supporting the Anglican Church, and Maryland recognized the right of all Christian churches to be supported with tax money. By 1789, every state except Connecticut adopted a constitutional provision protecting religious freedom. Maryland and Delaware, however, specifically confined this right to Christians. Massachusetts, New Hampshire, New Jersey, Pennsylvania, and North Carolina did not extend it to atheists or nonbelievers. Vermont, which in 1891 became the fourteenth state to join the union, guaranteed freedom of conscience, yet insisted that every Christian sect must support some form of worship.

Through the end of the eighteenth century the local option system of tax support for churches prevailed in New England and the South. At the time the First Amendment was ratified, seven states authorized the use of local taxes for worship, with the privilege extended exclusively to either Protestants or Christians. Jews were so few in number that they rarely attracted much attention. In places where they congregated, like Savannah and Charleston, Jews were neither allowed to assign tax dollars for their own religious purposes, nor expected to contribute to Christian congregations. Muslims, Hindus, and those who followed other Eastern traditions were rare to nonexistent. Laws enforcing the Christian Sabbath were common throughout the states. Blasphemy and profanity were punished. An individual who was not a Christian in good standing, and preferably a Protestant, could be subject to numerous civic disadvantages with regard to voting, office holding, or jury membership.

This is the world that the founding generation had inherited: Religion was ingrained in the American civic consciousness,[5] to the point of being more or less oppressive at certain times and places, often at the whim of popular majorities, against the will of resentful minorities. There was also a growing spirit of liberty: on the one hand spread by a religious awakening that challenged established beliefs; on the other, nourished by political ideas transposed from the European continent that inspired men of knowledge to create a new governmental order.

Enlightened Minds

The European Enlightenment was constructed around a fundamental belief, a belief in the power of the human mind to resolve the mysteries of life and advance civilization to a higher level. In England, Francis

Bacon posited the idea that reason could provide a more reliable path to human discovery than either faith or inspirational revelation. Rather than rely on abstract premises, the New Learning was to proceed on the basis of empirical observation—a scientific method of investigation in which laws of nature could be induced from the accumulation of hard data, the classification of information, and the repetition of experiments.

Isaac Newton's elaborate scientific inquiries into the laws of motion and gravity, expressed in mathematical formulations, would explain an exquisite natural order. But instead of enlisting reason as a tool for rejecting the existence of God, Newton was convinced that the "clockwork universe" he had discovered was evidentiary proof of a "primordial architect" who is an "intelligent and powerful being." For him, reason and religion were compatible, in fact complementary.

Newton's work would inspire social philosophers to search for natural laws of politics through the study of history. If scientific knowledge could help man manage the physical universe, then an understanding of politics and history could be used to develop a sophisticated statecraft for fashioning a better democracy. No political writer exerted more influence over the founding generation than John Locke.[6] His theory of natural rights had an especially profound effect on the thinking of Thomas Jefferson and James Madison. Locke had witnessed the religious strife that divided England and the rest of Europe through the seventeenth century. His first reaction to the turmoil, recorded in his early writings,[7] was to support a state-enforced religious orthodoxy that would crush dissent. He then came to realize that faith could not be imposed by government decree, that true faith was based on genuine belief.

Locke emphasized in his Letter Concerning Toleration that "true religion consists in the inward and full persuasion of the mind; and faith is not faith without believing."[8] Not only was religious coercion by the government a violation of human rights, it was a senseless use of power that could only breed resentment and rebellion. Diversity of opinion cannot be eliminated, he advised; discrimination can be. According to Locke, the function of government, formed on the basis of a social contract among free and equal individuals, is to protect individual freedom. Liberty of conscience is paramount. In Locke's governmental arrangement, individuals would forgo a degree of freedom to public authority, which in return would ensure a larger complement of natural rights.

Locke's response to religious conflict was to envision two distinct, though not entirely separate, societal institutions in church and state. One was concerned with spiritual affairs and the "acquisition of eternal life," the other with temporal affairs and the business of government. Freedom of conscience empowers the individual to hear "the voice of God"[9] through reason, enabling a person to develop into a moral self. A person might be inclined to proselytize on the basis of individual moral conviction, but in a free society the truth must be conveyed to nonbelievers through persuasion rather than the force of law. As Locke put it, "The churches are to have no authority over civil government; that is churches are to have no jurisdiction over worldly matters."[10]

But what if an individual's faith-based convictions are incompatible with the laws of government? And who is to decide on the proper boundary between church and state in matters of public concern? Locke was clear on both questions in deferring to the will of political majorities. He made a distinction between belief and behavior. The former was protected by government; the latter could not be protected in circumstances where it compromised the functioning of the state. A person of faith might be expected to follow the dictates of his conscience, but he must also be prepared to accept the consequences of recalcitrant actions and the attendant penalties.

Locke's conception of religious freedom did not extend to Catholics, who were believed to be loyal to a foreign power. Nor did it include atheists, who could not enter into covenants or take an oath before God. Locke accepted the establishment of the Anglican Church and public support of it. Locke's definition of religious freedom was generous for his time, but it was far from absolute. In his mind, the legitimate authority of the state, the ultimate protector of all freedom, had to be preserved. Granting religious freedom to dissenters did not require disestablishment.

Locke's formulation did allow for rebellion in instances where the government did not act in the best interests of the people or acted without their consent. This notion, along with his emphasis on natural rights and human equality, explains his appeal to colonists living under British rule. Among those who took up Locke's writings was Thomas Paine, the revolutionary pamphleteer who has become an intellectual hero of contemporary secularists. Notwithstanding his condemnation of organized religion, Paine was not an atheist. He in fact considered Christianity a "species of Atheism" for its glorification of a man rather than God.

Raised by Quaker parents, Paine was a deist whose belief in God was as genuine as his suspicion of ecclesiastic authority.[11] As he himself indicated, "I believe in one God and no more. . . . My own mind is my own church." All the same, Paine faced social ostracism for his criticism of Christianity. The European Enlightenment equipped the founding generation with an intellectual framework for challenging traditional assumptions about the structure of society, and the distinct prerogatives of the church and the state within it. Their thinking did not give rise to a secular society in any sense of the word.

Many of the leading lights of the founding generation have been referred to as deists. Then, as now, deism means different things to different people. Most deists valued reason over the authority of the Scriptures. Some did not belong to a church; others belonged to several churches, not necessarily of the same denomination. Some attended services regularly, others did not. Most rejected the claim that Jesus Christ was God, or that he could perform miracles. Most questioned particular tenets of Christianity, such as the Holy Trinity or the Holy Eucharist. Some did not believe in the power of prayer, or that a Divine Being intervenes in human affairs. But all deists shared one belief in common; all deists believed in God.

At age eighty-two, Benjamin Franklin was the senior member of the delegation that assembled in Philadelphia to write the Constitution. He was also the most famous, and probably the wisest.[12] By the time the Constitutional Convention met in 1787, Franklin had already distinguished himself as a coauthor of the Declaration of Independence, a widely read essayist, and a witty commentator on life, love, and politics. His bawdy, mischievous *Poor Richard's Almanac* was an influential best-seller up and down the eastern seaboard.

An artful diplomat, Franklin had helped to secure France's alliance in the war and negotiated peace with Britain. The self-educated savant and bon vivant had also achieved world renown for his achievements in science. Before setting foot on European soil as a diplomat, "Doctor Franklin" had been honored by the prestigious scientific academies of England, France, Italy, and Germany for his experiments on electricity. He was also known for his inventions. They included the lightning rod, a stove, a cooling device, a musical instrument, a timepiece, seafaring vessels, and bifocals. Pot-bellied stoves, cast in iron to resemble Franklin's pear-shaped body, remain popular today.

Benjamin Franklin was a genuine celebrity. He personified the spirit of the Enlightenment more than any American in his time, and all but a few Europeans, for that matter. Like his contemporary Thomas Paine, Franklin distrusted the clergy, and was not fond of organized religion. One of seventeen children raised by Calvinist parents in Boston, he was happy to leave their orthodox ways behind when he headed south for New York and Philadelphia. For Franklin, religious and political dogmatism was a form of self-love that exceeded human capabilities. Such certitude was also divisive.

Young Benjamin was instinctively irreverent and earthy. After reading the Old Testament as a teenager, he wondered why God, given all the options, chose to speak to a wandering tribe living in the desert. In later years the lovable sage admitted to having a weakness for "low women" and other worldly pleasures. He fathered an illegitimate child whose mother was unknown, and kept a common-law wife with whom he had a son and a daughter. He seldom showed up in church. A clever pragmatist, Franklin did, however, appreciate the utility of religion.

As the elder statesman of Pennsylvania, Benjamin Franklin was the official host of the Constitutional Convention that met in Philadelphia. After a month of deliberation, when the discussion hit a stalemate over the composition of the national legislature, Franklin suggested a three-day recess and proposed that they hire a chaplain to begin each day with a prayer. He reminded his colleagues that from the outset of their hostilities with King George, the Continental Congress, meeting in the same room, had made it a daily practice to request God's help in their arduous struggle. Quoting from the Scriptures, he declared, "Our prayers were heard."

Would the founders of the new nation heed the advice of the wise Solomon who sought the Lord's assistance in building his mighty house, Franklin asked, or imitate Babel, whose tower was built with no recognition of God? Acknowledging a "superintending Providence in our favor," Franklin offered, "The longer I live, the more convincing proofs I see of the truth, that God governs in the affairs of men."[13] The good doctor's advice was never taken, but the episode has since fed the speculations of numerous biographers about the place he afforded religion in public life, as well as in his own.

Some observers have concluded that by rejecting Franklin's prayer proposal, the authors of the Constitution had signaled a change in thinking from the early days of the Revolution, towards a more secular frame of mind. They did, after all, outlaw religious tests for officeholders in the new national government, still enforced in the states. And there was no mention of God whatsoever in the document.[14] But what did the episode tell us about the aged man of the Enlightenment?

Had the colonists' improbable victory over the most powerful empire in the world demonstrated to him the positive influence of divine intervention, the power of prayer, the possibility of miracles?[15] Or was the prayer proposal a convenient distraction from the differences that divided the convention? Franklin did seem to enjoy communal worship, yet his precise viewpoint on religion is somewhat inscrutable. At minimum, it seems fair to discern that he genuinely believed in God. He said as much in a letter to his friend Ezra Stiles, the president of Yale College, stating, "I believe in one God creator of the universe. That he governs it by his providence. That he ought to be worshipped."[16]

Franklin wrote the letter to Stiles towards the end of his life, suffering from debilitating pain, dependent on opium to relieve it, preparing to meet his maker. In the same letter, he expressed doubts about the divinity of Jesus Christ, but acknowledged that if people's belief in Christ caused them to live by his teachings, it was to good effect. Like many of his generation, Franklin held that public morality was a necessary condition for a decent civil society. He was never convinced that organized religion was a prerequisite for morality. He, however, understood the possible connection, and was somewhat persuaded that church membership had a positive influence on those from the lower rungs of society.

Even in his greatest moments of doubt, Franklin was reluctant to offend the religious sensibilities of his contemporaries, for he appreciated how important faith was to many of them and was ever cognizant of the positive role it could play in society. He contributed to a number of churches in Philadelphia, and rented a bench in Christ Church. It would be an overstatement to suppose that Franklin's attitude towards religion was entirely utilitarian, but pragmatism was certainly an essential part of his worldview. In the Age of Reason, faith and realism were wholly compatible.

With no more than a few years of formal education, George Washington was among the least bookish of the Founders. A man of action, he had a keen sense of history, his place in it, and the weight of political precedent that the first generation of Americans would leave for posterity.[17] As he admitted in a letter drafted in 1797, he preferred "rather to let my designs appear from my works than my expression." That being said, he left a fairly substantial written record on the issue of religion.[18]

The gifted group of men who collaborated to form the nation paid the charismatic Mr. Washington an unusual measure of deference. There was never any doubt among them as to who would be the first president. He was a natural leader, albeit an overrated general. After commanding the Continental Army, he presided over the Constitutional Convention. He embodied the courage of the Revolution and the hopes of the fledgling government.

If the rejection of Franklin's prayer proposal signaled a new secularism among those assembled in Independence Hall, it did not register with Mr. Washington. As we have seen from his inaugural and farewell addresses and two Thanksgiving proclamations, Washington assumed that religion, morality, and good government were inextricably intertwined, and he was not bashful about saying it publicly. In his words, "Reason and experience both forbid us to expect that National morality can prevail in exclusion of religious principle. . . . morality is a necessary spring of popular government."[19]

Washington was comfortable with his public benedictions to a "Supreme Being." He had followed form in his farewell to the governors of the newly independent states in 1783, shortly before he gave up his military commission, thinking that he would never return to public life. He also seemed convinced that the providential hand of God was instrumental in mapping the destiny of the new republic. Throughout his lifetime, Washington used more than a hundred different terms to refer to Divine Providence.[20]

George Washington gave meaning to the term *ceremonial deism*, but for Washington the religious rituals he followed in public were more than utilitarian tools to bring people together in the formation of a common identity. As commander of the Continental Army, Washington had petitioned Congress to appoint military chaplains, ordered his troops to attend church, and purchased twenty thousand Bibles for their use. In his second inaugural address, Washington focused on the solemnity of the ceremony and the sacredness of the oath, which to early Americans was still deemed a covenant with God that underwrote the integrity of civic relationships.

Although Washington was an irregular churchgoer and refused to take Holy Communion, he did serve as a vestryman in the Episcopal Church of Virginia. Whether or not he believed in the divinity of Christ, Washington, as did many of his contemporaries, virtually equated religion with Christianity. In 1779 he urged the Chiefs of the Delaware Tribe to learn "the religion of Jesus Christ"[21] as a way to improve their position in life, reflecting the common notion that religious conversion could serve to acculturate the savage population. In his 1783 circular to the governors, he referred to Jesus Christ as the "Divine Author of our blessed religion."[22] In a letter from 1787 designed to assure his friend Lafayette of his open-mindedness on matters of faith, he wrote, "Being no bigot myself to any mode of worship, I am disposed to indulge the professors of Christianity in the church, that road to Heaven, which to them shall seem the most direct plainest easiest and least liable to exception."[23]

After all was said and done, the Father of Our Country expressed a genuine commitment to religious freedom. Following his election, Washington corresponded with a number of religious leaders, occasioned by their concern that the original Constitution, absent the Bill of Rights, had not afforded sufficient protection to minorities. Washington was direct and unambiguous on the matter. In a letter from 1789, he assured Baptist leaders that he would "never had placed my signature on it" if that were so. He further proclaimed that "every good citizen . . . ought to be protected in worshiping the Deity according to the dictates of his own conscience."[24] And Washington's conception of religious freedom did not just apply to Christians.

In separate communications, Washington offered assurances to the Hebrew congregations of Savannah, Philadelphia, New York, Charleston, Richmond, and Newport. Writing to the latter in 1790, he noted that the government of the United States "gives to bigotry no sanction."[25] He emphasized that the new constitutional order (now protected by the First Amendment) goes beyond the sort of "toleration" that prevails when one class of people indulges another in the "exercise of their natural rights."

Washington gave similar assurances to Catholics, Quakers, and evangelicals who had been the targets of persecution. He apparently saw no contradiction between his open embrace of Christianity and his commitment to religious equality. While contemporary commentators might view his utterances on Christian citizenship as insensitive or exclusionary, Washington felt confident speaking his mind as a Christian, while simultaneously standing by his commitment to nondiscrimination.

George Washington had no desire to involve himself in the doctrinal disputes that separated religious denominations; but one does get a clear sense from reading his remarks that he would have drawn the line with religious groups whose beliefs might cause them to undermine the principles of the government he so loved. He did not dwell on the question, though. He preferred to assume that religion, in its many manifestations, would nourish the attributes of character that were conducive to responsible citizenship.

It would be difficult to find an individual more different from Washington than his own vice president, John Adams.[26] Washington was a military man, Adams was a scholar. Washington was calm and calculating, Adams was explosive. Washington was strong and statuesque, Adams was short, round, and sickly (dubbed "His Rotundity" by detractors). Washington was confident about his place in history, Adams was insecure. He once pouted, "Popularity was never my mistress."[27]

Adams seemed destined to play second fiddle, always overshadowed by giant personalities: Washington in the executive branch, Franklin in diplomacy. He was locked in a lifelong rivalry with Jefferson, which lasted till the day they both died on the Fourth of July, fifty years after the signing of the Declaration of Independence. Adams had chaired the committee that drafted the Declaration and presented it to the convention, because he was deemed a more capable speaker than Jefferson, its principal author. Adams was denied a second term in the White House after Jefferson, his own vice president, defeated him in a brutal election.

John Adams was notoriously cantankerous, yet he shared a famously affectionate marriage with his wife Abigail. Bright, charming, literate, dedicated to her husband and her country, Abigail Adams was the most impressive American woman of the period.[28] Her correspondence with her husband during his years of public service provides us with one of the period's most complete historical records. If Adams's strict Puritan upbringing made him seem inflexible at times, it also left him highly principled. After the Boston Massacre of 1770 left five patriots dead and the city enraged, Adams agreed to represent the British soldiers who were charged with the murders. Adams's dazzling courtroom performance got six of the eight accused men acquitted, and many of his own friends and neighbors angry with him. Still, the thirty-four-year-old lawyer was not deterred; he insisted that the troops deserved a fair trial.

The parents of young John had groomed him for a career in the ministry, but law and politics eventually won out. Adams remained a practicing Christian throughout his adulthood, and attended services in a variety of Protestant churches. He understood both the practical uses of religion and the dangers that follow when relationships between the government and the church are too intimate. His approach to writing the Massachusetts constitution seems to reflect the tension between his Congregational upbringing and his Enlightenment view of the world.[29] Reminiscent of provisions enacted by the Puritans in the Bay Colony, Adams's first draft of the 1780 constitution read, "It is the Duty of all men in society, publickly, and at stated seasons to worship the supreme being, the great Creator and preserver of the Universe." It was later reworded at the convention to read, "It is the right as well as the duty."

Adams's charter also stipulated that only Christians should be eligible to serve as governor, lieutenant governor, or in the legislature. He moved to require all state officers to take an oath, "I believe in the

Christian religion and have firm persuasion of its truth." An early draft, opposed by Adams, had required the payment of taxes in support of Congregational ministers. Adams supported an amended version that empowered the legislature to levy taxes for the support of "public worship of god, and the teachers of religion and morals." It allowed citizens to apply such funding to Protestant denominations of their own choice. Although freedom of religion was not included among the "natural" and "inalienable" rights specifically listed in the state constitution, the final 1780 version granted all subjects liberty for "worshipping God in the manner and season most agreeable to the dictates of his conscience" provided that "he doth not disturb the public peace, or obstruct others in their religious worship."[30]

John Adams was convinced that a knowledge of and belief in God were necessary characteristics of good citizenship. He was also persuaded that requiring individuals to practice religion in a Christian tradition as a condition for public office is compatible with religious freedom, at least as he saw it. He was serious about forcing the government to retreat from the theological quarrels that separated Protestant sects, including the Congregationalists, who were still a majority. At the same time, he was comfortable prescribing oaths for the profession of Christianity as a necessary foundation for democratic government. In the course of the convention, Adams opposed provisions in the Massachusetts constitution that discriminated against Catholics, but he was unsuccessful. While Adams occasionally spoke up for the rights of atheists, the truth is that his definition of the right to practice religion as one saw fit did not offer much protection to those citizens who chose not to practice religion at all.

In 1820, when Adams reached the ripe age of eighty-five, he was asked to serve as a delegate to a state convention that had been called to revise the constitution he had written. By then the feeble old man was a revered statesman, without peer in his home state. He had been selected unanimously, and received a standing ovation when he entered the convention chamber. As the meeting came to order, Adams rose to offer one bold amendment that would have guaranteed complete religious freedom in Massachusetts. What he had in mind was the predicament of the Jews, and his good friend Mordecai Noah, a New York editor who had frequently visited the old man in his retirement. Noah had written Adams to remind him that the freedom of conscience outlined in his constitution did not apply to people who were not Christians. Adams took up the cause, but his proposal did not carry. The elderly gentleman from Braintree, who had grown past his Puritan roots, was too far ahead of his time.

Two Gentlemen of Virginia

Thomas Jefferson and James Madison are cited with such regularity by the Supreme Court that it would constitute gross scholarly negligence to overlook their contributions when studying the First Amendment. The infatuation that writers and readers of history have with Jefferson is unparalleled. More is written about the "Sage of Monticello" than any of the Founders. He was a brilliant visionary, whose thoughts on politics, education, and architecture still command attention. His words have been an endless source of inspiration for Americans of different political persuasions, including adversaries on opposing sides.

Jefferson was also the most enigmatic figure of his generation.[31] As we have seen, the man who wrote the Declaration of Independence had a somewhat elitist approach to education by today's standards, and his views on women and people of color were astonishingly regressive. In 1775 the aloof Virginia squire arrived at the Philadelphia convention in an ornate carriage, having traveled the distance with four horses and three slaves in his entourage. He was hardly the personification of revolutionary egalitarianism.

Jefferson's attitudes and behavior towards religion were not entirely consistent either. Yet Americans, especially constitutional separationists, turn to him to derive meaning from the First Amendment as though he were the reigning authority. There is a bit of irony in all of this. Aside from his own vanity, which was sizable, Jefferson probably would not have approved of our looking back to him and his contemporaries for guidance in resolving our own legal quarrels. He believed that each generation of people should write its constitution anew. As he put it, "The earth belongs to the living."[32] Moreover, he had no direct role in drafting either the Constitution or the Bill of Rights. He was out of the country for both projects. Nor was he enthusiastic about the original document, which concentrated federal power in such a way as to undermine the localism that he deemed essential to democratic rule.[33] During his time in the Virginia legislature, however, Jefferson articulated core philosophical themes that would later inform the constitutional assignment taken up by the First Congress.

James Madison was not nearly so glamorous as his intellectual mentor and political collaborator. He enjoyed a more conventional lifestyle as a wealthy tobacco farmer in Orange County. Montpellier, the stately home that Madison inherited from his family, was less flamboyant than the magnificent Monticello mansion that Jefferson built for himself. Happily married to Dolley for over forty years, there were no secrets of slave mistresses or illegitimate children in his story like the ones that spiced the reputation of his Virginia neighbor. Madison just never captured the popular imagination as Jefferson has.

James Madison in many respects, though, was the most important of the Founders.[34] He was the chief architect of our government, the principal author of the Constitution and the First Amendment. If John Adams was the most learned political theorist of the bunch, Madison was the supreme political scientist who could adapt principles of governing to the needs of the new nation. He would draw on the enlightened thinking of Locke, Hume, and Montesquieu to construct an elaborate yet elegant system of separated powers that resembled Newton's celestial universe, invested with movement, balance, and order. Unlike Jefferson, who saw constitutions as temporary arrangements, Madison hoped that the compact made in Philadelphia would provide stability to the young country and continuity through the ages.[35]

By the end of the eighteenth century, a second religious revival had come to Virginia. Its effects were especially evident in the central Piedmont, where ethnic and religious diversity flourished. The picturesque area that stretches from the James and Rappahannock rivers in the east to the edge of the Blue Ridge Mountains was populated by English, Scotch-Irish, and German settlers, forcing loyal Anglicans to share the religious landscape with Presbyterians, Baptists, Methodists, and independent Episcopalians. The Piedmont was also home to Thomas Jefferson and James Madison, who would represent the territory in the legislature. An odd combustion of evangelical worship and enlightened reason created a climate in the region that was uniquely suited for the cultivation of religious tolerance and cooperation. Rational deists tended to be drawn from the gentry, evangelicals from more modest folk, but a common animosity towards English rule and its Anglican church kept the alliance intact.

While initially raised in Anglican households, both Jefferson and Madison were influenced by Scottish Presbyterian tutors. Madison's most renowned teacher was John Witherspoon, the Scotch Presbyterian minister who was a signer of the Declaration of Independence, and subsequently became president of Princeton University. Jefferson was a serious student of the Bible. He once assembled his own version of the New Testament, later dubbed the "Jefferson Bible," from cutouts of passages he favored.

Jefferson admired Christ as a great teacher, but denied his divinity and routinely dismissed references to mysticism and miracles that enchanted other Christians. For him, the life of Jesus was a model of good conduct that Christians should emulate rather than worship. The trinity that enamored Jefferson consisted of Bacon, Newton, and Locke. Their painted portraits were among his prized possessions, and still hang in the parlor of his Monticello mansion. His unorthodox views led some of Jefferson's enemies to denounce him as an "infidel" and an "atheist" when he sought the presidency in 1800, but the allegations were unfair.

Between 1776 and 1780, twelve of the fourteen states wrote new constitutions. Jefferson was a member of the committee appointed to revise the colonial laws of Virginia. In this capacity, Jefferson wrote his famous Bill Number 82, the Virginia Statute for Establishing Religious Freedom. Jefferson was so proud of the statute that he had it listed on his tombstone as one of his three great lifetime achievements. (The others were the Declaration of Independence and the University of Virginia). The bill declared that "Almighty God" had "created the mind free," and denounced the corrupting influence of "imperious" rulers who would interfere with individual religious thought. It further read:

> No man shall be compelled to frequent or support any religious worship, place or ministry whatsoever, nor shall be enforced, restrained, molested, or burdened in his body or goods, nor shall

otherwise suffer, on account of his religious opinions or beliefs; but that all men shall be free to profess, and by argument to maintain their opinions in matters of religion.[36]

The passage is notable for two reasons. First for its limitations: In Lockean fashion, Jefferson's explicit reference to beliefs and opinions suggests that the religious freedom he embraced did not necessarily apply to individual actions. As he wrote later to the Baptist ministers, "The legislative powers of government reach actions only and not opinions."[37] This distinction was not unusual for the time. Religious liberty was not ordinarily conceived of as a license for exemption from laws that all citizens were supposed to observe. Following this blueprint, people were free to believe or not believe what they chose, but everyone was expected to obey the law regardless of their faith. Several of the new state constitutions, however, included "free exercise" clauses, which were generally understood to provide a wider scope of protection than freedom of thought, belief, or opinion.

Second, Jefferson's attention to compelled support was written in response to petitions by dissenters, who sought to undo the Anglican establishment and share the privileges enjoyed by the old church.[38] The provision was a clear break with Lockean liberalism. Not only did it oppose establishment, it sought to resolve that nobody should be compelled by the government to give support to any church. The proposal proved to be too ambitious for even the relatively diverse political setting of Virginia. While Jefferson's proposal was supported at the committee level, the legislature chose to enact a compromise measure that exempted members of dissenting sects from supporting the Anglican Church. The bill's support on the committee served to differentiate the more liberal political climate of Virginia from that of New England, where the Puritan culture carried a strong expectation of subsidized religiosity. But its defeat in the legislature also illustrated how out of step Jefferson was with the leaders of his own state.[39]

It is understandable why contemporary opponents of public support to religious institutions gravitate to Jefferson's famous enunciation, but the analogy is flawed. It applies neatly to proposals that would use public money for the direct support of churches, which would impose extra burdens on taxpayers. It might also be applied to challenge tax exemptions for church property, a privilege Jefferson happened to support. The application is problematic, however, when it is directed at faith-based institutions that deliver educational or social services in context of the modern American state. We will return to this question in a later chapter.

Jefferson wrote his oft-quoted letter to the Danbury Baptists in 1802 after his presidential election to reassure the dissenters that he disapproved of the subjugation they suffered under the Congregationalists in New England. The twenty-six Baptist churches in the Connecticut Valley were an important part of Jefferson's political constituency. The Congregationalists were his opponents. Congregationalist ministers had taken Jefferson to task for his liberal religious views, throwing their support behind John Adams and the Federalists. The letter conjured up animosities that arose in Jefferson's ugly battle for the presidency. When President Adams called for a "day of solemn humiliation, fasting, and prayer" in 1798, his Republican opponents accused him of trying to establish a national church. Jefferson invoked the symbolic "wall of separation" to explain why he was abandoning the practice followed by his two predecessors in the White House. His employment of the metaphor was political as well as philosophical, rhetorical as well as reasoned.

In fact, a complete separation of church and state was unfathomable in Jefferson's day. Historians of the period have noted that the Baptists themselves had no such expectation.[40] For them, a better world meant having privileges similar to those enjoyed by the Congregationalists, not complete separation. Jefferson and the Baptist leaders also understood that Jefferson's interpretation of the First Amendment had no direct bearing on church-state relations in Connecticut, other than to help influence public opinion in their favor. Jefferson, in particular, would have had it no other way. The Bill of Rights was designed to protect the states from encroachments of federal power.[41] The constitutional bargain prohibited the national government from establishing a church, but left it to the states to work out their own arrangements regarding religion.

At the end of the eighteenth century, the heart of American civic life remained concentrated at the state and local levels. It was not secular in spirit, nor did it prescribe separation. In Virginia, where the movement for religious freedom moved at a more hastened pace than elsewhere, the protocols of government were still soaked with religious symbols. In 1779, when he was the governor of Virginia, Jefferson decreed a day of "public and solemn thanksgiving and prayer to Almighty God." He had earlier helped draft a similar resolution as a member of the House of Burgesses. The proposal was presented to the legislature by his close ally James Madison. Even Jefferson's Bill for Establishing Religious Freedom began by acknowledging the "Almighty God." His letter to the Baptists ends by pledging to "reciprocate your kind prayers for the blessing of the common Father and Creator." Jefferson had also written Bill Number 84, which would punish Sabbath breakers. Madison put it before the legislature on the same day that he introduced Bill Number 82.

Despite the fuss he made over the Thanksgiving proclamation as president, Jefferson's speeches were consistently laced with references to a "Creator," a "Deity," a "Supreme Being," and even a providential "Superintending Power." Two days after he dispatched his Danbury letter, Jefferson attended church services in the House of Representatives, which he continued to do over the next seven years. In his first inaugural address, Jefferson paid homage to an "overruling Providence" who "rules the destinies of the universe."[42] In his first annual message to Congress, Jefferson expressed gratitude to "the beneficent Being" for the gift of peace.[43] His second annual message to Congress began with a reference to the "goodness of that Being." He concluded it by asking the nation to join him in prayer, once again acknowledging the "Being in whose hand we are."

As a thinker, Jefferson was among the most nonsectarian of the Founders. As such, his ideas do not provide us with an accurate measure of their opinions on church and state. His animosity towards the clergy was widely known, especially as it was directed to those outspoken ministers who were his political enemies. His own actions in both the federal and state government, however, did not comport with his reputation as a strict separationist. This disparity between thought and action is not easy to reconcile, and we do not need to do it here. Perhaps Jefferson kept his own counsel, and was able to separate his personal convictions as a man of reason from his public actions as a representative of the people. Or maybe he was just a political pragmatist, who was not above pandering to the majority when it suited his purposes. If such were the case, it would tell us as much about the age in which he lived as it would about Jefferson himself.

Or perhaps the discerning Mr. Jefferson was capable of making a substantive distinction between the phenomenon of religion and the institution of the church: one being an intellectual and spiritual perspective that gives meaning to life in the context of a larger, divinely scripted, reality; the other being an organizational structure that brings like-minded people together under one roof, separates them from others, and produces the lifeblood of politics. Under this construct, the latter was to be treated with more suspicion than the former, while it was understood that neither could or should be entirely driven from public life.

MADISON AS METAPHOR

In 1784 Patrick Henry proposed a bill in the Virginia Assembly to levy a general assessment on property that would allow the state to support "Teachers of the Christian Religion." The bill counted among its original supporters George Washington and John Marshall, who would later serve as the nation's fourth chief justice of the Supreme Court. Advocates of the assessment were worried that the disestablishment of the Anglican Church had contributed to a general decline in public morality, and wanted to counter the effect it could have on the quality of civic life in the new nation. In the fall of 1784, the legislature adopted a law that incorporated the Episcopal Church, granting the church certain legal privileges but not full establishment. It also postponed action on the assessment bill.

With Henry in control of the key legislative committees, it seemed only a matter of time before the gifted orator would have his way on the surtax. In a moment of despair, Jefferson turned to God and wryly suggested to Madison that they pray for the early death of their powerful adversary. Madison instead took advantage of the legislative delay to rally opposition among religious dissenters. He then threw his support behind Henry for the governorship as a ploy to remove him from the legislature before the bill came up for approval. Henry was elected. Sensing strong legislative support for the surtax even in Henry's absence, Madison took his case to the public in 1785, when he anonymously wrote his "Memorial and Remonstrance Against Religious Assessments." George Mason had hundreds of copies printed up, and circulated them throughout the state.

Madison's essay emphasized the risks that presumptuous government power can pose to religion. In Lockean fashion, the grand architect of the constitution recalled that religion "can only be directed by reason and conviction, not by force and violence." He referred to freedom of conscience as "inalienable." In a departure from Locke, he further explained:

> It is the duty of every man to render to the creator such homage and only such as he believes to be acceptable to him. This duty is precedent, both in order of time and in degree of obligation to the claims of Civil Society. Before any man can be considered as a member of Civil Society, he must be considered as a subject of the Governour of the Universe.[44]

The scope of religious liberty defined in the "Memorial and Remonstrance" vis-à-vis the government even exceeded the standard set by Jefferson, who was more inclined to abdicate to public authority. The essay also introduced egalitarian concerns that are central to Madison's thinking. To give Henry his due, it is noteworthy that the benefits of the proposed bill would have accrued to a variety of Christian sects, not just the incorporated Episcopalian Church to which he and his allies belonged. Quakers and Mennonites were exempted because they maintained neither clergy nor churches. But the proposal did not take into consideration the preferences of non-Christians, who at the time would have included tiny populations of Jews and Muslims. Nor did it consider atheists, agnostics, or deists, all of whom would be required to render financial support to a local church. Madison properly saw the measure as a step towards a loosely assembled Christian establishment. He insisted that "the Bill violates that equality which ought to be the basis of every law" because it subjected some people to "peculiar burdens."

Madison's appeal resonated with Baptists, Presbyterians, and Methodists, who were a sizable minority. George Washington, surprised by the negative reaction to the assessment bill, backed off from supporting it, convinced that it was not worthwhile to provoke political bitterness in the Old Dominion, especially over religion. With Henry absorbed in the duties of the executive branch, Madison deftly substituted Jefferson's Bill for Establishing Religious Freedom in place of the original assessment proposal. Seven years had passed since Madison first put Bill Number 82 before the legislature, and by now Jefferson was off on a diplomatic mission to France. But its final passage was a source of great pride to the two friends, and it cemented a political alliance that lasted a lifetime despite differences they had over the new Constitution.

The egalitarian concern introduced by Madison underscores the problems that arise when contemporary opponents of aid to faith-based institutions cite the "Memorial and Remonstrance" as a philosophical reference point in support of their arguments. Most of the current aid programs in question are designed to support secular functions, such as education and social services, and they are not usually restricted to any one religious denomination. Following present legal standards, the Supreme Court would have also struck down the assessment bill opposed by Madison, but the same contemporary standard of neutrality allowed it to approve school vouchers in the *Zelman* case.

The second Madisonian document that contemporary separationists are fond of citing is his "Detached Memoranda" from 1817. Written by Madison in his retirement, it challenged the president's reading of Thanksgiving proclamations and the appointment of congressional chaplains. Here again Madison's egalitarian concerns are brought to fore in objecting to the latter, knowing full well that not all religions would be fairly represented in a country that still harbored deep prejudices against certain groups. As he indicated:

> The establishment of the chaplainship in Congress is a palpable violation of equal rights. . . . The tenets of the majority elected shut the door of worship against the members whose creeds & consciences forbid a participation in that majority. To say nothing of other sects, this is the case with that of Roman Catholics &

Quakers who have always had members in one or both of the legislative branches. Could a Catholic clergyman ever hope to be appointed a Chaplain? To say that his religious principles are obnox-
ious or that his sect is small, is to lift the evil at once and exhibit
in its naked deformity the doctrine that religious truth is to be
tested by numbers, or that the major sects have the right to govern
the minor.[45]

As the fourth president of the United States, Madison did not oppose the use of congressional chaplains. It was he who reinstituted the
custom, interrupted by Jefferson, of delivering a Thanksgiving proclamation. What are we to make of this discrepancy? Had the "Father of
the Constitution" become more separationist in his old age? Had the
elder statesman acquired a new wisdom with time that had alerted him
to the increased dangers of religious rivalry? Or had he let his fear of
political discord get the better of him, as with some secularists presently
on the Supreme Court, leading him to prescribe a stricter separation
as a remedy for religious pluralism and its attending conflict?

I have always been inclined to view Madison as more accommodationist than Jefferson, although there are authorities on the subject
who would differ, or perhaps suggest that I have overstated the difference between the two men.[46] It is not our task here to determine who
the real Madison was, so much as to glean something from his nimble
mind that can be helpful to us in managing our own disagreements.
This brings us back to his essential egalitarianism. It was already evident in 1776, when the twenty-five-year-old Madison, fresh out of
Princeton, was elected as a delegate to the Virginia constitutional
convention.

After the convention had refused to disestablish the Anglican
Church, Madison respectfully took exception to draft language that
the more senior George Mason had proposed for the Declaration of
Rights. Mason's wording read, "All men should enjoy the fullest toleration in the exercise of religion, according to the dictates of conscience." Madison, again rejecting a Lockean construct, persuaded
the convention to adopt alternative language that read, "All men are
equally entitled to the free exercise of religion, according to the dictates of conscience."[47]

Mere "toleration" was not sufficient to suit Madison's taste for free-dom. "Tolerance" suggested a set of privileges that citizens derived at the sufferance of state authorities, privileges that could be withdrawn when politicians saw fit. "Equality" denoted a sense of fairness to which all citizens were entitled as a matter of human right, whatever their religion. Madison introduced similar language when the First Congress met to compose the Bill of Rights, which would have required "full and equal rights of conscience."[48] After some discussion, he proposed the language contained in the present Establishment and Free Exercise clauses. As we have already seen, these provisions were designed to protect the states from federal power as much as they were to protect the rights of citizens.

If Madison had his way, the First Amendment would have also gov-erned the states. The constitutions adopted in most states after 1776 allocated inordinate power to the state legislatures. Madison was wary of this power and the tendency of popular majorities who controlled legislatures to act carelessly with the rights of minorities. This fear of "majority tyranny," conditioned by a healthy dose of egalitarianism, instructed the statecraft behind his writing of the federal Constitution. Madison accepted interest and factionalism as basic facts of political life, laws of human nature. The genius behind Madison's thinking was his ability to convert the base instincts of human actors into a formula for democratic governance. This would be achieved in part by an elabo-rate architecture of institutional design, in part by letting the forces of politics run their natural course.

Anti-federalists contended that creating a more centralized system of government in place of the loose confederation of states that existed under the Articles of Confederation posed a danger to individual free-dom. Madison turned their argument on its head, maintaining that a larger "extended republic" provided a greater safeguard to freedom.[49] As he outlined in Federalist Paper No. 10, the threat of majority tyr-anny can be remedied by a diverse political landscape composed of many competing groups and interests. A thriving pluralism would make it difficult for any one group or coalition to dominate politics. The same held true with regard to religion, which, Madison appreciated, was a source of division and conflict in politics. He explains in Federal-ist Paper No. 51:

In a free government, the security for civil rights must be the same
as for religious rights. It consists in the one case in the multiplicity
of interests, and in the other in the multiplicity of sects. The degree of security in both cases will depend on the number of interests and sects.[50]

For Madison, a robust pluralism was an antidote to tyranny. While
Locke had hoped to contain the political turmoil that flowed from
religious differences through the authoritative establishment of a state
church, Madison's prescription called for a large measure of freedom.
Freedom would lead to greater pluralism, which in turn would shelter
freedom. This was a natural process discoverable through the careful
study of history. This was a constitutional formula that had already
been validated by experience in the colonies. His plan of governance
would incorporate a system of separated or shared powers permitting
the executive and judicial branches to check and balance the popularly
elected legislature. Even within the legislative branch, an appointed
Senate with longer terms of office, insulated from popular pressure,
would act to restrain the "passions" of mischievous majorities. As Madison put it, "Ambition must be made to counteract ambition."

Persuaded that neither the executive nor the judicial branch was
adequately equipped to contain the power of a popular legislature,
Madison had recommended the creation of a joint council of revision
from the two branches. This council would have been empowered to
both veto and revise laws written in the legislature. In his later years
Madison insisted that the judicial branch, more detached from ordinary
politics than either of the others, would serve as the "surest expositor
of the Constitution."[51]

But whose vision of the Constitution and the First Amendment
would their principal author have had the independent judiciary enforce: that of the young egalitarian who had drafted the Virginia Declaration of Rights, that of the mature pluralist who had composed the
Federalist Papers, or that of the older separationist who had written the
"Detached Memoranda"? Madison was in some sense a combination of
them all. One, however, could draw different implications from his
works depending on the point of emphasis. While his egalitarian and
pluralistic instincts converge in common cause to protect minorities,

together they do not necessarily command a strict separation. Madison's approach to governing requires that believers and nonbelievers be treated alike. It leaves somewhat unsettled exactly where the line between church and state should be drawn.

Like Jefferson and Franklin, Madison distrusted the clergy and was fearful of the contaminating effect it could have on politics and on religious freedom. In a letter written to his friend William Bradford in 1774, he referred to "pride ignorance and Knavery among the Priesthood."[52] On another occasion in 1787, he warned, "When indeed Religion is kindled into enthusiasm, its force like that of other passions, is increased by sympathy of the multitude."[53] Unlike Washington and Adams, Madison was not inclined to prescribe religion as a foundation for civil society, but at the age of seventy-five he opined that "the belief in a God All Powerful, wise and good, is so essential to the moral order of the World and to the happiness of man, that arguments which enforce it cannot be drawn from too many sources."[54]

Taken together, these statements reveal both a liberal and a republican strain in Madison's thinking. He was reluctant to rely on human character in casting a vision of the good life, but hopeful about the prospects for cultivating civic character. He identified religious belief as a necessary if not sufficient part of the societal equation. In his own education, Madison had felt the influence of two intellectual traditions, a liberal rationalism he absorbed from the Enlightenment, and a classical republicanism he acquired by studying Greek and Roman philosophy.[55] The apparent dichotomy in his thinking suggests that Madison, like Jefferson, like most of the Founders for that matter, viewed religion from two distinct perspectives: as a divinely inspired moral order that could strengthen civic cohesion, and as a politically engaged institutional entity that could weaken it.

Madison was more alert than most of his contemporaries to the religious prejudices of his own age, a set of biases that favored certain kinds of Christians and consigned other persons, believers and nonbelievers alike, to the sidelines of democracy. He also knew that government, with all its power, could not force citizens to believe or not believe anything against their own inclinations. But like the others of his generation, Madison had faith in God, and during the most public aspects of his life in government showed a willingness to invoke religious references in the form of ceremonial deism without fear that his utterances would offend those who did not share his form of religiosity. Unlike many in our own time, neither he nor the great majority of his renowned colleagues equated faith with ignorance or disbelief with reason.

In its best light, there was a healthy portion of humility, born of doubt, that shaped eighteenth-century American liberalism. Madison wrote in Federalist No. 10, "As long as the reason of man continues fallible, and he is at liberty to exercise it, different opinions will be formed."[56] Notwithstanding obvious blind spots that led them to favor Christianity and suspect atheism, there was an appreciation among the Founders, on some level at least, of how oppressive certitude could be on matters of faith and reason. Even when one was convinced about the erroneous ways of his neighbor, conviction was tempered by a cautious acceptance of everyone's (almost everyone's) right to be wrong.

Madison was prescient in foreseeing how American religion would diversify with time, but even he could not have imagined to what degree. Nor could he have fathomed in his day how secularism itself might become a force for abridging the rights or interests of religious minorities as the modern nation became more suspicious of all references to religion and God. Is our overarching secularism an acquired wisdom gained from the passage of time? Or is it an unwitting fear that will generate its own evils? How might we reconcile it with the rights and interests of that minority of citizens who want to live their lives according to their faith without endangering those who do not?

8

AMERICAN LANDSCAPE

WITH JAMES MADISON'S wise counsel, the American Founders created a system of government fashioned to meet the needs of a religiously plural society. As Madison originally saw it, this pluralism would help protect society from religious tyranny. But questions about it remain. Today as the country realizes an unprecedented level of religious diversity, Americans wonder whether the differences among them are a true source of strength or a danger to the very fabric of the society in which they live. Members of the United States Supreme Court openly disagree over the level of religiosity that can be safely accommodated in the public square, and whether its presence is cause for celebration or strife.

When Robert Putnam completed his monumental study of American civil society in 2000, his conclusion about the place of religion confirmed what scholars had already surmised. In his words, "Religion is today, as it has traditionally been, a central fount of American community life and health."[1] Other than education, religiosity is the most important predictor of civic engagement for an individual or group.[2] Putnam's research, however, pointed to an erosion of civil society during the latter half of the twentieth century, and a "hollowing out" of the institutions that compose it. Churches were no exception. Other research had shown that between 1957 and 2000, the number of people who responded "none" to questions about their religious affiliation rose from 3 percent to 14 percent.[3] The change wasn't devastating for congregations, but it was significant.

The general pattern of civic disengagement mirrored a growing disenchantment with political life, most evident in a steep decline in voter turnout since the 1960s.[4] The voluntary associations that form the texture of civic life in local communities have always played a vital role in American democracy. On the one hand, the churches, clubs, labor unions, neighborhood councils, softball leagues, and other local associations that compose it are important training grounds for capable citizenship. They are the places where people learn how to work together towards positive social ends. Joining these organizations, men and women acquire skills that enable them to collaborate, trust, compromise, organize, give, get, lead, follow, and think beyond themselves. These voluntary associations also provide an important institutional buffer between the individual and the government, the midpoint between a private existence and a public existence, a sphere of personal freedom within the context of a chosen group.

Putnam cites historical research indicating that church membership was quite low in 1776, accounting for only 17 percent of the population.[5] Despite the fact that political life in early America was saturated with religious reference points, most people did not go to church regularly. It could be difficult getting there in those days. Eighteenth-century roads were poor, and the rural terrain could be challenging, worse still during the harsh winter months. But prayer and Bible reading were common activities in the home, especially among the more literate. It seems that as Americans began to observe religion in designated houses of worship, they ushered it out of the public square. Putnam finds that religious observance reached a peak in the 1950s, when, as we saw earlier, a loose consensus around Judeo-Christian beliefs wrapped itself in the American flag to ally faith with patriotism. He records a 10 percent falloff in church membership over the last four decades of the twentieth century, and a 25 percent to 50 percent (quite a range) drop in church activities.

Putnam also observes a growing division in the country between the devoutly religious and those who are entirely unchurched. These polar opposites have attracted the lion's share of attention in the media, not to mention the courts and the political arena. But the real story of American religion is found in what I would call the "hollow middle." It is this larger, passive, undecided, ambivalent sector of the American populace that sets the terms of religious freedom at the beginning of the twenty-first century. This population was already evident in the 1950s, when religion stoked nationalism and the average person's knowledge of matters pertaining to faith was shallow and inconsequential. It is this hollow middle that protects the country against the ascent of religious radicalism in politics and government. It is also this hollow middle that leaves the deeply religious vulnerable to extreme secularism, which when left unchecked can also compromise rights protected by the Constitution. I will return to these points later. First, I need to more fully explain who inhabits the hollow middle, and why they play such a significant role in mediating our political differences over religion.

We got an early glimpse of this population in chapter 2, when we looked at polling data on American public opinion. The surveys revealed a wide dissonance in public attitudes about the role of religion in political life. There is a strong consensus in the country on the importance of protecting religious minorities. Americans also seem to like politicians with religious convictions, and agree that religious leaders should stand up for their beliefs; yet they want public officials to compromise on matters of faith, and they are skittish about the participation of organized religious groups in politics. Although the great majority of Americans believe in God and claim some kind of church affiliation, most say that religious beliefs do not shape their political opinions. They endorse government support for faith-based institutions, but are worried that such support may lead to proselytizing and discrimination in hiring.

Their ambivalence about the role of religion in public life was again apparent in a survey conducted by the Pew Forum in 2006.[6] Fifty-nine percent of those polled said that the influence of religion in American life is declining, compared to 34 percent who said that the influence of religion is increasing. Seventy-nine percent of those who said its influence is declining (50 percent of all those polled) indicated that this declining influence in American life is a bad thing. Forty-five percent believed that the influence of religion in government was decreasing, while 42 percent believed it was increasing. A slight majority of those who said that the role of religion in government is declining agree that it is a bad thing. Nevertheless, the great majority (63 percent) of those polled said that the will of the American people should have more sway in the making of laws than the Bible does. While a significant minority (32 percent) of Americans favor letting the Bible hold more sway than the popular will, the vast majority, by a margin of two to one, hold that democracy should override religious conviction when it comes to making public policy. Although 51 percent of those polled agreed that houses of worship should be able to express their views on politics, 46 percent said that religious institutions should stay

out of politics. Like many of the founding generation, Americans distinguish between the positive role that religion can have on individual
and community life and the negative effect it can have on organized
political life.

Most Americans abide by a hollow faith. They keep it as one of the
many attributes that form their overall identity. It does not play a decisive role in shaping their political views or how they run their lives.
And they more or less expect the same from their government. There
are sharp clashes of opinion within the population, most pronounced
between those who inhabit the extreme right and the extreme left of
the political landscape. We should be reminded, however, that not
all Americans who inhabit the edges of the religious landscape are
comfortable at the edges of politics. Most religiously devout people do
not want to use the government as a tool to impose their beliefs on
others, and most unchurched people are not ideological secularists.

In this chapter we will take a closer look at the religious landscape
in America. A review of the relevant research shows that the country
is not only experiencing a growing diversification in religious affiliation
by denomination, but also a diversification in the way people choose
to worship. We will also examine what it is that religious congregations
do beyond bringing people together to worship. This investigation will
give us better insight on the role these organizations play in civil society. It will provide us with a more intelligent basis for determining the
risks and rewards they present in American public life.

DIVERSIFICATION

Two key factors have contributed to the diversification of religion since
the 1960s: a decline in mainstream (especially Protestant) denominations, and immigration from Asia and Latin America. Mainstream
Protestants—Methodists, Presbyterians, Episcopalians, Lutherans,
American Baptists, and the United Church of Christ—lost membership, while evangelical groups gained. Again, this was not a devastating
shift for mainstream churches, but it was significant. The number of
evangelicals among Protestants grew from 56 percent of the total in
1974 to 63 percent in 1991.[7] The latter include members of the South-

ern Baptist Convention, the National Baptist Convention, independent Baptist churches, and such denominations as Pentecostal, Holiness, Assemblies of God, Evangelical Free, and Missionary Alliance churches. Evangelical congregations draw their membership from a poorer, less educated population. They are also more likely to be composed of racial minorities. While many evangelicals became politicized in the 1980s by affiliating with the Moral Majority, a 1991 survey indicated that 28 percent of evangelicals are African-American, many of whom belong to Baptist and Pentecostal churches.

Despite the gains by evangelicals, mainstream churches still dominate the overall landscape. Because many evangelical churches are independent from national organizations, there is more diversity within their ranks. For example, there are thirty-one Pentecostal and twenty-one Baptist denominations. Diversity also exists within mainstream traditions. There are fourteen Methodist and nine Presbyterian groups. Smaller denominational traditions also diversify. Thus, there are twelve Mennonite and six Quaker groups. If all the unaffiliated groups were combined, they would be the third largest denomination in the country, behind Roman Catholics and the Southern Baptist Convention.

The National Congregational Study (NCS) lists the denominational breakdown of church attendees by percentage as follows: Roman Catholic (28.6), Southern Baptist Convention (11.2), no affiliation (9.7), United Methodist Church (9.2), Evangelical Lutheran Church of America (4.4), other Baptist denominations (3.1), three black Baptist conventions (3.0), Presbyterian Church (USA) (3.0), Episcopal Church (2.5), United Church of Christ (2.0), other Pentecostal denominations (1.9), Lutheran Church Missouri Synod (1.9), Jewish (1.6), non-Christian and non-Jewish (1.6), Assemblies of God (1.5), other or unknown Lutheran denominations (1.3), Jehovah's Witnesses (1.1), Church of God (various denominations) (1.0), American Baptist churches (0.9), Church/Churches of Christ (0.9), Church of Nazarene (0.8), three black Methodist denominations (0.7), Latter Day Saints (0.7), Eastern Orthodox denominations (0.7), Disciples of Christ (0.7), Unitarian Universalist Association (0.5), Church of God in Christ (0.5), Church of the Brethren (0.5), Evangelical Church (0.5), Seventh-day Adventist (0.5), Two Mennonite denominations (0.3), Reformed Church of America (0.3), Christian and Missionary Alliance (0.3), other Methodist denominations (0.3), other Presbyterian denominations (0.3), other Christian denominations (2.0).[8]

One of the most interesting developments to occur on the American religious landscape is the introduction of Eastern religious traditions from Asia that fall outside the "homogenized" Protestants, Catholics, and Jews that Will Herberg wrote about in the middle of the last century.[9] The largest components of what sociologist Robert Wuthnow describes as the "new diversity" consist of Hindus, Buddhists, and Muslims.[10] We do not know how receptive Americans will be to these new arrivals, now composing less than 1.6 percent of those who attend services, as they continue to grow and change the face of religion. Because of tensions in the Middle East and the identification of the Islamic faith with terrorism, Muslims present a unique test for the depth of religious toleration in the Unities States. While all three of these major groups represent a bold contrast to the European religions that historically have defined American culture, they also maintain distinct traditions among and within themselves.

There are an estimated 1.3 million Hindus in the United States. Unlike Christians who believe that they are made in the image and likeness of God, Hindus hold that the deity is beyond human comprehension. Unlike the monotheistic religions of the West, Hindus worship many forms of the deity—some resembling animals, some humans, and others taking on a combination of forms. Lord Ganesha, the god of learning, has the head of an elephant and four hands. The god Siva, a symbol of creative energy, is represented in the form of a phallus. Because of wide variations in the languages and culture of India, Hinduism itself is quite diverse. While most Hindu sects recognize the sacred ancient texts known as the Vedas, each also has its own scriptures. Immigration to the United States has muted some of these differences. Many temples celebrate specific traditions within Hinduism; others have served as gathering places for people of Indian extraction who worship different gods and perform different rituals. Hinduism is not dogmatic, so it is possible to follow one or more paths without rejecting another. In this sense Hinduism is a model of doctrinal tolerance.

The ethnic clustering seen among Indians is very much in keeping with the American immigrant experience. Living and worshiping in ethnically defined communities has always given newcomers a sense of belonging in a land where they are perceived as different. It is an important transitional phase in the process of American assimilation. But even as a way of connecting with the more familiar, this process of ethnic or religious self-identification involves a certain amount of change and flexibility that was not required in more homogeneous settings that thrived in the old country. For Italian immigrants, it required overcoming regional distinctions between Sicilians and Neapolitans that were enforced by local dialects in order to form a common Italian, eventually Italian-American identity. Membership in the Catholic Church gradually led to coexistence and intermarriage with the Irish, who were quite different culturally. Among the Jews, forging a common religious identity would mean crossing national and language boundaries so that immigrants from Poland, Russia, and Germany could form a single religious community.

As a group, American Hindus tend to be well educated. Many possess advanced degrees and are employed in the professions, distinguishing them from the European immigrants of the nineteenth and twentieth centuries. Such entrée into well-paying jobs could make it easier for them to assimilate. Their appearance, culture, and traditions still separate them from others, however, and language boundaries force many to be underemployed in jobs that are not commensurate with their training. In New York City, the old image of the Jewish cab driver wearing a flat tweed cap has given way to the Indian driver wearing a white turban—better educated, if not so easily adapted to the treacherous traffic of the city streets. Besides India, many Hindu immigrants originate in Pakistan, Bangladesh, Sri Lanka, and Nepal.

Buddhism began as an alternative to Hinduism. The historical Buddha, or "Enlightened One," lived in northeast India sometime between the sixth and fifth centuries B.C., before his teachings spread to central and southeast Asia. Buddhism has held a certain exotic attraction for Americans since the mid-1960s, and the expansion of Buddhism in the United States has been somewhat propelled by the conversion of Westerners. According to Wuthnow, estimates of their number range from 2.5 million to 4 million. Meditation centers have sprung up all over the country, accommodating Westerners who value Buddhism as much for its spirituality as for its religiosity. Because Buddhism can be found in so many Asian countries, it has spawned a variety of distinct followings. Buddhism has recently been introduced into this country by immigrants from Vietnam, Cambodia, Thailand, and Sri Lanka. Here again immigration has brought changes. In Vietnam, for example, meditation was something practiced only by monks, who stood aloof from the rest of the population. In America, Vietnamese Buddhists participate in meditation exercises and enjoy more personal relationships with the monks.

Shin Buddhism was introduced to California in the late nineteenth century by Japanese workers. When World War II broke out, its followers began to imitate Western religions as a way to emphasize their American kinship. This attempt to accelerate assimilation did not halt discrimination or internment, but it has had a lasting effect on the way Shin Buddhists practice religion today. Places of worship are called churches rather than temples; services are conducted in English by a minister who meets with his congregation on Sunday mornings. There are distinct branches within the Shin tradition. While the Buddha is recognized as a source of inspiration, Shin Buddhism is not theistic and does not follow a body of teaching based on the written word. Zen Buddhism, an offshoot that traces its origins to China, Japan, Vietnam, and Korea, emphasizes meditation as a tool for personal growth and is more individualistic. Drawing on Hinduism, Taoism, Confucianism, and Shintoism, Zen is popular with American converts who like to practice their faith in places called temples. Because of the popularity of the Dalai Lama as a spiritual and political figure, Tibetan Buddhism also enjoys a following among American converts.

Notwithstanding political animosities between Americans and the Arab world, the Islamic faith has more in common with the Judeo-Christian tradition than either of the aforementioned religions. To begin with, it is monotheistic. All Muslims worship Allah as the true God who created and sustains the world. Their faith is also based on the written word, as revealed in the Koran, supposedly the last of the divine scriptures, following the Torah and the Gospels. Muslims, therefore, trace their origins to the Old and New Testaments. According to their teaching, Allah had revealed his divine message to Mohammed, a holy man born in Arabia in 570 who was the last of the great prophets, completing a lineage the included Adam, Abraham, Moses, and Jesus.

Muslims follow strict dietary rules that prohibit the consumption of pork or alcohol, and require fasting during the Islamic holy season of Ramadan. Observant Muslims are also required to pray five times a day, which can make it difficult for them to adapt to Western life.

Muslims began to migrate to the United States after World War II in order to escape repressive regimes in the Middle East. Their population grew with liberalization of the immigration law in 1965. Today most American Muslims are from Pakistan, India, Bangladesh, Indonesia, and Africa, rather than the Middle East. Estimates of their numbers vary from 2 million to 7 million. Despite different points of origin, religious practices among Muslims tend to be less diverse than those in other Eastern faiths. Congregations tend to form around ethnic and socioeconomic clusters, as is common among American immigrants.

Here again immigration to the United States has exerted an influence on traditional ways. Wuthnow observes that 78 percent of those attending Friday prayer services are women, and he cites research indicating that two-thirds of the mosques allow women to serve on their governing boards—practices that are uncommon in the homeland. Although prayers are always said in Arabic, an increasing number of mosques use English to conduct business and deliver sermons. Some Islamic leaders in the United States claim that coming to America has made members of their congregations more religious than they were in their home countries, again as a way to claim identity in a foreign land and find fellowship with people who share their culture. Others claim that the younger generation is assimilating too quickly, acquiring American ways of dress and behavior that are disrespectful of family traditions.

Separate studies show that the functioning of the mosque itself is becoming more Americanized.[11] Once dedicated solely to prayer, Islamic centers now increasingly offer educational, counseling, and recreational programs. The role of the clergy also has expanded. Whereas in Asian and Arab cultures the role of the imam was usually limited to presiding over prayer services, in the United States these clerics assume a more pastoral role, forming personal relationships with families in their communities. In response to American work schedules, there are more religious activities taking place on Sunday now. There is also some evidence of changing viewpoints on issues such as abortion and gender roles.

As was the case with previous generations of immigrants who came here from elsewhere, America will change the newcomers as they change America. But the question remains how well America will receive them. Generally speaking, theirs has been a mixed experience. At times, Muslims have been singled out with suspicion in the aftermath of the World Trade Center bombings. That being said, researchers tend to agree that the most recent arrivals have not been subject to the same kinds of organized persecution that greeted Catholics and Jews in the nineteenth and early twentieth centuries, not to mention Baptists, Quakers, and Mormons in earlier times. The general assessment is that Americans have become more receptive to and tolerant of religious minorities.[12]

Robert Wuthnow's "Religion and Diversity Survey" was designed to examine how Americans are responding to the "new diversity," with particular attention paid to the attitudes of people who identify themselves as Christians, representing the largest religious tradition (or traditions) in the United States. The survey was administered between September 2002 and February 2003. Wuthnow concluded from the surveys that "pluralism exists in the United States, broadly enough to embrace the new religious diversity" but "not deeply enough to be genuinely satisfactory."[13] His survey indicates that while 64 percent of the American public would support a law curbing immigration, 51 percent said they would welcome a stronger Muslim presence; 58 percent said the same (stronger presence) for Hindus, as did 59 percent for Buddhists. In all, Americans were more likely to view Muslims (47 percent) as "fanatical" than they were Hindus (25 percent) or Buddhists (23 percent). Only 5 percent said they were very familiar with the teachings of Islam or Buddhism, and 3 percent with Hinduism.[14]

As it turns out, 80 percent of the respondents in the Religion and Diversity Survey claimed to be Christians. Approximately three-quarters of those surveyed thought that all major religions—including Christianity, Hinduism, Buddhism, Islam—contain some truth about God, and only one in six disagreed. In all, 79 percent thought that God's truth is revealed in many ways, including history, culture, nature, and tradition; only 18 percent agreed that God's truth is revealed just in the Bible. Forty-four percent of the respondents held that Christianity is the only way to have a true relationship with God, while 53 percent disagreed. Given that the great majority of those surveyed were Christian, it stands to reason that many (a large minority) believed Christianity was the only true way to connect to God, but the great majority also found value in all religions.

Wuthnow's diversity survey gives us another glimpse at the hollow middle of the American landscape. Once again we see evidence of dissonance and ambivalence—a desire to embrace new minorities, yet a fear of the unknown; a willingness to see truth and good in all faiths, yet strong feelings about the authenticity of one's own beliefs. It is not surprising that a year after the tragic events of 9/11, many Americans viewed the Islamic faith as fanatical. It is notable that a majority did not, and that a substantial minority expressed receptivity to a larger Muslim presence. As these new groups work their way into the American mainstream, perhaps familiarity with them and their ways will bring greater acceptance from the mainstream. Historically, such acceptance has carried the expectation of change and adaptation. American assimilation has always been a two-way street. The acquisition of a new American identity has typically involved some abandonment of old ways.

Wuthnow probes further by asking those surveyed whether they agreed or disagreed with the following paired statements: "(1) Christianity is the best way to understand God. (2) All major religions, such as Christianity, Hinduism, Buddhism, and Islam, are equally good ways of knowing about God." On the basis of their answers, Wuthnow sorts the respondents into four groups: *spiritual shoppers* (31 percent) who disagree with the first statement and agree with the second, *Christian inclusivists* (23 percent) who agree with both, *Christian exclusivists* (34 percent) who agree with the first but disagree with the second, and 11 percent who could not be classified on the basis of the two questions posed. The substantial minority that falls into the exclusivist category points to the right side of the religious landscape. A closer examination of the group, however, reveals some interesting insights with political significance.

Sixty percent held that God's word is revealed only in the Bible. This is somewhat implicit in a defined group that includes religious fundamentalists who rely on a literal interpretation of the Bible to form their beliefs. A slight majority (54 percent), however, thought that all religions contain some truth about God. For the purpose of our own analysis, we might refer to the latter as the more *open-minded* of the exclusivists. And again, it should not be assumed that the 33 percent of the exclusivists who disagree with the former assertion (that all religions contain some truth about God)—let's call them the *purists*—would want the government to use its authority to enforce their beliefs. From a political perspective, I would suggest that a sub-stantial portion of the open-minded exclusivists and some portion of the purists would refrain from using the government as a tool for reli-gious dogmatism. When combined with the great majority of those counted as spiritual shoppers (31 percent) and Christian inclusivists (23 percent), and some portion of the remaining unclassified (11 per-cent), we get another glimpse at those who inhabit the middle ground of the American landscape.

I don't mean to overstate this observation or misapply the survey. There are limits to the diversity survey, inherent from its stated objec-tives. It focuses on Christian attitudes towards specific minorities who are identified as Hindu, Buddhist, or Islamic. We don't learn a lot about the attitudes of other religious groups or nonbelievers. We don't learn as much as we might about the attitudes of Christians towards other groups, or even towards certain types of other Christians. Although the survey does a fine job sorting out the population of Christians among shoppers, inclusivists, and exclusivists, we know that Christians are quite diverse. This fine study, nevertheless, provides us with another perspective on American attitudes towards religion.

SWITCHING AND SLIDING

Alan Wolfe has completed two major investigations that are helpful in furthering our understanding of the middle landscape. The first, pub-lished in 1998, is an examination of what Americans think about a variety of issues, including, as he lists them, God, country, family, rac-ism, welfare, immigration, homosexuality, work, the political right and the political left. It is focused on middle-class people who live in the suburbs. The research was prompted by a concern, shared by many, that the country had become politically polarized and radicalized to the right.

The portrait of American religion that Wolfe draws is one he describes as a "Quiet Faith."[15] It confirms a high level of religiosity across the country when compared to other modern societies, specifically defined in such terms as a proclaimed belief in God (94 percent), in the Bible as the actual word of God (82 percent), in an afterlife (80 percent), heaven (70 percent), and hell (57 percent). A slight majority (51 percent) of his respondents claimed to pray every day, 45 percent claimed that they watch or listen to religious programming, 79 percent said that God has guided them in making decisions, and 63 percent thought that religion can answer all or most of today's problems.

Despite high levels of religiosity, Wolfe reports, "There is not much support out there in middle America, at least among our respondents, for the notion that religion can play an official and didactic role in guiding public morality." Politically speaking, Americans seem to have a laissez-faire attitude towards religion. This is possible because most ignore religious sectarianism and dislike doctrinal strife. Wolfe observes a growing religious diversity and a wider acceptance of it among middle-class Americans. Only 19 of 200 respondents disagreed with a statement reading, "There are many different religious truths and we ought to be tolerant of all of them." These surveys were admittedly conducted prior to the 9/11 bombings and the Bush elections, casting some doubt on their continued accuracy; but the findings are not naive. Wolfe acknowledges a devout population who holds that confining religion to the private sphere does not allow them to be true to the commandments of their faith. For them, compromise and conviction can be antagonistic.

The larger profile reveals a growing public acceptance of a morality "writ small." For Wolfe, the "ultimate test" for tolerance concerned the issue of homosexuality, with which the great majority of middle-class Americans were uncomfortable, overshadowing negative responses on race, ethnicity, immigration, and politics. Roughly 70 percent of his sample population opined that sex between people of the same gender is wrong. Forty-two of the respondents condemned homosexuality, using terminology such as *abnormal, immoral, sinful, sick, perverted,* and *unacceptable*. Nearly twice this number (78), however, supported the notion of teaching toleration for homosexuals in the schools. This may be a small comfort to gays and lesbians, but it depicts a growing trend towards greater tolerance that cannot be ignored. Noting a liberal trend on the issue, a survey released by the Pew Forum on Religion and Public Life in August 2006 indicated that 35 percent of Americans support gay marriage and 54 percent favor allowing gays to enter legal arrangements that would carry many of the rights enjoyed by married couples.[16]

Wolfe's second study focuses on the "transformation of American religion." It reveals that Americans are not only shopping when it comes to religious affiliation, they are actually switching. A Gallup Poll conducted in 1955 had found that only 4 percent of Americans practiced a faith different from that of their parents. By the mid-1980s, one-third of the population had taken on a religious affiliation different from their parents.[17] Religious identity has become more a matter of choice than inheritance. Wolfe attributes this pattern to a rise in individualism and a growing tendency of people to intermarry. The practice of religious switching is less prevalent among certain groups, however. Jews (85.1 percent) and Mormons (81.4 percent) were especially likely to maintain their original religious identities through the 1990s.[18] More recent studies reveal that intermarriage is increasing among Jews, although intermarriage does not necessarily require switching.

Beyond the conversion of traditional Protestants to evangelical denominations, Wolfe observes other groups abandoning their cultural roots as a function of assimilation. For example, many Latinos are leaving the Catholic Church to form Pentecostal churches in their communities, which allow laypeople and married clergy to take leadership roles that are restricted to priests in the Catholic Church. Some Latinos also find the emotionally expressive services of Pentecostal churches more gratifying than the formal rituals of Catholicism.[19] Many Chinese and Koreans have switched to Christianity. Among the latter, the process of switching to the Presbyterian Church began in Korea, where conversion tends to be associated with modernity and middle-class status. Half of the Korean immigrants who come to the United States are Presbyterian prior to immigration; half of the others convert after they arrive.[20] Korean-Americans practice a conservative form of Christianity, with attention to Bible study and a commitment to spreading the word of God. Perhaps when they get more settled here, Koreans will learn to associate modernity and Americanism with a more moderate form of faith. Perhaps they or their children will switch again.

Overall, switching among religions is symptomatic of other behavioral characteristics that increasingly define the way Americans practice their faith. It points to a declining emphasis on creedal doctrine, tradition, moral judgment, and the notion of sin. Wolfe cites a Notre Dame study from 1987, which found that even active Catholics are not traditional in their attitudes towards church teaching, policy, and priorities.[21] While Wolfe associates the overall softening of religious attitudes with tolerance, respect, and fairness, he acknowledges that devout religious observers see it as an alternative to true religious belief. His general assessment of the situation, nonetheless, is optimistic. He writes, "Americans love God and love democracy and see no contradiction between the two, which is why they clothe their public life in the language of faith while they bring God down to earth and seek salvation through personal choice."[22]

At the end of 2004, Anna Greenberg, a private pollster, conducted a national survey of young people between the ages the ages of eighteen and twenty-five. The "Oh My God" (OMG) survey, named for an expression popular among youth, was sponsored by a consortium of groups and foundations.[23] It was designed to determine, as the subtitle of the survey puts it, "how Generation Y is redefining faith in the iPod era," when "every listener can be their own DJ." As implied by the subtitle, the study found a high level of individualism among respondents, which analysts associated with open-mindedness and tolerance, and a belief that "people should do their own thing, even if it seems strange to others." It found that Generation Y seeks to find community and meaningful involvement with their fellow human beings, but in informal and nontraditional ways. The same population does not feel that it is necessary to belong to a church, synagogue, or mosque to be religious or spiritual. It was marked by a growing diversification caused by immigration from Asia and Latin America. Fifteen percent of the participants were African-American, 18 percent Hispanic, and 4 percent Asian.

When forced to identify themselves, 44 percent classified themselves as religious, 35 percent as spiritual but not religious, and 18 percent as neither. The OMG survey revealed three distinct groupings with regard to the practice of religion: the *Godly* (27 percent) for whom religion and God are a central part of their lives, the *God-less* (27 percent) for whom religion plays a little role, and the *Undecided* (46 percent), who are uncertain yet positive about their religious identities. We are told that the Godly are more comfortable with traditional forms of religious practice, the God-less have spiritual and ideological aspects to their religious identity, and the Undecided lean towards informal and expressive religious practices rather than formal or institutional involvement. The report found a surprisingly high level of religiosity among the population in the sense that 68 percent claimed to talk about religion informally with their friends, 64 percent claimed to occasionally pray before meals, and 55 percent claimed to occasionally read religious materials. Yet religion is found to be personal in the sense that 23 percent of those polled do not identify with any denomination.

According to the OMG poll, young people are less concerned about their relationship with God than they are about other things, such as personal and sexual relationships, jobs, and grades. Politics comes out at the bottom of the things that Generation Y thinks about. As is found with the general adult population, OMG discovered a strong correlation between religiosity and a broad range of volunteer activity. Seventy-nine percent of the most religious among the young had participated in volunteer activity during the prior twelve months, compared to 43 percent among the least religious. Religion was less closely aligned with political involvement. Religious youth seemed to have a distinctive worldview and approach to life—being more connected to family and community, having higher self-esteem and a sense of self, and having more traditional views about family, sex, and marriage.[24] Generally speaking, Generation Y is found to be more liberal than the older generations on social issues. A slight majority (51 percent) says it is not necessary to believe in God to have good values (but 47 percent differ). Fifty-three percent favor gay marriage, and 63 percent favor a woman's right to have an abortion.

I was somewhat surprised to discover that as late as November 2004, a bare majority of the younger generation supported gay marriage. The percentage that supports a women's right to have an abortion is higher than that of the general population but not overwhelming. A national survey of high school seniors released in early 2006 by researchers at Hamilton College in New York gives a slightly different picture of a population that was younger than the OMG group.[25] While 62 percent wanted the Supreme Court to preserve *Roe v. Wade*, 67 percent said that they thought abortion was always or usually morally wrong. Sixty-seven percent would also require parental permission before a woman under the age of eighteen could have an abortion.

Support for the right of abortion varied with the circumstances: when pregnancy is a threat to woman's life (88.9 percent), when the pregnancy is a result of rape (80.9 percent), when the woman is under eighteen and unmarried (49.2 percent), when the baby will probably be born with a serious birth defect (48.2 percent), when the family can't afford more children (39.8 percent), when a married woman doesn't want more children (28.5 percent). Thus while these high school seniors supported *Roe v. Wade*, they had conservative moral views on abortion, and seemed to want women to take responsibility for actions that lead to pregnancy. This is a generation of young people, we should note, who has benefited from sex education programs, preparing them to avoid unwanted pregnancy.

Among the high school seniors in the Hamilton survey, 53.6 percent supported gay marriage and an additional 20.1 percent expressed support for civil unions. Sixty-three percent supported adoption by same-sex couples. One needs to be cautious about overstating the predictive value of the OMG and Hamilton surveys in forecasting the future American landscape. Individuals tend to become more religiously, socially, and politically conservative as they acquire age, a spouse, children, and money. Perhaps many of the "Religion-less" and Undecided in OMG will eventually identify with a particular denomination, though not necessarily the one of their parents. The results do correspond to a general moderating trend in public attitudes that points to greater tolerance. It remains to be seen how tolerant a generation of people with such nontraditional religious viewpoints will be of individuals who are devout and somewhat idiosyncratic about their faith.

Social Services

In 1996, President Bill Clinton signed a welfare reform law that in-cluded a charitable choice provision. It required the states to permit religious organizations to share in federal funding made available to other nonprofit organizations for social services. It also forbade the states from obliging religious institutions to alter their internal gover-nance, remove religious symbols, or modify the expression or practice of their religious beliefs as a condition of participation. Liberals criti-cized the law as an affront to the principle of separation between church and state. Conservatives greeted the measure as a correction of long-standing policies that discriminated against faith-based institutions.

In 2001, a newly elected President George W. Bush signed two exec-utive orders that established a White House Office of Faith-Based and Community Initiatives and created administrative units in five federal agencies to facilitate the flow of social service funds to religious institu-tions. Liberal Democrats denounced the action as a reward to religious fundamentalists who had supported the president's election campaign; many African-American and Latino clergy who had not voted for Bush welcomed the initiative, anticipating benefits for their own congrega-tions. It is probably too early to assess how these recent changes in federal policy will affect the boundaries between church and state; however, there is a good deal of research available on how religious institutions expend their time, energy, and resources that cast light on the present situation.

In 2005, Mark Chaves published the results of the National Congre-gation Study (NCS), designed to examine the involvement of religious congregations in a range of private and public activities. The research focused on churches, synagogues, mosques, and temples, of which there are more than three hundred thousand in this country. He found that their most significant role in society is cultural—what he referred to as the trafficking of ritual, knowledge, and beauty through worship, reli-gious instruction, and the arts. Contrary to popular notions, he ob-served, "Congregations are not, in general, social service organiza-tions," and "Only a minority . . . participate in politics qua congregations." Therefore, "Congregations play only a small role in society's political system."[26] Chaves cites research by Putnam and others documenting a significant decline in church participation during the later part of the twentieth century, paralleling what was occurring in other civic institutions. Chaves also found variations in the activities of congregations that were related to individual characteristics such as size, resources, and tradition.

While most congregations are small, most of the faithful belong to big congregations. According to the NCS, 71 percent of the congregations in the United States have fewer than one hundred active adults, but the biggest 10 percent of them contain about half of all churchgoers. The average annual budget for a congregation is $56,000, yet the average churchgoer belongs to a congregation with a budget of $250,000. Fifty-seven percent of the congregations containing 75 percent of all members participate in some form of social service activity.[27] The most popular congregational activities involve programs that supply food (33 percent), housing or shelter (18 percent), and clothing (11 percent) to the needy.[28] The incidence of social service programs is correlated with the size, wealth, education, and location of congregations.[29] The biggest 1 percent of the congregations spends 20 percent of all the money spent on social services; the biggest 10 percent spend more than half. Large, middle-class congregations located in or near poor neighborhoods tend to be more active in social programs. Moderate or liberal Protestant, Catholic, and Jewish congregations are more involved in social services than conservative Protestant ones (which are also smaller). Most (84 percent) of the activity is collaborative with other government, nonprofit, or religious organizations. Therefore, rather than offering an alternative to the secular network of service providers, religious congregations are part of the same network.

Religious tradition is a factor in determining the kinds of functions congregations perform and how they do so. According to the NCS, large, mainline Protestant congregations with better-educated, theologically liberal members are more likely to collaborate with other organizations and agencies. Moderate-liberal Protestant organizations are more likely to give money to an institution of higher learning and support education-related programs—a pattern somewhat related to wealth. Catholic congregations are more likely to organize volunteer work and run their own elementary and secondary schools. The Missouri Synod Lutherans also run many schools. Education has long been part of the social ministry operated by the Catholic and Lutheran churches, once devoted to their own members, and now extended to a broader population of urban children that is religiously diverse. Research cited in an earlier chapter also points to a significant increase in the number of Christian academies since the 1960s.[30]

In a review of the research on faith-based services, Robert Wuthnow cites a number of studies that suggest a higher level of social service activity among religious congregations than that found by Chaves, most of the gap is attributable to differences in methodology.[31] Wuthnow calculates that Chaves may have underestimated by about 10 percent the proportion of congregations that formally sponsor programs. He nevertheless refers to the NCS as "the gold standard as far as current research is concerned." He agrees that congregations are more likely to help other organizations provide services than to invest heavily in separate initiatives.

Wuthnow's own research confirms conclusions drawn earlier by Putnam and others indicating that people who are more actively and traditionally religious are more prone—twice as likely in his estimation—to volunteer their personal services than others. His surveys further demonstrate a strong correlation between various forms of religiosity and participation in volunteer activities. For example, individuals are more likely to volunteer their services to the poor, the sick, and the elderly if they read the Bible regularly, attend church frequently, pray daily, and value spiritual growth. As he sees it, "Doing work to help the needy is reinforced by . . . spiritual practice."[32] He explains that religious instruction inculcates compassion; it teaches people that unconditional love is a legitimate human sentiment. Moreover, this sense of love cultivates feelings of respect and acceptance that are appreciated by those who are cared for, thereby having a positive effect on the quality of the services rendered.

Wuthnow's research in this domain distinguishes between the social services that are formally organized by religious congregations (churches, synagogues, mosques, temples) and the individual works of people who are religious. The latter, according to him, do not get captured in congregational research. Many of these services are coordinated by large faith-based organizations with philanthropic and service missions, such as Catholic Charities, the Federation of Protestant Welfare Agencies, and the UJA-Federation. Others are made available through more informal networks that recruit volunteers to work in hospitals, soup kitchens, tutoring programs, clothing drives, and the like. In Wuthnow's assessment, activities based outside the congregations themselves are more significant and ultimately more effective. Wuthnow was especially impressed with the informal circles that constitute caring communities and create face-to-face relationships with service recipients.

Wuthnow's interviews with clients revealed that they had higher levels of trust in faith-based providers than in providers who were from government agencies. Clients identify personal qualities in these (faith-based) caregivers that include affability, sincerity, competence, faith in God, familiarity, affinity, empathy, and accessibility. All of these attributes were facilitated by the common religious identity frequently shared by the caregiver and the client, even though faith was rarely discussed in service settings.[33] The great majority of social service recipients preferred to deal with faith-based organizations (63 percent) rather than non-faith-based (13 percent). Twenty-three percent expressed no preference. They report that relationships tend to be more personal and familiar with faith-based providers, rather than organizational and bureaucratic. These general characteristics, according to Wuthnow, enhance the capability of specialized faith-based networks to contribute to civil society.[34]

The complex profile Wuthnow offers from his data seems incongruous, almost paradoxical in light of previous discussions about religious conservatives. It is difficult to reconcile the image of Bible-thumping Christians with his notion of "unconditional love." It is they, after all, who are prone to moral judgment. It is they who oppose homosexuality and abortion. It is they who resist public policies that force people of faith to compromise their consciences. Are they the same folks that Wuthnow has in mind when he speaks of compassion and unconditional love? They are, to some extent, and he gives examples.

Wuthnow specifically mentions the Salvation Army, one of the largest faith-based organizations in the country, which is an evangelical arm of the Universal Christian Church.[35] The Salvation Army operates community centers, thrift shops, group homes, housing programs, and day care centers. Over the years, it has stubbornly held on to its religious roots.[36] As an organization it asserts a belief in "the sanctity of human life," and expresses dismay over the high rate of abortion. Yet it does not condemn abortion outright, nor does it refuse its services to people who might have had or are contemplating having one. Wuthnow might have also mentioned the Catholic Church, which has an official position against homosexuality and opposes gay marriage politically, yet operates a huge network of health care and counseling centers for victims of AIDS.

A lesson to be drawn here, if we believe the research, is that American religion is complicated; it is full of contradictions. Official organizational positions can be translated into different forms of institutional and personal behavior. While the stereotypes we are presented with in the media can carry some truth, they do not tell the entire story. Even the religious eccentrics among us can have a viable middle. Conscience and compassion are not incompatible.

POLITICS

Politics is the other side of public life. If civil society is the channel through which individuals and groups give to the common entity, politics is about getting something from it. Civics is a manifestation of generosity; politics is about self-interest. The former is cooperative, the latter competitive. When politics is taken to a higher level, it can engage the players in a quest for the common good. However, since different participants have a different understanding of what that is, even such high-minded discussions lead to conflict. Because the more religious among us are prone to have very definite ideas about what is good, they often find themselves at the center of such conflict, as we have seen. A central question before us now is how far the devout are willing to go to use politics to impose their ideas on others, and more importantly, when it becomes problematic for the rest. But of course, religious people are not the only ones with strong convictions in politics, so they need protection also. Certitude is a condition that afflicts people of many stripes.

According to the National Congregation Study (NCS),[37] the majority (58 percent) of religious congregations in the United States do not
engage in political activity; but, taking the size of congregations into
consideration, a majority of those Americans (60 percent) who participate in religious services belong to congregations that engage in some
form of political activity. Twenty-six percent of the congregations informed their members about opportunities for political activity, and 17
percent distributed voter guides. Thirty-seven percent of the congregational members were told of opportunities for political activity, and 39
percent received voter guides. Twenty-one percent of the members
were in congregations that had meetings to organize a demonstration,
get people registered to vote, discuss politics, or lobby public officials.
(Nine percent of the congregations organized for the same reasons.)

As with social services, the kinds of political activities that congregations engage in vary by denomination, which is a function of the
combined effects of tradition, size, wealth, education, and other social
factors. The biggest congregations engage in lobbying at about the
same rate as other nonprofits (20 percent). A large proportion of people who belong to congregations identified as Jewish (90 percent),
black Protestant (71 percent), and Catholic (68 percent) report at
least one kind political activity. A smaller proportion belonging to
moderate-liberal white (57 percent) and evangelical-conservative
white Protestant (52 percent) congregations do. It is notable that
with all the hoopla in the media about the political ascendance of
Christian Right in American politics, members of their congregations
were the least likely to be engaged in some form politics. That might
have changed somewhat with the formation of the Bush coalition in
2000, which came together after the NCS was conducted.

According to the testimony of their members, denominations
seemed to focus their attention differently, and some were inclined
towards a wider range of activities. Jewish congregations, the most active group, informed their members about political opportunities (60
percent), held group discussions (45 percent), invited elected officials
(37 percent), invited candidates (35 percent), distributed voter guides
(25 percent), lobbied officials (20 percent), and registered voters (20
percent). Black Protestants informed their congregations about opportunities (47 percent), registered voters (35 percent), distributed voter
guides (28 percent), invited candidates (27 percent), and invited

elected officials (25 percent). Catholics informed people of opportunities (45 percent), organized demonstrations (42 percent), distributed voter guides (26 percent), and lobbied elected officials (23 percent).

According to reports by congregational members in the NCS, white Protestants, the least active of groups, tended to be the most focused in their political activities. Liberal-moderates among them informed people about political opportunities (34 percent) and distributed voter guides (20 percent). Conservative Protestants distributed voter guides (32 percent) and informed people about political opportunities (28 percent). The NCS gave an inordinate amount of attention to the fact that evangelical-conservative Protestants distributed voter guides, and that 70 percent of their guides could be identified as Christian Right voter guides. This emphasis in the analysis was puzzling. Although evangelical conservatives tended to distribute the voter guides more frequently than other groups, their attention to guides (32 percent) was not extraordinary compared to the others: black Protestants (28 percent), Catholics (26 percent), Jews (25 percent), moderate-liberal Protestants (20 percent). Nor should it come as a surprise to anyone that evangelical-conservative Protestants favored the Christian Right (I actually wonder about the 30 percent that did not).

There was no indication in the NCS, however, of whether any of the other groups favored liberal candidates or causes. Groups that self-identify as a minority tend to act as a block. Christian conservatives do it the same way that African-Americans and Jews do. Perhaps the most interesting fact uncovered from the Christian Right designation pertaining to the voter guides is that 33 percent of the moderate-left Christians indicated that they received such literature in their churches. This may be due to the fact that the moderate-left congregations did not exclude Christian Right materials from among all those that they distributed. The designation also serves to highlight the degree to which other denominations did exclude Christian Right materials, which is also unsurprising. Of those who distributed voter guides, 8 percent of the black Protestants, 14 percent of the Catholics, and 17 percent of the Jews included Christian Right materials among them.

We have already discussed the unique role that the church plays in the African-American community. This is not a myth; it is borne out in the empirical research. Commenting on the NCS results in the context of a larger literature, Chaves writes, "African American congregations have embraced electoral politics more than white congregations, and even explicitly partisan involvement in elections seems more common and more accepted among African-American churches than among white churches."[38]

Wuthnow found that African-Americans (50 percent) were twice as likely as any other group (white 23 percent, Hispanic 26 percent) to favor government support of faith-based service programs. Differences by race were even more dramatic than differences by political identification, although the two sets of factors overlap. Support on the basis of political identification was recoded as follows: very conservative (33 percent), very liberal (30 percent), conservative (29 percent), moderate (24 percent), liberal (22 percent). Support by party identification was as follows: Republicans (28 percent), Democrats (26 percent), independents (26 percent); those who voted for Bush (26 percent), those voted for Gore (23 percent).[39] It was mentioned in an earlier chapter that African-Americans are also more likely to support school vouchers than any other group.

In 1995 Sidney Verba and his colleagues published the results of an extensive survey on civic voluntarism in America, which today remains the seminal empirical analysis on the relationship between civic activity and political activity.[40] The study confirmed generations of research in political science establishing that participation is related to education, income, family background, and skills, once again demonstrating the social roots of political inequalities among demographically defined groups.[41] These inequalities are expressed most conspicuously in terms of race and class. Social scientists had known for some time that voluntary civic associations serve as workshops for democracy. One of the signal contributions of the Verba study was to explain how voluntary civic institutions that prepare people for political life also function to moderate, if not correct, political inequalities stemming from social inequalities.[42] The explanation brings us back to the topic of religion, and more specifically the role of the black church.

As in previous research, the "civic voluntarism" survey documented a high level of religiosity among people who engage in various forms of activity. The great majority (69 percent) of those who are civically involved are members of a local religious congregation, and those who attend services more frequently are more active. It further showed that of the various forms of voluntary activity, church involvement was the least stratified in terms of income and race. Contrary to the pattern in other kinds of civic associations where Anglo whites predominate, African-Americans are the most religiously active, followed by Latinos.

Part of the explanation for this pattern is historical, since the church for many years was one of the few civic institutions open to poor minorities.[43] Verba and his associates also attribute it to organizational characteristics, especially in the black church. The mostly Protestant churches that African-Americans belong to are not hierarchical in their governing structures, so they provide many opportunities for members to participate in leadership roles, preparing them for civic and political engagement on the outside. While Latinos exhibit high levels of church attendance, they are more likely to be Catholic. Catholic churches, where leadership is dominated by the priesthood, are more hierarchic, making them less useful as training grounds for politics. This factor may be undergoing some change because of the growing shortage of clergy in neighborhood parishes. As already mentioned, many Hispanics are also turning to evangelical churches.

The finding with regard to black churches is profound. On the one hand, it suggests that religious institutions—specifically the African-American church—have a positive influence on the life chances of disadvantaged populations. Verba and his team write, "Religious institutions play a much more important role in potentially enriching the stockpile of participatory factors for those who are otherwise disadvantaged."[44] On the other hand, these same institutions have a salutary effect on the quality of American democracy by promoting equality, which is so essential. Thus the authors explain, "Although the democratic polity is the domain of human endeavor founded on the equality of all citizens, the religious domain is in fact a more democratic area of activity."[45] These findings must be taken into consideration when evaluating the impact of religion on civic and political life.

THE HOLLOW MIDDLE

The term is not meant to be derogatory, although it carries both positive and negative implications. When I refer to the hollow middle, I am picturing religious life for the great majority of Americans who express a belief in God and attest to some form of congregational affiliation. What I see are a people whose faith shapes neither their lives nor their politics. They are a people whose faith is not characterized by deep doctrinal commitments or pangs of conscience dictated from the pulpit. Their faith lacks density and depth, the pervasive quality associated with the deeply religious whose beliefs define their individual and communal existence. They believe in God and they go to church, but for the most part they live secular lives and see no problem with doing so.

I can't help but to analogize them to their great forefathers who called themselves deists—God-loving individuals who were inured to the idea of a divine being, who were comfortable with public testimonials thereof, who were not ill-disposed towards prayer, who were sometimes inclined to worship in more than one house or denomination, and whose sense of toleration grew with the realization of a more diverse world around them. They seem to believe that religion can have a positive effect on public life, but are suspicious of it as an organizational force in politics. The tolerance of the early generation ran shallow when it came to those who strayed from the mainstream Christian fold; the tolerance of the latter runs shallow when it comes to those who take religion more seriously than they do.

Although contemporary Americans shun religious dogma, they are not unprincipled. They have an allegiance to their democracy. They understand that in order for their great experiment in government to succeed, they must be ready to accept differences among themselves. They are prepared to compromise. And they have. They are not so inclined to rid religion from the public square as are adamant secularists; however, as they watched through the latter part of the twentieth century, the Supreme Court and the popular branches of government invoked the Constitution to engineer the secularization public life and public schools.

The picture that emerges from the empirical research on religion is consistent with a larger profile of the American populace drawn by Morris Fiorina, who concludes from his own surveys that the vast majority is philosophically moderate.[46] Fiorina argues that the fabled culture wars that writers and newscasters obsess over are a myth. When he examines blue states and red states, he finds only shades of difference between them. When he examines hot-button issues such as abortion and gay marriage, he finds a large consensus at the center of political life that has endured for more than three decades.

While Fiorina does not deny political discord, he claims that differences are outweighed by wider agreement. Yes, he concedes, Americans disagree over abortion, but less over whether it should be legal (80 percent agree it should), and more over the conditions under which it should be allowed. As he puts it, the United States is a "closely divided" rather than a "deeply divided" nation.[47] Americans gravitate toward the middle; they are "largely centrist" in their political leanings. This analysis is confirmed in a Pew survey from 2006, which concluded that most Americans favor "no clear ideological approach to most social issues." It elaborated, "Despite talk of 'culture wars' and the high visibility of activist groups, on both sides of the cultural divide, there has been no polarization of the public into liberal and conservative camps."[48]

The moderation that abounds, according to Fiorina, is symptomatic of an ambivalence towards political issues and a growing disenchantment with politics, evidenced by the decline in voting already mentioned. He tells us that the simplistic notion of a polarized electorate is fed by the media, which prefers to cover highly charged conflicts that attract larger viewing audiences. Coupled with negative campaigning and reporting, these stories of pitched battle breed cynicism among people, begetting a withdrawal from politics.[49] The situation is compounded by a political party system that caters to ideologues on the left and the right, and nominates national candidates who are out of touch with popular sentiment.[50] These high-profile leaders personify American politics, but they do not accurately represent it. Yet, I might add, they and the organized groups that support them enjoy undue influence over public policy.

Fiorina's survey was administered after the midterm elections of 2002, yet his conclusion about the distance between party leaders and the people is corroborated by subsequent polls. A Pew poll conducted in the middle of 2005 found that a substantial number of Americans believe ideological extremists have too much control over the two major political parties—with 45 percent expressing concern that "religious conservatives" have too much clout among the Republicans, and 44 percent saying the same about "secular liberals" among the Democrats.[51]

In 2006, 69 percent of the respondents in a similar poll said that liberals "go too far" in trying to exclude religion from schools and government; 49 percent said that conservative Christians "go too far" in trying to impose their religious values on the country. It is notable that more Americans, the great majority, see a greater danger looming on the left than the right—supporting the underlying premise of this book. In the same survey, only 26 percent of the respondents indicated that the Democratic Party is friendly towards religion as compared to the Republican Party (47 percent, a decline of eight points from the previous year).[52]

There is a basic intelligence to the American disposition towards religion. Generations of social science research has informed us of the positive effect that religion has on civic and political life. It is indispensable in both spheres. It has always served as a source of strength for those who are otherwise disadvantaged. The same religious convictions that incline people towards moral judgment (which is not necessarily bad) incline them to do good deeds. While there is some evidence from the last presidential election that conservative Christians are coming into their own politically, the most politically active congregations in the United States—Jewish and African-American—move politics to the left, although African-Americans tend to be more conservative on cultural issues like abortion and homosexuality. Catholics, the largest denominational group, are divided on such issues and are reluctant to take political direction from the church hierarchy.

Immigration to this country tends to have an Americanizing, moderating influence on the religious practices of people, including those whose traditions are foreign to the Judeo-Christian way of life. We can only imagine what effect assimilation will have on second- and third-generation Asians who identify themselves as Hindus, Buddhists, or Muslims, but history does point clearly in one direction. The American political process might also have a moderating effect on the politics of conservative Christians. Here again history is instructive. As Alan Wolfe once remarked, "We cannot know what the future will bring, but if the past is any indication, most religious movements, no matter how traditional their origins, moderate over time. American democracy 'softens' religious purism far more often than strict religious movements 'harden' American democracy."[53]

I do not mean to suggest that left-leaning religious observers should be afforded greater tolerance than those on the right; although there are those, I am sure, who would argue just that because they are convinced that conservatives pose a greater danger to the American way of life. That, of course, is not the way to conceive a constitution for a free society. We cannot assign rights and protections on the basis of whether we agree with someone, or whether we like them. Laws are written to protect some kinds of behavior and to discourage other kinds of behavior, a subject we will take up in the next chapter. Wolfe's astute observation is reassuring to a point, but it does not address the central problem at hand; it just assumes the problem will fade away. It may, but not altogether; and the more it fades, the more vulnerable it will leave idiosyncratic religious minorities who choose to live their lives differently.

I would define the religion problem as a duality: on the one hand protecting the rights of the many from the designs of religious extremists, on the other protecting the rights of a devout minority from the designs of extreme secularists. As Madison had foreseen and history has shown, in a democracy minorities are more vulnerable than the majority. Although the popular inclination towards the center and its awareness of the dangers posed from both the left and the right is heartening, it may provide a shallow defense for religious freedom. As we become more religiously and politically moderate, the barrier of protection provided for the more peculiar among us becomes increasingly thin.

I assume that most of the respondents in the Pew survey from 2006 had a moderate form of religiosity in mind, much like their own, when they spoke of the dangers posed to religion. Theirs is not a faith that would cause them concern with the mores set by the popular culture. Theirs is not a faith that would cause them to resist teaching about birth control in the public schools, or object to literature that some devout observers find inappropriate for young children. I wonder how far this moderate majority would go to protect the prerogatives of devout oddballs to live their lives according to the dictates of their consciences.

We should be reminded that the moderate attitudes of the American populace are to some extent built on a foundation of ambivalence and uninterest concerning matters political. The busy, self-absorbed, twenty-first-century American who is preoccupied with work, family, and other demands may not share the same passion for freedom as his forefathers, whose politics were driven by the harsh experience with colonial oppression. Nor is religion as important to him. Contemporary Americans have had the luxury of remaining aloof from politics without a noticeable effect on their lifestyles. I suspect they are more likely to be moved by the kinds of threats posed from the right, which would compromise their understanding of the proper relationships between church and state and offend their taste for moderation.

The chasm between political elites and the citizenry that was evident through the latter part of the last century remains. The gusts that move politics to the edge blow from both the left and the right. But, I would argue, the wide center, the hollow middle of America politics, is more likely to check a drift to the right. This is admittedly speculative on my part. We do not have a firm grasp on what the future brings. History informs us; but when it comes to politics and religion, our fears often guide us, much as they did the elder Mr. Madison. These fears are mine. Others would disagree, I am sure. They would point to an assumed rightward shift on the Supreme Court as a sign of things to come. They might recall, however, that the appeals court that ruled against Vicki Frost in the *Mozert* case was dominated by appointees of President Ronald Reagan. More recently, a federal judge appointed by President George W. Bush vigorously decided that the teaching of intelligent design in the public schools of Dover, Pennsylvania, is an unconstitutional imposition of religion.

Notwithstanding the shrieking alarm he sounded over the emergence of an "American theocracy," political analyst Kevin Phillips tells us that America in the twenty-first century is "too big and too diverse to resemble the Massachusetts Bay colony of John Winthrop."[54] After dissecting years of election returns, including those of the past two presidential contests, the wary Mr. Phillips concludes, "Bluntly putting it, I believe that a careful electoral analysis shows that what can be called the Bush coalition is too narrow to govern successfully and was empowered to win only by a succession of odd circumstances in both 2000 and 2004."[55]

Phillips's analysis is borne out by the results of the 2006 mid-term elections, which ended with the Republican Party losing control of both houses of Congress, as President Bush's approval ratings plunged. It is equally notable that profiles of the new Democrats entering Congress suggested a movement to the political middle rather than the political left, reinforcing profiles of American centrism and moderation.[56] The operative word among the new freshman was "collaboration" rather than "conflict," holding out the possibility of a new politics during the closing years of the Bush administration.

Whatever the future brings, we would hope that it promises a commitment to freedom that protects the religious and the nonreligious alike. This will require an American consensus that allows religious people to live their lives as they see fit, and prevents the most political among them from imposing their beliefs on others. The consensus I have in mind must be shared widely by the American populace, the political branches of government, and the courts of law. This brings us to the final chapter.

9

CONSCIENCE AND COMPROMISE

WE BEGAN THIS BOOK with a discussion about religious bias and its legitimization in the United States. This temperament, identified with an element on the political left, not only allows its purveyors to indulge their prejudice with impunity; it moves them to engage the government as a partner to enforce their perspective through a narrow interpretation of religious rights. Since the middle of the past century, those so inclined have had a certain measure of success in advancing their cause. Theirs is not the kind of bias directed at any one denominational group, so much as it is expressed towards the idea of religion itself and members of society who take their faith more seriously than the rest of us do—like the people profiled in the *New York Times Magazine* on the eve of the 2004 election: the ones who pray, the ones who feel close to God, the ones who wear their religion on their shirtsleeves, who arrange the details of their lives to fit their faith, rather than the other way around.

This bias is not pervasive. Most Americans are religious, in a manner of speaking. Although they do not practice their faith with the same vigor as those who are vulnerable to bias, they do not respond to the devout with alarm. Nor do they perceive religion in the same way as some activists on the political right who have claimed with some exaggeration that they were responsible for the presidency of George W. Bush. The determination of these religious activists to use their new-found power to impose their faith on others is partly responsible for the animosity towards religion of which we speak, giving some credence to the concerns raised by Ron Suskind in his provocative *Times Magazine* article from 2004.

This final chapter will draw on the materials covered earlier to present an approach to religious freedom designed to protect all Americans. There has already been notable progress in this direction, but not enough. Over the past twenty years the Supreme Court has modified its restrictive standard of church-state relations as it was once defined by the so-called *Lemon* test.[1] In doing so, it has assumed a more accommodationist position that reached its apex with the *Zelman* ruling of 2002.[2]

Both rulings inquire as to whether state action with religious implications has a secular public purpose. But where the *Lemon* test would focus on whether the action in question advanced religion or led to excessive entanglement between church and state, the *Zelman* standard emphasizes the need for evenhandedness or neutrality in the treatment of secular and religious institutions, and asks whether the use of a religious institution to carry out a general governmental function involves an element of choice on the part of service recipients.

Distinguishing clearly between religious and secular purposes is difficult enough in a country where the two have historically been intertwined. Trying to measure the differences and disentangle them leaves us with a standard of review that can be both ambiguous and arbitrary. The equanimity of the neutrality standard is unassailable on its face. The alternative would be to either favor or disfavor religious people and institutions. Introducing the notion of volition goes to the heart of the freedom that we are trying to protect.

We saw this factor in play when comparing the National Cathedral question raised by Susan Jacoby on behalf of secularists, and the Pledge of Allegiance challenge initiated by Mr. Newdow before the Supreme Court. What made President Bush's participation in the post-9/11 prayer service at the cathedral acceptable was that it was private and voluntary. Prohibiting it would have compromised the rights of those who wanted to be there, including the president. What ultimately gave Mr. Newdow the right to let his daughter refrain from reciting the Pledge (although he was not satisfied with the option) was that it took place at a public school where attendance was compulsory. Since 1943, conscientious objectors have enjoyed the right to sit out the exercise, but not the power, as Mr. Newdow has sought, to prevent others from partaking in it who wish to do so.

Despite the progress made by the post-*Lemon* Court in defining religious rights more broadly, the standard of religious freedom now operable still leaves the most religious among us legally vulnerable to the litigation-prone whims of ardent secularists. The "play in the joints" between the Establishment and Free Exercise clauses to which Chief

Justice Rehnquist alluded in *Locke v. Davey*[3] still favors the former. Most legal discourse on the First Amendment, including that which Chief Justice Rehnquist shepherded towards greater accommodation during his career on the court, remains fixated on what the Establishment Clause permits rather than what the Free Exercise Clause protects. And when this second question comes up, the restrictive standard set by Justice Scalia in the *Smith*[4] ruling does not leave much room for maneuvering.

It should not go unnoticed, by the way, that the two justices who were instrumental in setting these boundaries are usually associated with the conservative wing of the Court. If the Court is going to grant devoutly religious people the protection they deserve, it must take religious freedom more seriously than it has. Such a shift may be on the horizon with the new composition of the Court (a matter I will get to a bit later). That being said, even if the Court did become more accommodationist, it would not be able to afford the most devout among us the freedom they need to live their lives in complete harmony with the dictates of their consciences.

There are necessary limits assigned to religious freedom in a constitutional democracy. Some of these limits can be ascribed to the nature of religion itself; others have to do with the demands of constitutional democracy. Coming to terms with these limits is useful in helping us to appreciate how precious the remaining freedom really is, and why it is worthy of protection.

The first of these limits is imposed by the conflict that can exist between religion and reason. This is not to say that faith and reason are categorically incompatible, as do some secularists like Sam Harris, the best-selling author of *The End of Faith* we met in the early part of the book, who compared all religious observers with terrorists in their proclivity towards irrationality.[5] At times, however, faith and reason can be irreconcilable. This is best explained by way of example.

Consider, for the purpose of illustration, the Catholic doctrine of transubstantiation. Based on the biblical story of the Last Supper, it refers to the miracle in which a priest is said to transform bread and wine into the body and blood of Jesus Christ. The doctrine is the central premise of the mass that is attended daily by millions of Catholics all over the world. Catholics accept it as a matter of faith; for the nonbeliever it is problematic. After the consecration part of the mass is over, the wafer distributed to the congregation still has the physical characteristics of bread; the substance in the chalice, which sometimes is also consumed by the faithful, has all the tangible qualities of wine. In this instance faith and reason cannot be easily reconciled.

Transubstantiation is not a matter of faith that typically comes up in the public forum. For most non-Catholics it is too far-fetched to warrant serious discussion, thereby reasonably excluding itself from common discourse. There are other matters of faith, perhaps not so profound to the true believer, which do arise in popular discussion. Among the more prominent is that of creationism, which arose in the debate about teaching evolution in public schools. Despite the best efforts of intelligent design (ID) theorists, there is no scientific way to demonstrate the existence of a divine creator. Yet most Americans, not to mention mainstream theologians, hold that the theory of evolution is compatible with the existence of God.

No less a scientist than Isaac Newton believed in a Prime Mover, although Newton was never faced with the empirical reality of evolutionary theory. The passage of time has brought mounting evidence to support evolution. So why does the idea of divine creation have such currency in the modern world, years after scientists were able to demonstrate that we are, so to speak, accidents of nature whose ancestors were apes? There are several possible explanations—cultural, religious, and epistemological, not to mention human vanity—all of which can be linked without much imagination.

Americans are taken with the story depicted in the Book of Genesis because it is part of their upbringing, whether they are Jewish, Christian, or Muslim. There is also something appealing about a tale that traces our beginnings to a man and a woman created by a Supreme Being. While most Americans, especially the educated, are "too smart" to reject the teaching of mainstream science, they are inclined to accept it with a grain of salt because they do not really understand the regimen of proofs that prompts scientists to endorse evolution with such certainty. As I stated earlier, most Americans accept evolutionary theory as a matter of faith, much as they accept some version of the creation narrative. Unlike transubstantiation, Adam and Eve, whether literally or metaphorically, have a popular following in America.

It seems that creationists were in a better position when they argued their case on the basis of religion rather than science. Although our system of government has not always been as tolerant as it should be, it is capable of accommodating religious belief. The attempt by ID theorists to convert creationism into a campaign against evolution was a step backwards. It was more prudent to accept compromise in the form of a plain vanilla version of church-state separation.

The job of the state through the instrumentality of the public schools is to teach science, and religion cannot stand in the way of it. The state, however, has no business officially using science as a tool for refuting religion. Acknowledging the existence of a religious position outside the providence of science does not detract from the validity of the scientific theory; it simply recognizes that people have different ways of comprehending the world around them—ways that are not entirely compatible, ways that are not wholly convincing as a matter of objective truth. Religion and science, like church and state, are different if not entirely separable spheres. Religion instinctually resists compromise; democracy requires it. In the company of reason, compromise is the second limit imposed on religion in a constitutional democracy.

Most Americans appreciate that in order for democracy to function peacefully, citizens must be willing to negotiate their differences. Although the constitutional arrangement allows individuals wide latitude to believe what they want to believe, the government at times needs to draw the line when it comes to actual behavior. Both Locke and Jefferson were cognizant of the distinction between thought and action and the kinds of protections that can be afforded them by government. In many instances the government can accommodate the demands of conscience without interfering with the rights of others or the general public order. For example, without much disruption to the rest of us, conscientious objectors can be excused from the obligation to serve in the military during wartime or from saluting the flag in a public school. In different situations, accommodation to the demands of conscience can seriously intrude on the rights of nonbelievers.

Let's return here, by way of example, to the contentious issue of abortion. There are some people—many I should say—who believe that abortion is the taking of an innocent life, not unlike an act in which one person assaults another with a lethal weapon. There are several legal avenues open to a citizen who morally opposes abortion in that way. She may speak out in the public forum; she may lobby the government to make laws against it; she may run for office with the hope of passing such laws; or she may picket a health center that performs the act with the hope of discouraging it.

There is a legal limit, however, to how far she can go to stop it. She cannot physically intervene to prevent the performance of the act as she might to prevent a deadly assault, even though she perceives the victims in the two situations to be equally worthy of her intervention, even though she feels a similar moral compulsion to prevent the act from happening. That kind of compromise is necessary if our democracy is to work; yet it should not be taken lightly by the great majority who can readily accept it without making the same moral concession.

The abortion opponent who is prevented by law and popular convention from taking the matter into her own hands does not stop believing that what occurs on the operating table at the clinic is murderous. The demand for compromise that underlies our democratic system not only prevents her from forcing other people to behave as she would, but it prevents her from doing what in her mind is the right thing for her to do. The price she pays in the democratic bargain is dearer than it is for the person who does not share her moral perspective.

Our religious freedom is not only a limited freedom; it is unlike any other that we value as Americans. It is least satisfying for those to whom it matters the most, the devoutly religious. Conversely, it works best for those to whom it matters the least, the great majority who practice religion more casually, or, as Stephen Carter once wrote, who follow popular manners and treat religion "as a hobby."[6] Imagine for a moment, a similar conception of freedom applied to other values that we cherish as Americans. Imagine a definition of free speech formed around the needs of the quiet, or of a free press formed around the needs of the illiterate, or the right to assemble around the habits of the shy.

I do not mean to be facetious about this. I want to highlight the limited degree of protection our democracy can afford the deeply religious.[7] Not only is our democracy incapable of guaranteeing the devout a scope of freedom to practice their faith and live their lives as they see fit. At times the government must use its authority to force the most religious among us to compromise their own sense of right and wrong. That is a significant price to pay for the opportunity to exist peacefully in a pluralistic society, and it is important to recognize the exchange.

An explicit recognition of the democratic compromise marks an appropriate starting point for our closing discussion on the place of religion in American public life. When the state uses its authority to stand between a citizen and her conscience, it better have a good reason. As some constitutional lawyers, excluding the majority in the *Smith* case, would say, there ought to be a compelling public interest at stake. As any good liberal knows, the rights of conscience preceded the existence of the state, and cannot be revoked by the state too lightly without damaging the original social contract. Of course, what constitutes a compelling public interest can be a matter of debate in itself. The courts have not been especially helpful in this regard.

Compelling government interest is a term of art in the legal profession for a standard of judicial review that triggers "strict scrutiny" of a governmental action that may compromise constitutional rights. The concept is a sound one, but the courts at times have been irrational in their interpretation of it. A case in point is an eight-to-nothing decision the Supreme Court handed down in 2006 concerning enforcement of the federal Controlled Substance Act (CSA) of 1970.[8] As a matter of law, the *Boerne*[9] decision of 1997 that struck down a provision of the Religious Freedom Restoration Act (RFRA) incorporating free exercise protections against the states, where the bulk of litigation takes place, let stand the requirement that a compelling government interest must be present before the federal government can burden religion.

In 2006 the Court ruled that federal law enforcement officers had not demonstrated a compelling government interest when they confiscated an illegal hallucinogenic drug from a religious group called the Uniao do Vegetal, translated "Union of the Plants." The group had claimed that the use of the drug brought them closer to God. In reviewing the case, the Court observed that since 1994 Congress had granted an exemption to the federal drug law to thousands of Native Americans who ingested peyote as part of a religious ritual. The Court's reasoning was a classic example of two wrongs making a right.

Some observers might cite such a case as an illustration of the risks incurred from a robust interpretation of religious rights (here defined statutorily through RFRA).[10] I would be more inclined to describe the above case, and the precedent set in the peyote exception, as an abuse or misinterpretation of robust religious rights. Of course there is a compelling public interest at stake when the federal government enforces a drug law that conflicts with religious practices. Despite what the Court said in this particular case, most reasonable people would see it that way. The government should control the consumption of dangerous drugs, for whatever reason they are used.

And yes, the state should step in when parents put their children at risk by refusing medical treatment for religious reasons.[11] And yes, pedophile priests should not be allowed to abuse privileges associated with religious sanctuary to avoid criminal prosecution. There is nothing inherently erudite about these propositions that is beyond the grasp of ordinary citizens capable of sound moral judgment. It is unfortunate that such matters have become a serious source of debate among legal scholars, but the confusion among the lawyers is not sufficient reason to abridge legitimate constitutional rights.

The notion of religious liberty I have in mind would grant people of faith the most generous scope of freedom possible without infringing on public order or the rights of others to practice or not practice religion as they choose. My preference is to maximize the freedom of every individual to be the best person he or she, according to the dictates of conscience, can possibly be.[12] I want to minimize situations in which the state uses its authority to force people to do something they think is wrong, because I believe that doing so is neither good for the individual nor good for the state. I say this knowing full well that individuals have different understandings of what it means to be good, and that not all notions of goodness are derived from religion.

Two centuries ago the Founders had a difficult time separating conscience from religion—or Christianity for that matter. In the more secular world of the twenty-first century, we must protect the genuine instincts of people to be good, whether they are religious or not. The Founders not only appreciated the moral necessity of protecting the right of individuals to follow their conscience, they also understood the futility of exercising state power to alter it, a lesson contemporary partisans on both the left and the right come to rather slowly.

If a constitutional convention were called today to modernize the esteemed document, we might consider revising our conception of the First Amendment from a set of rights designed to ensure "freedom of religion" to one more broadly focused on "freedom of conscience" to mark the uncoupling of morality from religion (and Christianity) that has occurred in a more pluralist America. It is more than a little ironic that, as a newly constituted Supreme Court may finally stand ready to energize the Free Exercise Clause, it may be time to de-emphasize the benefits it brings to religion.

My suggestion is not meant to diminish the importance of religion so much as to ensure the protection afforded to all people of conscience. The Supreme Court has already moved in this direction through constitutional interpretation. But as we will see, even so-called secular notions of morality can be traced to religious tradition. The potential for disagreement is enormous here, and it requires the state through its institutions to set rules determining how citizens are permitted or expected to behave in the context of their own moral judgments.

These are not easy boundaries to draw. The most skilled draftsmen will wind up with imprecise lines of demarcation in attempting to reach a fair definition of religious freedom for all concerned. Just for beginners, it might be useful to note some general distinctions mentioned earlier to help structure the discussion: distinctions between private life and public life, between political speech and political action, between politics and government, those pertaining to education of the young, and those pertaining to the roles of the distinct branches of the government.

Private Life and Public Life

Religious institutions have always been at the heart of American civic life, serving as incubators for social activity that benefits society and maintaining a sphere of individual and group freedom outside the control of public authority. Religious institutions are also a source of civic strife. As political actors, they have not only accentuated our divisions; when empowered by the arm of the government, they have been discriminatory and oppressive towards minorities with whom they disagree. At times the religious derivation of unjust treatment by the government has been explicit, as was the case of the Puritans in the eighteenth century, and the Protestant majority in the nineteenth century.

At other times, religion's role in perpetuating policies that are unfair to particular groups has been more distant because religious teaching was so much a part of the common-law practices formally codified over time. Laws regulating marriage are a particular case in point, and help explain why the American sense of tolerance has moved so haltingly on the issue of gay marriage. While private religious practice is worthy of protection by the law, it becomes problematic when it has the force of law. But how does one know the difference and, therefore, where to draw the line?

Let us start with the simple item of religious speech, and trace the path in which it moves from the private to the public realm and why it matters. Other than the confines of the home, the most private expression of religious speech occurs in houses of worship. Congregations are voluntary communities of like-minded people who share a common set of beliefs and traditions. Their coming together on regular occasions is a form of self-affirmation that has no direct impact on the outside world. Once religious speech moves into the public arena, it can have different implications, depending on the intent and the circumstances.

A troupe of Hare Krishna members singing to tambourine music on the sidewalk is one form of religious speech familiar to most of us. It is an expression of faith and a form of proselytizing. Passersby may find their presence to be anything from amusing to annoying. A disgruntled pedestrian could be forced to walk around them or to cover his ears to avoid their message. The troupe is afforded the same constitutional protections as other groups who follow local ordinances governing public demonstrations. Their activity is protected by the speech, assembly, and religion clauses of the First Amendment.

If an interdenominational group of Christians, Jews, and Muslims assembled on the same sidewalk to protest abortion, the implications of the gathering would be more political. Their purpose would be to influence public opinion and to pressure political actors to adopt policies that would end or limit legal abortion. If successful, this could have an effect on the lives of other citizens. Their action is a form of religious speech. The Founders were well aware of the difference between using religion as a framework for understanding the world and using religion as a framework for changing it, as well as the risks that arise when an individual or group moves from one framework to the other.

Generally speaking, pedestrians on the sidewalk are likely to find the abortion protesters more disturbing than the Hare Krishna celebrants, especially if they believe that imposing legal constraints on abortion violates a woman's right to make her own decision on the matter. The gathering, nevertheless, is also protected by the Constitution, as any form of political speech would be. While their political argument against abortion is rooted in religion, one does not need to rely on religious teaching to have a morally based position against abortion. Here the religious and secular arguments can converge as well as clash, especially when the interest of the unborn fetus is factored into the discussion.

Now let us consider political argumentation that is grounded in a purely religious perspective. While few would argue that faith-colored positions should be legally banned from the public square, some secularists might be inclined to treat such argumentation with strong suspicion, as is their prerogative. They are not altogether comfortable with religious argumentation in the public square, because of concerns about where these arguments might lead government decision-makers. But political argument, if it is to be effective, must be public.

Religious people cannot easily divorce their moral concerns from their faith. Although religious speech can lead to government action, they are not one and the same. Government action is binding on citizens; political speech by religious people is not. It should also be noted—perhaps with only modest relief to ardent secularists—that when political argument relies entirely on religious reasoning, it is not usually effective in the halls of government. It lacks the secular currency needed to be persuasive. It is in most instances a benign political tool.

For example, a Muslim may urge his neighbor to pray in a prostrate position five times a day in order to meet his holy obligation to Allah, as a Catholic might urge the same neighbor to venerate the Eucharist to thank God for his redemption, but these admonitions are unlikely to influence nonbelievers or their representatives in the government. They are likely to fall flat in a democracy that rejects the idea of a religious establishment. Then again, there are exceptions to this general rule, and in such cases the consequences can be significant and the dangers real. At what point should the alarm be sounded? What types of defenses can be mobilized, assuming the problem is easily detected?

As legal philosopher Michael Perry has explained, most conventional morality has its origins in religious tradition, and laws are made to reflect moral standards.[13] We have already noted the problem of separating secular laws and conventions from their religious origins in the case of marriage. Until today most legally binding marriage vows are administered by a member of the clergy. Sometimes the religious roots of public policy are more easily identifiable than in others, and some faith-based positions have no apparent secular justification for serving as a basis for policy.

In the very early history of our nation a man had to be a Christian to hold public office. This restriction remained in place in most states well after religious tests were banned at the national level with the adoption of the federal Constitution. The assumption behind the practice was that only men of the Christian faith were worthy of the public trust. (Women of course were entirely excluded.) Its purpose and outcome were patently discriminatory.

Up until 1965 Connecticut had a law that prohibited the use of contraceptives. The law dated back to 1879, when clergymen and leaders in the medical profession spearheaded a campaign to clean up the loose sexual morality they feared had infected the nation.[14] Congress had passed a law six years earlier that prohibited sending obscene materials in the mail. Birth control paraphernalia were among the banned materials. Many states followed suit with their own statutes that prohibited birth control. In the early part of the twentieth century these laws ran into opposition by eugenicists. The latter groups embraced birth control as a technique to curb the procreation of inferior races of people who were migrating to America from southern and eastern Europe. Later on, birth control was recognized more broadly as a civil rights issue.

By the middle of the twentieth century, Connecticut and Massachusetts were the only states in the union to retain laws against birth control.[15] In 1958, at the urging of Catholic bishops, Connecticut toughened its statutes to make it an offense for any person, including a physician, to "aid, abet, or counsel" a woman regarding the use of contraceptives. According to the teaching of the church, birth control is the moral equivalent to abortion in its obstruction of human life. Between 1923 and 1964, there were twenty-nine attempts in the Connecticut legislature to remove birth control laws from the books, all of which failed. In the latter years, the Catholic hierarchy remained the single most important obstacle to eliminating the statutes.

Viewed from a secular perspective, the policy against birth control was difficult to justify. It not only infringed on the intimate relationships of couples, it increased the risk of sexually transmitted disease and teenage pregnancy. While legal scholars quibbled over the Court's reasoning, there was not much of a public outcry in 1965 when the United States Supreme Court in *Griswold v. Connecticut* struck down the law for its intrusion into the privacy of marital relationships.[16]

Seven years later, the Court, in *Eisenstadt v. Baird*, extended the protections articulated in *Griswold* to cover nonmarried persons, again without much public reaction.[17] Most people understood the religious motivation behind the law, and the practice of birth control was common even among Catholics. The *Griswold* and *Eisenstadt* rulings were subsequently used as precedents for expanding the privacy doctrine to establish a woman's right to an abortion in *Roe v. Wade*,[18] which proved to be much more divisive.

The progression from *Griswold* to *Roe* is instructive for a number of reasons. It once again underscores the political vulnerability of government actions that are based almost entirely on religious reasoning as opposed to those that have moral currency in the secular world. It also highlights the special role that the federal judiciary plays in ensuring that religious doctrine is not used as a basis for setting policy. Furthermore, examining the path from *Griswold* to *Roe* is useful in defining an approach for distinguishing between a moral position that is essentially religious and a moral position that is religiously relevant. Rather than pretend that hard boundaries exist between the two, it is better to view such questions on a continuum that requires the application of that rare commodity called "disinterested human judgment."

While it is certainly possible for one to have a secular position against birth control, the position is more readily associated with a religious point of view—not only attributed to the teaching of the Catholic Church but also associated with the Orthodox Jewish and Muslim faiths. Although much of the political opposition to abortion is religiously based, one does not need to rely on religious reasoning to challenge the morality of abortion once the interest of the unborn child is taken into account.

Looking at the issue on a continuum from religious to nonreligious argumentation, the question becomes clearer when we factor into consideration a number of other contentious issues having to do with human life. For example, one might view embryonic stem-cell research as more analogous to contraception, while viewing euthanasia and the death penalty as more analogous to abortion, when weighing the religious content of moral considerations. The latter are more arguable on wholly secular grounds considering the competing rights of individuals.

Again, I do not want to overstate the ease with which such distinctions can be made. The analytic distinctions made here with regard to the issue of human life are not meant to set down hard-and-fast rules for the settlement of any particular policy issue so much as to introduce considerations that are pertinent when making policy judgments. The validity of policy judgments pertaining to religion will inevitably rely on the circumstances surrounding a particular case, such as the two Ten Commandments cases that were recently decided simultaneously and differently by the Supreme Court on the basis of distinct fact patterns.

The need for such fine-line distinctions in political inquiry illustrates not only the distinct role played by the courts compared to the other branches of government, but also the special role of judges compared to elected officials. The role of elected officials is to represent the viewpoints of their constituents. Especially as it pertains to questions of morality, some of these views may be more or less grounded in a religious perspective, or in fact may be entirely based on religious convictions.

The probability of the latter succeeding in a political chamber is relatively low because, as we saw, policy positions articulated purely on the basis of religious argumentation are not especially persuasive to most citizens and their representatives. But success is possible. A representative elected by an orthodox Jewish, Catholic, or Muslim constituency may genuinely believe that the use of contraceptives compromises human life. As self-defeating as his religious position may be in a legislative body composed of nonbelievers or religious moderates, he has every right to promote his position among his legislative colleagues. Depending on how committed he is to his position as a matter of conscience, one might even say that he has a moral obligation to try to pass a law that reflects his position on the issue.

The alternative is to expect the elected official to act in a way that he believes is unethical or immoral. Again, this is not an easy call. As was true with several politicians mentioned earlier, a morally reflective elected official might also be expected to factor into his or her calculation the important role that compromise plays in our democratic process, as well as a consideration of the demands of conscience (both religious and other) that motivate his or her adversaries.

Given the health risks associated with unprotected sex, one could certainly make a moral case against the banning of contraceptives. Given the significant health benefits that can result from stem-cell research, one can reasonably make a moral argument in its support. Even when these considerations are taken seriously, however, the elected official is not automatically obliged to betray his sense of morality in the fulfillment of his governmental responsibility. He is the representative of a political constituency. He is a political actor with independent judgment, and politics is ultimately a dispute over values, some of which cannot easily be severed from religious contexts.

The role of the judge is quite different. She too may be expected to come to the governmental table with a moral position that is more or less informed by religion. But unlike the elected official, she is granted a smaller window of opportunity to legitimately indulge that position in her work as a governmental actor. Enabled by life tenure (if she is a federal judge), her first duty is to protect the Constitution from the excesses of the political branches. She is expected to interpret the law based on her understanding of the Constitution and judicial precedent.

The discussion that accompanied the recent appointments of Chief Justice John Roberts and Associate Justice Samuel Alito to the Supreme Court is illustrative of the complex role played by the judiciary.

The process of selecting federal judges is a highly political one involving nomination by the president and confirmation by the Senate, both of which demand a high level of partisan scrutiny. Once a candidate is approved, though, he has a special obligation to protect the Constitution free from political and personal considerations. The judge is the last line of protection against government action that compromises individual rights.

In the most recent confirmation hearings, some members of the Judiciary Committee sought assurances that the two nominees, when on the Court, would act in one way or another when it came to certain controversial issues like abortion or executive privilege. Reasonable people can differ over the wisdom of forcing judicial nominees to telegraph their positions on contentious issues that may eventually come before them. It is fair, however, to ask how diligent a nominee will be in sorting his religious convictions from his jurisprudence. It is appropriate to determine whether a candidate for the bench can distinguish between a moral position that flows primarily from a personal religious viewpoint and a position that has merit in a more secular context because the court is the ultimate safeguard against the improper mingling of law and religion. The Constitution that the federal judge or justice swears to protect is a higher law than the statutes passed by legislative bodies.[19]

The stakes can also be high when one moves from the establishment side of the First Amendment to the free exercise side, which is less concerned with the legitimate authority of the government and more concerned with the rights and privileges of citizens. Take, for instance, cases in which religious observers, as a matter of conscience, seek exemptions from general laws. Why, we might ask, should religious observers be exempted from laws that are generally applied to all citizens?[20] What about the neutrality principle that we embraced just a few pages ago?

Well, the most compelling argument for such exemptions has to do with the nature of religious belief and the commands upon the conscience it makes when it is genuinely felt. This is in part a concession to an age-old American premise, which held that religion can have a positive influence on moral character and that there is a correlation between personal character and civic virtue, both of which contribute to the quality of American democracy. Put another way, it is generally better for the state to avoid using its authority to compel a citizen to perform an act the citizen genuinely believes to be wrong. At a time when Americans are more apt to separate moral conviction from religion, however, one does not need to abandon the neutrality standard to protect rights of conscience.

The Supreme Court, or at least some of its members, made a noble attempt to incorporate protections to a broad range of conscientious objectors in a series of cases that had to do with military service. Instead of admitting outright that some objectors were not relying on religion to formulate their moral perspectives, the Court adopted a wide-ranging definition of religion.[21] When the selective service law was first enacted in 1948, it exempted persons who were conscientiously opposed to war by reason of their "religious training and belief." It defined the latter as "belief in relation to a Supreme Being involving duties superior to those arising from any human relation, but [not including] essentially political, sociological, or philosophical views or a merely personal moral code." The law seemed to be fashioning a twentieth-century notion of rights to an eighteenth-century notion of conscience.

When the pacifist Daniel Andrew Seeger sought conscientious objector status in 1965, the Court chose to define religion in terms of a broad inclusive category.[22] Seeger, an outspoken opponent of the Vietnam War, claimed to believe in "goodness and virtue for their own sakes" and admitted to having "a religious faith in a purely ethical creed [without] belief in God except in the remotest sense." In reviewing Seeger's case, Justice Clark opined, "The test of belief 'in relation to a Supreme Being' is whether a given belief that is sincere and meaningful occupies a place in the life of the possessor parallel to that filled by their orthodox belief in God of one who clearly qualifies for exemption."[23] He further noted "the richness and variety of spiritual life in our country."

Five years later, in another conscientious objector case, Justice Harlan wrote that it would violate the Establishment Clause to limit the exemption only to conscientious objectors who oppose war for "theistic beliefs."[24] He elaborated that Congress "cannot draw the line between theistic and nontheistic beliefs on the one hand and secular beliefs on the other." The Court was not in complete agreement on this holding.

In 1972, Justice Douglas appeared to retreat from this broad definition of conscience in a partial dissent in the *Yoder* case, which exempted the Amish from compulsory education laws in Wisconsin. In that most potent of free exercise cases, Justice Douglas made it a point to distinguish between a conventional religious viewpoint and a pacifist position of the sort that writer Henry David Thoreau articulated on more secularist grounds. That interpretation put the definition of conscience back into the eighteenth century.

In this day and age, the Constitution should not restrict conscientious objector status exclusively to religious people. Faith is relevant in a court of law because it is more easily associated with an integrated lifestyle that speaks to the level of conviction for which one is seeking the exemption. A Quaker who is an active member of his meetinghouse is a more convincing conscientious claimant than someone who arrived at his position while on his way to the military draft board (when there was such a thing). A more dramatic example of what I have in mind was the claim by the Amish in the *Yoder* case that sending their children to high school with other children would compromise their way of life, involving customs and values that were deep-seated and distinct.

There were so many visible manifestations of their religious conviction that it was difficult to challenge the sincerity of the Amish. Besides that, their way of life did not pose any burden to society. Some constitutional scholars have contended that the Supreme Court inadequately protected the interests of the children in the *Yoder* case. Their assumption is that our majority way of life is better than the simple life the Amish have chosen for themselves. Their point is arguable, but in the end it comes down to a dispute over values rather than the sheer interest of the children that is so obvious in the medical assistance and pedophile situations.

Amish society has survived and prospered for many years. One does not need to be a foolish romantic to appreciate a lifestyle that rejects violence, materialism, and competition in favor of a life that is peaceful, modest, and community-minded. Their ways are conspicuously different, but the Amish would represent a reasonable alternative to popular norms whether or not their ways were rooted in religion. Given the high school graduation rate in the general population,[25] perhaps growing up in Amish society, where young people learn a trade, is not as striking a disadvantage as it might seem. Moreover, because the Amish way of life is a matter of private choice, men and women who reach the age of adulthood reserve the right to leave their community and join the mainstream society if they wish.

These are difficult questions to sort out. In order to approach the task judiciously, we need to be able to step back from a preconceived notion of the good life that is informed by our own preferences and biases. Compare the Amish case with the nineteenth-century *Reynolds* case involving the Mormons. All indications seemed to suggest that Mr. Reynolds's religious convictions were deep-seated and genuine. A large part of the animosity towards the Mormons stemmed from the fact that their polygamy offended conventional public mores that were rooted in Christianity and its notion of a proper marital relationship. Unlike the Amish, who were perceived as being wholesome, decent, law abiding, and hardworking, the Mormons were viewed as sexual deviants.

Inherent in the mainstream religious traditions that were then operable were legitimate concerns involving the personal interests of individuals who lived in Mormon society, which the state had a duty to protect. While polygamous marriages were supposedly entered into on a voluntary basis, there were signs that these arrangements exploited women, even when judged by the archaic standards of the nineteenth century. Beyond that, many young women were prematurely encouraged or forced into marriage with predatory older men. There were no comparable interests at stake in *Yoder.* The Amish case was primarily a dispute over social and educational values, whereas the Mormon case allowed the government to intervene in relationships that compromised rights and interests worthy of state protection. The state had a duty to intervene in *Reynolds* regardless of whether the polygamous arrangements were based on religious beliefs.

CHILDREN AND SCHOOLING

There is nothing more basic to parenting than a mother and father's desire to pass on their values to their children.[26] So when deeply religious parents whose values fall outside the mainstream send their children to public school, they enter into a relationship that is inherently fraught with conflict. Public schools, after all, are governmental institutions that transmit the values of the common culture to the minds and souls of children. Because compulsory education is a matter of law across the country, public schooling is a subtle act of state coercion. Most families have no choice but to send their children to public schools, because they do not have the financial means to send them to private or religious schools. The arrangement works for the great majority, which is part of the problem if you are in the minority. The rights of the latter must be protected. Before schools require children to absorb material that undermines values taught in their homes, school officials should be expected to show that they have a compelling educational reason for doing so.

Given the stakes, a reasonable person might expect decision makers in a democracy to be sensitive to the needs of families whose religious values are vulnerable in the school environment, or at least willing to grant these families the same deference afforded nonreligious conscientious objectors. But that has not always been so. Leave aside the specific case of Vicki Frost and the dissenters in the *Mozert* case for the moment. Although the Court eventually allowed students to refrain from saluting the American flag, it refused to grant them released time to take religious classes at their schools. Granted, one case involved a claim based on the rights of conscience, while the other involved a mere accommodation; yet the differing responses by the Court suggest a general insensitivity towards religious people. The appeal by a small minority of children to opt out of the Pledge of Allegiance exercise was accommodated as a basic right of conscience, as it should have been. The appeal by a larger minority of students, perhaps a majority in places, to be released from classes to take religious training was treated as a disruption.

It wasn't the number of students involved in either situation that was decisive. If a majority of students wanted to refrain from saluting the flag, their request would be granted. The plea by students who wanted to take religious instruction at their schools was evaluated differently, not just in terms of the needs of the students making the request, but also with regard to the purported needs of those who did not. Justice Frankfurter in particular was concerned that the latter would feel marginalized, even though marginalization was never suspected as a motive behind the released-time program.

In the flag case, being different was interpreted as a right; in the
released-time case, being different was interpreted as a form of exclusion. It would not have been entirely unreasonable to introduce the
question of student perceptions in the flag case. Justice Frankfurter
was consistent on that point in his opposition to exemptions in the
flag case. Public schools are supposed to instill a sense of citizenship
and common identity. Permitting students to reject a popular patriotic
ritual can readily be interpreted by impressionable students as a challenge to those unifying objectives. Nonetheless, individual conscience prevailed.

The decisive consideration in the released-time case was the presence of religious instruction on the premises of a public school. The
Court took care of that with an eventual compromise that allowed
students to take their religious instruction off campus. The net effect
of the new "accommodation" was to make it more inconvenient for
students to take religious instruction. Concerns for the marginalization
of those who abstained from taking the instruction faded out of focus.

Religion would later reappear in the public schools with the passage
of the Equal Access Act, and recognition by the courts that religious
groups must be afforded the same rights and privileges as others. Some
after-school activities brought in under these auspices include an element of religious instruction. Released time itself does not seem to be
a burning issue anymore. If it were reintroduced in the public schools
today, it would attract considerably fewer students than it did in the
1950s. The contemporary popular culture is more secular. As shallow
as American religiosity was after World War II, parents were more
prone to go through the motions and keep up appearances. No need
for that anymore.

In recent years public school districts have become more amenable
to the introduction of religious subjects into the curriculum.[27] Well-
respected constitutional scholars who would ordinarily be identified
with a separationist posture have encouraged schools to improve instruction about religion as a historical and cultural phenomenon so
that young people can better appreciate the role religion has played
in human and moral development.[28] This is all well and good. The
programs under way can enrich the public school curriculum, but they
are not an accommodation to religion. They are meant to guarantee
that schools cover subjects that ought to be taught. They put back

lessons that should have never been removed in the days of ardent secularism and incorporate much-needed materials that were omitted from the basic curriculum.

School prayer remains more contentious. It is not an academic subject, but a form of worship. It has come up in the classroom, at graduation exercises, and during athletic events. The courts have moved towards a reasonable philosophical position on the question by permitting moments of silence and distinguishing between student-led prayer and exercises organized by school officials. The former are private, the latter are a manifestation of government policy. But as a practical matter, the agreed-upon compromise can be difficult to implement. Sometimes it is hard to tell whether students initiated the prayers or whether professionals at the school were involved. Very young students at elementary schools are incapable of organizing such an activity. Even when students are the source, school officials must assume responsibility for overseeing the prayers, sometimes creating the impression of official sanction.

In the end, these well-meaning efforts at accommodation may prove to be inadequate for deeply religious people whose faith is more central to their existence. Devout observers may prefer to pray on their own, using designated texts rather than the homogenized scripts that emerge from political consensus. A mere moment of silence might be insufficient for them to meet their spiritual obligations. Faithful adherence to traditions may involve praying several times a day. Additionally, their religion may call for special dietary restrictions, the observance of special holidays, the learning of a particular language like Hebrew or Arabic, or the separation of the sexes during certain school activities like physical education classes. Then, there is the ever-volatile issue of the school curriculum.

To a large extent the case of Vicki Frost and her friends in the *Mozert* case turned out to be more controversial than it needed to be. The appeals court was more determined to enforce the majority will of the school board than to appreciate the religious sensibilities of the families. What made the ordeal so ridiculous was that after the parents were forced to accept the reading series, the publisher (McGraw-Hill) decided that the materials in question were not essential to the lessons after all. There was no real compelling education issue at stake, and therefore no good reason to make these particular materials compulsory for all students.

In this situation a mechanism also existed to accommodate the minority students without any great disruption to others. Tennessee had a home-schooling law that would have made it possible for parents to offer their children instruction from a state-approved reading list while excluding the materials mandated by the school board. The appeals court rejected the compromise Judge Thomas Hull had negotiated at the trial. Judge Hull was later vilified in the press for his effort to reach a fair resolution. Parents were told to take it or leave it. The *Mozert* case was a prime example of how the common school can breed discord rather than harmony.

The dispute that erupted in *Mozert* was essentially a clash of values. It is similar to the kind of disagreement that arises when children are required to take a sex education class that conflicts with the religious beliefs of their parents. These parents deserve the same kind of accommodation afforded conscientious objectors who refuse to salute the flag. Sex education is no more central to the public school mission than is saluting the flag. In fact a parent should not have to resort to a religious claim if for some reason she believes that a particular piece of literature or classroom lesson promotes values that she finds offensive, especially when younger children are involved.

These disagreements over values, however, should not be confused with the kind of debate that has emerged over the teaching of evolution. Evolutionary theory is a definitive scientific paradigm that is an essential aspect of teaching and learning. To omit it from a science curriculum is to diminish the curriculum, and schools should not be expected to exempt students from it. There is a difference between truth and values. Public schools serving diverse populations must be prepared to compromise on the latter, not the former.

But even if a public school were willing to accommodate a deeply religious family by providing a convenient time for taking religious instruction, or excusing students from value-based instruction that offends their faith, or arranging for periods of voluntary prayer, or making provisions for special dietary needs in the cafeteria, or pardoning students from following the school dress code, such accommodations might not be sufficient to serve the needs of the deeply religious. For some families it may not be enough to avoid offense. Deeply religious families may want to educate their children in an environment that openly conveys and supports faith-based values. In a state where education is compulsory and supported through public funding, the genuine concerns of these families must be taken seriously by state authorities. Provision should at least be made for those who cannot afford to assume the financial burden of private school tuition.[29]

For too long, the courts have indulged the naive assumption that the best way to avoid political or religious conflict is to force children to attend schools together following the same general formula with regard to the values conveyed. As we saw in *Mozert*, this very proposition has been a source of disagreement.[30] Imposing a monolithic system of education on a pluralistic population has brought dissention and resentment. Many defenders of the common school model have advanced the idea that allowing students to attend schools outside the public system fosters political fragmentation and prevents children from developing a civic consciousness.[31] There is no evidence to support such claims.

The existing evidence indicates that people who attend religious schools exhibit high levels of civic and political participation, which should not be surprising given the role that religious institutions play in promoting civil society.[32] A visitor to New York, and I would imagine many other American cities, is more likely to find children saluting the American flag and singing the National Anthem in religious schools than in the public schools. The notion of the common school is something of an American myth. Compulsory education laws are written to exempt students whose families can bear the cost of private school tuition. The principle of common education gets sacrificed on the alters of wealth and privilege. The demands of conscience are not so readily accommodated.

BEYOND TOLERANCE

It is not enough to tolerate deeply felt religious belief in a free society. As a twenty-five-year-old James Madison admonished his senior colleagues at the Virginia constitutional convention of 1776, all people should be "equally entitled to the free exercise of religion, according to the dictates of conscience." Once the state has determined that all children should be educated and that schooling is a public responsibility, forcing parents to assume a financial penalty for educating their children in an environment that supports their faith is a form of discrimination that violates the egalitarian premise. It burdens the free exercise rights of those who can afford it and revokes the rights of those who cannot. As a matter of public policy, an economically disadvantaged family that chooses to forgo a public school education as a matter of conscience—religious or other—ought to be provided with a level of public support equal to the amount they would receive in public school.[33] This arrangement would allow all parents to fulfill their responsibility to educate their children in accord with compulsory education laws as they choose.

The prospect of using tax dollars to pay for tuition at a religious school again returns us to the Virginia legislature of 1777 when Thomas Jefferson made his eloquent argument against compelled support. Judges, lawyers, and constitutional scholars regularly cite Mr. Jefferson's famous plea as an argument against school vouchers. The argument, which Mr. Madison endorsed, has more recently been used to oppose public support to faith-based social service organizations. In both cases the Jeffersonian reasoning does not hold up in its contemporary application.

Jefferson's bill was written against the direct support of churches, which were not significantly involved in the performance of secular functions. Religious institutions that are presently involved in the delivery of educational and social services are very much involved in the performance of secular functions long considered responsibilities of the state. Their religious identification does not add an additional burden to taxpayers so long as the cost of service delivery does not exceed the cost of providing the same services through government providers. Madison's widely cited "Memorial and Remonstrance" is one step further removed from contemporary concerns because it dealt with a bill that would have paid for the education of the clergy, and only the Christian clergy at that.

Obviously there are taxpayers today who object to the use of religious institutions to carry out public functions. But it has never been the prerogative of taxpayers to exercise veto power over government expenditures with which they disagree, whether their displeasure stems from the war in Iraq or the welfare state. The merits of a particular public policy must be measured on its own terms. In the present discussion about the First Amendment, the question concerns what rights are at stake, and what policy is more likely to protect and advance those rights.

Here the conflict between the *Lemon* and *Zelman* standards is especially acute. The secular relevance of educational and social services is indisputable. To the degree that these services are delivered in the spirit of a faith-based moral consciousness, they do advance a religious point of view and, in so doing, commingle the missions of church and state. But insofar as public funds are administered in a neutral fashion, their expenditure does not favor religion in general or any religion in particular, making the policy intrinsically egalitarian. And insofar as service recipients enjoy the option to choose their service providers, the policy advances the freedom of clients.

While the disgruntled taxpayer may be unhappy with the religious service provider his neighbor selects, he does not lose a morsel of freedom from the availability of a choice, once it is agreed that the service provided is worthy of public support and that the religious organization is meeting its secular responsibility. His loss is imaginary. There is a tangible margin of freedom realized when a service recipient has the opportunity to pick the school or the health center where she and her family will be served.

There is also a measure of equality realized when that educational opportunity is no longer defined as a function of economic privilege available only to families who can afford the cost of private tuition. Research cited in the previous chapter suggests that service recipients express higher levels of satisfaction when they are able to select providers that reflect their own values. Research from choice experiments in education consistently reveals higher levels of satisfaction recorded among parents and children who attend private, religious, and charter schools in comparison to those in public schools. Among other things, they appreciate the opportunity to choose.

The taxpayer has a right to dislike the religious institution his neighbor may choose, but the same taxpayer has no right to use the government as an instrument to indulge that dislike. What made the *Walz*[34] decision about tax exemptions for religious institutions so compelling in an era of jurisprudence dominated by the thinking of the *Lemon* court was its evenhandedness. Tax exemptions were allowed for religious institutions because they were allowed for other charitable institutions. Once tax exemptions were approved, all other arguments about indirect aid became trivial.

There are many commentators who fear that a publicly supported voucher program would put money into the wrong hands. For some the fear is genuine; for others it is a red herring in the voucher debate. Not so long ago when I took to the lecture circuit to discuss my book on school choice, I was repeatedly presented with the question, "So what do we do when the Ku Klux Klan or the Nazi Party decides to open its own schools?" By the time I finished my tour, I began to wonder whether the Klan and the Nazis maintained education development offices that were ready to spring into action the moment public funding became available.

On one rainy evening I was speaking to a group of neighborhood parents in the State Office Building on 125th Street in Harlem. A very distinguished gentleman who was well known in education circles and, like myself, an outsider to the community raised his hand to ask the inevitable question. Before I had a chance to respond a mother in the audience stood up and said she would take it. She told the gentleman not to worry. She said, "If the Klan and the Nazis decide to open a school in Harlem, we won't go." She told him that his time would be better spent worrying about the public school down the block, where only 20 percent of the children have been taught to read, and parents are reluctant to drop off their kids in the morning, fearing for their safety.

The mother's point is well taken: Parents will be discriminating about where they put their kids in school, if they are allowed to decide.[35] In order for a school to succeed, it must attract a clientele. But we need not rely entirely on parental discretion to guard against the misappropriation of public funds for purposes that undermine the public interest. Public funding should carry an expectation of public accountability. Private schools that accept indirect funding through choice programs should be expected to meet the same state academic standards that public schools are held to—not only with regard to basic skills such as reading, writing, and math, but also in other subject areas like science, history, and geography. And yes, the science curriculum should teach evolution. Furthermore, any school that teaches values that undermine the fundamental principles of American democracy (including tolerance) should not only be disqualified from receiving public funding, it should be closed down.

Beyond assuring that a religious school receiving indirect public funding meets its secular educational mission, state accountability should not serve as a vehicle for secularizing faith-based institutions. Although a school that accepts public funding should not be permitted to discriminate against applicants on the basis of religion, it should be permitted to maintain its character as a faith-based institution through the incorporation of religious instruction, prayer, exercises, and the observance of religious traditions. For the state to command otherwise would defeat the purpose of granting religious families the unburdened opportunity to choose religious schools.

Parents who do not want their children to participate in religious activity of this sort do not need to send their children to religious schools, nor should they be encouraged by the state to use open enroll-ment as a tool for diluting the religious character of these schools. The bottom line here is that once it is established that a religious school meets its secular educational responsibility, it should be treated as a self-governing institution with a legitimate religious purpose. It is here, I am afraid, that the American sense of religious tolerance comes up short. This is best illustrated by the public opinion surveys discussed in chapter 2.

According to the polls cited, the same American population that believes in God (96 percent), claims church membership (69 percent), agrees that church leaders should speak out on political issues (85 per-cent), feels that increased political involvement of church leaders would be good for politics (63 percent), and supports public funding for faith-based institutions (75 percent) gets cold feet when it comes to honoring the prerogative of the same institutions to govern themselves. Sixty percent worry that faith-based social service institutions might proselytize to their clients, and 78 percent are concerned that they would only hire their own members. The vast "hollow middle" of the American populace has its limits, when it comes to defining the proper

scope of religious freedom. The research in the preceding chapter suggests that not much proselytizing occurs at faith-based health and social
service organizations. Whether or not that is true, the instillation of
religious beliefs and values is a core purpose of religious schools.

In 1988 the Supreme Court approved a federal program that included religious organizations among the recipients of funds for premarital counseling.[36] A year earlier, the Court approved an exemption contained in the federal Civil Rights Act that allows religious institutions
to restrict hiring to employees of their own faith in positions where
faith is relevant to the performance of the job. Writing for the Court,
Justice Brennan declared that in the interest of autonomy religious
groups must be permitted to "select their own leaders, define their own
doctrines, resolve their own disputes and run their own institutions."[37]
In 2000, the Court applied the Freedom of Association Clause of the
First Amendment to uphold an employment policy of the Boy Scouts
that discriminated against homosexuals.[38]

It might not matter whether a clerical worker in a Catholic hospital
is a Catholic, but in a school or other institution that works with children, every adult is a potential role model who either advances or undermines the teaching of the institution in the way he or she behaves.
The question is how far a religious institution can go to maintain its
values, or more specifically, what kind of exemption it should be
granted from the enforcement of antidiscrimination laws. I would draw
the line somewhere between where the Court did in the Boy Scouts
case, and where the American public did in the Pew survey.

While faith-based institutions should be granted wide latitude for
adopting hiring practices that favor their own members, as a general
policy they should not be allowed to discriminate on the basis of race,
national origin, gender, or sexual orientation. Once religious identity
is established where it is relevant, other forms of identity are, except
in rare cases,[39] irrelevant so long as the employee agrees to abide by
the norms of the institution.

The employment policy proposed here presents a particular challenge with regard to gays. The first problem is that gays do not enjoy
the same constitutional and statutory protections as the other protected groups mentioned, so they are more legally vulnerable. On a
practical level, many religious groups categorically object to homosexu-

ality as a matter of faith. That being the case, these groups should not be legally permitted to discriminate against an individual solely because he is gay. If, however, an individual who is a role model at a school behaves in a way that undermines the values of the institution, the institution should retain the right to refuse hiring him (or to let him go), so long as the institution implements its standards of personal behavior evenhandedly with regard to all groups (homosexual and heterosexual). This may not seem like much protection for the gay employee of a religious school, but it actually is—as much as it is for anyone else at the school, which is all we can expect from an antidiscrimination policy.

The least intrusive approach to resolving a disparity between an employee's lifestyle and an institution's values is to expect the employee who is in a position to serve as a role model (whether homosexual or heterosexual) to exercise discretion, implementing a civilian version of the military's don't ask, don't tell policy on the school premises. If the institution, however, insists on enforcing a behavioral code consistent with its teaching, apart from the role model issue, it must do so evenhandedly with regard to gay or straight personnel. The private religious institution should retain the right to abide by its own values, but it should not be permitted to discriminate.

Here again, the use of a more detailed example can be helpful. Let's assume that Jack is gay, and he teaches at the Holy Smoke Orthodox Christian Elementary School. Let us also assume that Jack's sexual identity is known to his employer, and that Jack lives with another man. Jack's living arrangement should not be adequate grounds for dismissal. The question with regard to Jack is twofold. One, does Jack have a sexual relationship with his live-in partner that violates the teaching of the church? And two, how far is the school administration willing to go to ascertain that? Since the employer cannot go into Jack's bedroom at night, it has two options. It could either ask Jack directly what his relationship is with his roommate, or it can require him to sign a general employment agreement in which he declares that he is not living a life that contradicts the teaching of the school.

The operable rule for determining discrimination here should not be whether Holy Smoke asks Jack the question and/or acts on it. The operable rule should be whether the employer enforces its moral code towards its heterosexual employees with the same diligence. Does Holy Smoke inquire so vigilantly about the moral commitments of a heterosexual single person? Whether she has a lover? Whether she has ever had an abortion? Whether she engages in sodomy or mastur-bation? Whether the unmarried heterosexual has a sexual relation-ship? Whether the married couple practices birth control? Assuming that fidelity to the teachings of the faith is a crucial condition of employment at Holy Smoke, does the school administration try to ascertain whether a teacher attends church regularly? If the employer singles out gays for enforcing its religious teaching, it is discriminat-ing. If a homosexual or heterosexual person admits to or flaunts a lifestyle that openly contradicts the evenly enforced teaching of the religious organization, then the employer is entitled to let him or her go.

One would need to be an unusually devout religious observer to acquiesce to the kind of personal scrutiny that might exist at Holy Smoke, let alone follow the behavioral code that it enforces. Being so rigid, Holy Smoke's requirements could be a factor in dissuading potential clients who are not so observant of their faith. Many Chris-tian families might be inclined to send their children elsewhere. We might wonder why a person who is not inclined to accept such an orthodox form of religious observance would want to be associated with a place like Holy Smoke; but, in a free society, people who of their own volition want to work or send their children there ought to have the option.

A robust definition of religious freedom should allow religious institu-tions to be what their members want them to be within the constraints of the law. The law should function to protect individuals from unfair discrimination; it should not serve as an invitation to use litigation as an instrument to change a religious institution into something other than what it means to be according to its own teaching. Antidiscrimina-tion law should not be used as a lever for secularizing religious institu-tions. Antidiscrimination law should be enforced against discrimination.

This resolution to the problem at hand, I suspect, will not satisfy those on the far right or the far left of the political divide; but it may be the best we can do to protect a private sphere of autonomy for religious communities without seriously jeopardizing the rights of other vulnerable minorities—a challenge that remains at the center of the religion question.

• • •

As I put the final words of this book to paper, Democratic Party strategists around the country are gathering to plot how they might take back Washington from the Republicans. The word on the street is that they are aware of their missteps on the religion issue in 2004, and how their perceived animosity towards people of faith undermined their chances to win control of the White House and the Congress. In the meantime a lineup of Republican hopefuls is reviewing its notes from the last national contest, intent on maintaining its presumed advantage with people of faith so that it can repeat the victories of the Bush team.

I continue to wonder whether either side has figured out that the great majority of the American people are moderately religious; and that left to their own instincts, most voters would neither choose to drive religion from the public square nor wield it as a club for governing the nation. My advice to both sides, for what it is worth, is to refrain from grasping onto religion as an artifact of politics. It is much too important for that. Since the founding, religion has been a foundation for American civil society—that giant sphere of private life that exists beyond the reach of government and gives meaning to the word *freedom*. Our freedom is not without bounds. It does not entitle those who share its benefits to trample on the rights of others or disturb the public order. But to the vast extent that those who enjoy it contribute to the quality of democratic life, they deserve the opportunity to be the best people that they can be, unfettered by the rest of us.

NOTES

Chapter One: Fear and Loathing

1. Joseph P. Viteritti, *Choosing Equality: School Choice, the Constitution, and Civil Society* (Washington, D.C.: Brookings Institution Press, 1999).

2. Brown v. Board of Education, 347 U.S. 483, 493 (1954). See also Linda Greenhouse, "Win the Debate, Not Just the Case," *New York Times*, July 14, 2002, sec. 5, p. 4.

3. Milton Friedman, "The Role of Government in Education," in Robert Solo, ed., *Economics and the Public Interest* (New Brunswick: Rutgers University Press, 1955). See Joseph P. Viteritti, "Defining Equity: Politics, Markets, and Public Policy," in Alan Wolfe, ed., *School Choice: The Moral Debate* (Princeton: Princeton University Press, 2003).

4. Zelman v. Simmons-Harris, 536 U.S. 639 (2002). See Joseph P. Viteritti, "Reading Zelman: The Triumph of Pluralism and Its Effects on Liberty, Equality, and Choice," *Southern California Law Review* 76 (July 2003), pp. 1105–88.

5. Clint Bolick, *Voucher Wars: Waging the Legal Battle Over School Choice* (Washington, D.C.: Cato Institute, 2003).

6. Greenhouse, "Win the Debate," p. 4.

7. Although I did address the religious dimension of the voucher issue in my earlier book, one commentator in a comprehensive and generally positive review essay argued that the liberty argument in favor of vouchers deserved more emphasis. See Viteritti, *Choosing Equality*, pp. 117–77; Richard W. Garnett, "Brown's Promise, Blaine's Legacy," *Constitutional Commentary* 17 (2000), pp. 651–82.

8. Kevin Phillips, *American Theocracy: The Peril and Politics of Radical Religion, Oil, and Borrowed Money* (New York: Viking, 2006), pp. viii, 364–68.

9. Ron Suskind, "Faith, Certainty and the Presidency of George W. Bush," *New York Times Magazine*, October 17, 2004, p. 46 (sec. 7). Suskind later developed this theme in Suskind, *The One Percent Solution* (New York: Simon and Schuster, 2006).

10. Sam Harris, *The End of Faith: Religion, Terror, and the Future of Reason* (New York: Norton, 2004), p. 25. See also the best-selling book by Richard Dawkins, *The God Delusion* (Boston: Houghton Mifflin, 2006).

11. Harris, *The End of Faith*, p. 223. Harris's second book, *Letter to a Christian Nation* (New York: Knopf, 2006), is more moderate in tone and respectful of American religious traditions.

12. Phillips, *American Theocracy*, p. 237.

13. Jane Kramer, "Taking the Veil; How France's Public Schools Became the Battle Ground in a Culture War," *New Yorker*, November 22, 2004, p. 59.

14. Anthony Shadid and Kevin Sullivan, "Anatomy of the Cartoon Protest Movement, Opposing Certainties Widen Gap Between West and Muslim World," *Washington Post*, February 16, 2006.

15. Flemming Rose, "Why I Published the Mohammed Cartoons," *Spiegel Online*, May 31, 2006, http://service.spiegel.de/cache/international/spiegel/0,1518,druck -418930,00.html.

16. See generally Rosemary C. Salomone, *Visions of Schooling: Conscience, Community, and Common Education* (New Haven: Yale University Press, 2000).

Chapter Two: Religion and Public Life

1. Editorial, "Bishops at the Ballot Box," *Boston Globe*, June 16, 2004, p. A20; editorial, "Hustings and the Pulpits," *New York Times*, June 16, 2004, p. A22.

2. David Kirkpatrick and Laurie Goodstein, "Group of Bishops Using Influence to Oppose Kerry," *New York Times*, October 12, 2004, p. 1.

3. Alfred E. Smith, "An American Catholic Answers Back," reprinted in Kenneth J. Jackson and David S. Dunbar, eds., *Empire City: New York Through the Centuries* (New York: Columbia University Press, 2002), pp. 553–54. This essay was written in response to an accusatory article by Charles Marshall in the *Atlantic Monthly*, which described "the menace of a Roman Catholic in the White House."

4. Mario Cuomo, "Religious Belief and Public Morality: A Catholic Governor's Perspective," paper prepared for delivery to the Department of Theology at the University of Notre Dame, September 13, 1984.

5. Roe v. Wade, 410 U.S. 113 (1973).

6. Archbishop John O'Connor, "Human Lives, Human Rights," *Catholic New York*, October 18, 1984, p. S1.

7. Antonin Scalia, "God's Justice and Ours," *First Things*, May 2002, pp. 17–22. The remarks were originally made in a speech at the University of Chicago Divinity School in January 2002.

8. Joseph A. Califano, "Moral Leadership and Partisanship," *America*, September 29, 1984, 164–65.

9. In one poll, only 13 percent of Catholics said they believed abortion should always be illegal, 35 percent said it should be up to the woman, 17 percent said it should be legal in many circumstances, and 33 percent said it should be legal in few circumstances. For Latino Catholics the responses were less supportive of abortion: 18 percent always illegal, 26 percent up to the woman, 17 percent legal in many circumstances, 39 percent legal in few circumstances. John C. Green, "The American Religious Landscape and Political Attitudes: A Baseline for 2004," Washington: D.C., Pew Forum on Religion and Public Life, September, 9, 2004.

10. Alan Wolfe, *The Transformation of American Religion: How We Actually Live Our Faith* (New York: Free Press, 2003), p. 172.

11. Jodi Wilgoren and Bill Keller, "Kerry and Religion: Pressure Builds for Public Discussions," *New York Times*, October 7, 2004, A30.

12. See Ronald Dworkin, *Life's Dominion: An Argument about Abortion, Euthanasia, and Individual Freedom* (New York: Knopf, 1993).

13. Robert George, *The Clash of Orthodoxies: Law, Religion, and Morality* (Wilmington, Del.: ISI Books, 2001), pp. 75–89, 259–71. But see also Andrew Sullivan, *Virtually Normal: An Argument about Homosexuality* (New York: Knopf, 1995).

14. Toni Bentley, *The Surrender: An Erotic Memoir* (New York: Regan Books, 2004).

15. Tom Wolfe, *I Am Charlotte Simmons* (New York: Farrar, Straus and Giroux, 2004).

16. "Sexual Behavior and Selected Health Measures," prepared by the Institute for Social Research for the National Center for Health Statistics, Washington, D.C., September 2005.

17. Lawrence v. Texas, 538 U.S. 918 (2003). In 1996, the Supreme Court struck down a state constitutional amendment in Colorado that repealed all state and local laws banning discrimination on the basis of sexual orientation. Romer v. Evans, 517 U.S. 620 (1996).

18. See John M. Finnis, "Law, Morality, and 'Sexual Orientation,' " *Notre Dame Law Review* 69 (1994), pp. 1049–76.

19. Bowers v. Hardwick, 478 U.S. 186, 196 (1986) (Chief Justice Burger concurring).

20. Evan Gerstmann, *Same-Sex Marriage and the Constitution* (New York: Cambridge University Press, 2004).

21. Goodridge v. Mass. Department of Health, 440 Mass. 309, 798 NE 2d 941 (Nov. 18, 2003).

22. On September 30, 2004, the House of Representatives voted 227 to 186 in favor of the amendment, far short of the 290 needed for adoption under the two-thirds rule.

23. Hernandez v. Robles, 7N.Y.3d 338, N.E.2d1 (New York Court of Appeals, July 6, 2006).

24. Lewis v. Harris, No.A-68-05 (N.J. Supreme Court, October 25, 2006).

25. "First Inaugural Address," in W. W. Abbott et al., eds., *The Papers of George Washington* (Charlottesville: University Press of Virginia, 1987), vol. 2, p. 174.

26. Reprinted in Philip Kurland and Ralph Lerner, eds., *The Founders' Constitution*, vol. 5 (Chicago: University of Chicago Press, 1987).

27. "Farewell Address," in John Rhodehamel, ed., *George Washington: Writings* (New York: Library of America, 1997), p. 229.

28. Barry Alan Shain, *The Myth of American Individualism: The Protestant Origins of American Political Thought* (Princeton: Princeton University Press, 1994); John G. West Jr., *The Politics of Revelation and Reason: Religion and Civic Life in the New Nation* (Lawrence: University Press of Kansas, 1996).

29. "Letter from Thomas Jefferson to John Adams, 12 October, 1813," in Lester Capon, ed., *The Adams-Jefferson Letters* (Chapel Hill: University of North Carolina Press, 1959), vol. 2, p. 384, cited in Garrett Ward Sheldon, "Liberalism, Classicism and Christianity in Jefferson's Political Thought," in Garrett Ward Sheldon and Daniel L. Dreisbach, eds., *Religion and Political Culture in Jefferson's Virginia* (Lanham, Md.: Rowman and Littlefield, 2000), p. 98.

30. Alexis de Tocqueville, *Democracy in America*, ed. Phillips Bradley, vol. 1 (New York: Vintage, 1945), p. 317.

31. See Jean Bethke Elshtain, *Jane Adams and the Dream of American Democracy: A Life* (New York: Basic Books, 2002); James A. Morone, *Hellfire Nation: The Politics of Sin in American History* (New Haven: Yale University Press, 2003), pp. 52–89.

32. Morone, *Hellfire Nation*, pp. 119–215.

33. On Lincoln, see Mark A. Noll, *America's God: From Jonathan Edwards to Abraham Lincoln* (New York: Oxford University Press, 2002), pp. 426–37.

34. Brown v. Board of Education, 347 U.S. 493 (1954).

35. David Chappell, *A Stone of Hope: Prophetic Religion and the Death of Jim Crow* (Chapel Hill: University of North Carolina Press, 2004), pp. 107–8. See pp. 105–78 on the role of white churches in the South.

36. Benjamin Mays and Joseph Nicholsen, *The Negro Church* (New York: Institute for Religious and Social Research, 1933); E. Franklin Frazier, *The Negro Church in America* (New York: Schocken, 1964); Chappell, *A Stone of Hope*, pp. 44–104.

37. Chappell, *A Stone of Hope*, pp. 9–43. See also David Garrow, *Bearing the Cross: Martin Luther King, Jr. and the Southern Christian Leadership Conference* (New York: Morrow, 1986); Charles Marsh, *The Beloved Community: How Faith Shapes Social Justice, from the Civil Rights Movement to Today* (Boston: Basic Books, 2005); Albert Roboteau, *Fire in the Bones: Reflections on African American Religious History* (Boston: Beacon Press, 1995).

38. C. Eric Lincoln and Lawrence H. Mamiya, *The Black Church in the African-American Experience* (Durham, N.C.: Duke University Press, 1990).

39. Laurie Goodstein, "Conservative Churches Grew Fastest in 1990's, Report Says," *New York Times*, September 18, 2002, sec. A, p. 22.

40. Steven P. Brown, *Trumping Religion: The New Christian Right, the Free Speech Clause, and the Courts* (Tuscaloosa: University of Alabama Press, 2002), pp. 27–45.

41. Cited in Brown, *Trumping Religion*, p. 4.

42. George Gallup Jr. and Timothy Jones, *The Next American Spirituality: Finding God in the Twenty-first Century* (Colorado Springs: Cook Communications, 2000).

43. Andrew Kohut et al., *The Diminishing Divide: Religion's Changing Role in American Politics* (Washington, D.C.: Brookings Institution Press, 2000), pp. 26–33.

44. Steve Farkas et al., "For Goodness' Sake: Why So Many Want Religion to Play a Greater Role in American Life," Washington, D.C., Public Agenda, 2001.

45. Green, "American Religious Landscape."

46. These groups were defined as follows: traditionalist (strongly orthodox belief and high religious engagement), centrist (moderate relief and engagement), modernist (strongly heterodox belief and low levels of engagement). The other categories are supposedly self-explanatory.

47. "Pragmatic Americans Liberal and Conservative on Social Issues," Washington, D.C., "Pew Forum on Religion and Public Life," August 3, 2006.

48. "American Views on Religion, Politics and Public Policy," Washington, D.C., Pew Forum on Religion and Public Life, April 2001.

49. Michael Sandel, *Democracy's Discontent: America in Search of a Public Philosophy* (Cambridge: Harvard University Press, 1996), pp. 274–316.

50. See also Alasdair MacIntyre, *After Virtue: A Study of Moral Theory* (South Bend, Ind.: Notre Dame University Press, 1981); J. Donald Moon, *Constructing Community: Moral Pluralism and Tragic Consequences* (Princeton: Princeton University Press, 1993).

51. 42 U.S.C. Sec. 2000e-1(a) (2000).

52. Corp. of Presiding Bishop v. Amos, 483 U.S. 327, 341 (1987).

53. Stephen L. Carter, *The Culture of Disbelief: How American Law and Politics Trivialize Devotion* (New York: Basic Books, 1993).

54. See especially Richard J. Neuhaus, *The Naked Public Square: Religion and Democracy in America* (Grand Rapids, Mich.: William B. Eerdmans, 1984).

55. John Dewey, *A Common Faith* (New Haven: Yale University Press, 1934); Viteritti, *Choosing Equality*, pp. 157–61.

56. Stephen Holmes, "Gag Rules or the Politics of Omission," in Jon Elster and Rune Slagstad, eds., *Constitutionalism and Democracy* (New York: Cambridge University Press, 1988).

57. Susan Jacoby, *Freethinkers: A History of American Secularism* (New York: Metropolitan Books, 2004).

58. Jacoby, *Freethinkers*, p. 1.

59. Jill Lawrence, "Non-Believers Raising Their Voice in Capital," *USA Today*, September 21, 2005.

60. Elk Grove v. Newdow, 124 S.Ct. 21 (2004).

61. James Piereson, "Under God: The History of a Phrase," *Weekly Standard*, October 27, 2003, pp. 19–23.

62. According to Chief Justice Rehnquist, Woodrow Wilson solicited God's help when he asked Congress for a declaration of war against Germany in 1917. In his first inaugural address, delivered during the Great Depression, Roosevelt stated, "We humbly ask the blessing of God. May He protect each and every one of us. May He guide me in the days to come." In delivering his orders to the allied troops on D-Day, General Eisenhower declared, "Let us all beseech the blessings of Almighty God upon this great and noble undertaking."

63. It certainly can be argued that most moral positions can be traced to religious teaching, but some are more reliant on faith-based arguments than others. See Michael J. Perry, *Under God? Religious Faith and Liberal Democracy* (New York: Cambridge University Press, 2003), pp. 20–52.

CHAPTER THREE: TENNESSEE TALES

1. The most authoritative account of the trial and the events surrounding it is the Pulitzer Prize–winning book by Edward J. Larson, *Summer for the Gods: The Scopes Trial and America's Continuing Debate over Science and Religion* (Cambridge: Harvard University Press, 1997). For a more concise account that includes key documents, see Jeffrey P. Moran, *The Scopes Trial: A Brief History with Documents* (Boston: Bedford/St. Martin's, 2002).

2. Thomas S. Kuhn, *The Structure of Scientific Revolutions* (Chicago: University of Chicago Press, 1962).

3. Asa Gray, *The Elements of Botany for Beginners and Schools* (New York: Ivison, 1887).

4. Edward J. Larson, *Trial and Error: The American Controversy over Creation and Evolution* (New York: Oxford University Press, 1985).

5. Kenneth K. Bailey, "The Enactment of Tennessee's Anti-Evolution Law," *Journal of Southern History* 16 (November 1950), pp. 488–89.

6. Quoted in Larson, *Summer for the Gods*, p. 6.

7. Kevin Tierney, *Darrow: A Biography* (New York: Crosswell, 1979), p. 85. See also Clarence Darrow, *The Story of My Life* (New York: Grosset, 1932).

8. See Larson, *Summer for the Gods*, pp. 239–46.

9. See Larson, *Summer for the Gods*, pp. 37–41. See also Michael Kazin, *A Godly Hero: The Life of William Jennings Bryan* (New York: Knopf, 2006); Lawrence Levine, *Defender of the Faith: William Jennings Bryan* (New York: Oxford University Press, 1965).

10. Larson, *Summer for the Gods*, p. 7.

11. George Hunter, *A Civic Biology* (New York: American Book Company, 1914), pp. 195–96, reprinted in Moran, *The Scopes Trial*, pp. 186–87.

12. John W. Norris, "Evolution Not a Fact—The Bible a Fact," *AME Church Review,* October 1925, pp. 323–24.

13. Larson, *Summer for the Gods,* p. 27. See also Harry Bruinius, *Better for All the World: The Secret History of Forced Sterilization and America's Quest for Racial Purity* (New York: Knopf, 2006); Christine Rosen, *Preaching Eugenics: Religious Leaders and the Religious Eugenics Movement* (New York: Oxford University Press, 2004).

14. Hunter, *A Civic Biology,* pp. 195–96, reprinted in Moran, *The Scopes Trial,* pp. 185–86.

15. Reprinted in Moran, *The Scopes Trial,* pp. 74–75.

16. Epperson v. Arkansas, 393 U.S. (1968).

17. Edwards v. Aguillard, 482 U.S. 578 (1987).

18. Kuhn, *Structure of Scientific Revolutions.*

19. Larson, *Summer for the Gods,* pp. 173–74.

20. Mark Sappenfield and Mary Beth McCauley, "God or Science: Ninth-Grade Biology Teachers in Dover, Pa. Must Include 'Intelligent Design' in Their Instruction," *Christian Science Monitor,* November 23, 2004, sec. 2, p. 11.

21. Ariel Bailey, "Judge in Georgia Orders Anti-Evolution Stickers Removed from Textbooks," *New York Times,* January 14, 2005, sec. A, p. 1.

22. The most complete rendering of the story is contained in Stephen Bates, *Battleground: One Mother's Crusade, the Religious Right, and Their Struggle for Our Schools* (New York: Henry Holt, 1993).

23. Bates, *Battleground,* p. 31.

24. For a detailed analysis of the case, see Nomi Maya Stolzenberg, " 'He Drew a Circle That Shut Me Out': Assimilation, Indoctrination, and the Paradox of Liberal Education," *Harvard Law Review* 106 (1993), pp. 581–667.

25. Mozert v. Hawkins County Public Schools, 579 F. Supp. 201 (E.D. Tenn. 1984); Mozert v. Hawkins County Public School, 582 F. Supp. 201 (E.D. Tenn. 1984).

26. See Bates, *Battleground,* pp. 246–51, 277–78.

27. Bates, *Battleground,* p. 248.

28. Mozert v. Hawkins County Board of Education, 647 F. Supp. 1194 (E.D. Tenn. 1986).

29. Bates, *Battleground,* p. 277.

30. Bates, *Battleground,* p. 277.

31. Mozert v. Hawkins County Board of Education, 827 F.2d 1058 (6th Cir. 1987).

32. For an analysis of these opinions, see Salomone, *Visions of Schooling,* pp. 121–26.

33. For a similar case that took place in Bedford, New York, in 1995, see Salomone, *Visions of Schooling,* pp. 142–96.

34. Stolzenberg, "He Drew a Circle." See George W. Dent Jr., "Religious Children, Secular Schools," *Southern California Law Review* 61 (1988), pp. 863–941.

35. West Virginia State Board of Education v. Barnette, 319 U.S. 624 (1943).

36. Bates, *Battleground,* p. 277.

37. Smith v. Board of School Commissioners, 827 F.2d 684 (11th Cir. 1987).

CHAPTER FOUR: WHY SCHOOLS MATTER

1. Carl F. Kaestle, *The Evolution of an Urban School System: New York City, 1750–1850* (Cambridge: Harvard University Press, 1973), pp. 1–27.

2. Diane Ravitch, *The Great School Wars: A History of the New York City Public Schools* (New York: Basic Books, 1974), pp. 3–4.

3. "A Bill for the More General Diffusion of Knowledge," in Julien Boyd, ed., *The Papers of Thomas Jefferson* (Princeton, N.J.: Princeton University Press, 1950), vol. 2, pp. 526–33.

4. Cited in Garrett Ward Sheldon, *The Political Philosophy of Thomas Jefferson* (Baltimore: Johns Hopkins University Press, 1991), p. 130.

5. See Richard K. Matthews, *The Radical Politics of Thomas Jefferson: A Revisionist View* (Lawrence: University Press of Kansas, 1984), pp. 53–75; Sheldon, *Political Philosophy of Jefferson*, pp. 129–34; Winthrop D. Jordan, *White over Black: American Attitudes towards the Negro, 1550–1812* (Chapel Hill: University of North Carolina Press, 1968), pp. 429–572.

6. See Lawrence A. Cremin, ed., *The Republic and the School: Horace Mann on the Education of Free Men* (New York: Teachers College Press, 1957).

7. Stephen P. Erie, *Rainbow's End: Irish-Americans and the Dilemmas of Urban Machine Politics, 1840–1985* (Berkeley and Los Angeles: University of California Press, 1988), pp. 25–26.

8. Horace Mann, "Twelfth Annual Report," in Cremin, *Republic and School*, pp. 79–80.

9. Lloyd P. Jorgenson, *The State and the Non-Public School, 1825–1925* (Columbia: University of Missouri Press, 1987), p. 31.

10. See Charles Glenn, *The Myth of the Common School* (Amherst: University of Massachusetts Press, 1988), pp. 115–206.

11. Mann, "Twelfth Annual Report," p. 102.

12. See Diane Ravitch, *Left Back: A Century of Failed School Reforms* (New York: Simon and Schuster, 2000), especially chapters 2, 5, 6, 7.

13. See Alan Ryan, *John Dewey and the High Tide of American Liberalism* (New York: Norton, 1995); Steven Rockefeller, *John Dewey, Religious Faith and Democratic Humanism* (New York: Columbia University Press, 1991). While Ryan's intellectual biography highlights Dewey's growing disenchantment with and contempt for religion, Rockefeller holds on to the idea that Dewey, though disavowing organized religion, remained a religious humanist.

14. Dewey, *A Common Faith*, p. 7.

15. See Robert B. Westbrook, *John Dewey and American Democracy* (Ithaca, N.Y.: Cornell University Press, 1991).

16. John Dewey, "Education as a Religion," *New Republic*, September 13, 1922, p. 63.

17. John Dewey, "My Pedagogic Creed," *School Journal*, January 16, 1897, p. 80.

18. John Dewey, "Religion in Our Schools," *Hibbert Journal*, July 1908, pp. 806–7.

19. Ellwood Cubberley, *Changing Conceptions of Education* (Boston: Houghton Mifflin, 1909), p. 63.

20. Sol Cohen, ed., *Education in the United States: A Documentary History* (New York: Random House, 1973), p. 393.

21. Cohen, *Education in the United States*, p. 394.

22. William E. Sparkman, "Symposium: Issues in Education Law and Policy: The Legal Foundations of Public School Finance," *Boston College Law Review* 335 (May 1994), p. 572.

23. Lawrence Cremin, *American Education: The Colonial Experience* (New York: Harper Torchbooks, 1970), p. 207.

24. Cremin, *American Education*, pp. 15–16.

25. See David Tyack, Thomas James, and Aaron Benevot, *Law and the Shaping of Public Education, 1785–1954* (Madison: University of Wisconsin Press, 1986), pp. 154–62.

26. Tyack, James, and Benevot, *Law and Public Education*, pp. 157–58.

27. Cited in William O. Bourne, *A History of the Public School Society of the City of New York* (New York: W. Wood, 1870), p. 251.

28. Ruth Miller Elson, *Guardians of Tradition: American Schoolbooks of the Nineteenth Century* (Lincoln: University of Nebraska Press, 1964). See also John Westerhoff, *McGuffey and His Readers* (Nashville: Abington, 1978).

29. See John McGreevy, *Catholicism and American Freedom: A History* (New York: Norton, 2003), pp. 91–123.

30. See Ravitch, *The Great School Wars*, pp. 20–26.

31. Tyack, James, and Benevot, *Law and Public Education*, p. 164.

32. Otto Templar Hamilton, *The Courts and the Curriculum* (New York: Teachers College, 1927).

33. Donahue v. Richards, 38 Maine 379, 4409 (1854).

34. See Ravitch, *The Great School Wars*, pp. 27–76.

35. Michael Feldberg, *The Philadelphia Riots of 1844: A Study of Ethnic Conflict* (Westport, Conn.: Greenwood Press, 1975).

36. Ray Allen Billington, *The Protestant Crusade, 1800–1860: A Study of the Origins of American Nativism* (New York: Macmillan, 1938), pp. 388–89.

37. Abraham Lincoln, "Letter to Joshua Speed," in Roy P. Bashin, ed., *The Collected Works of Abraham Lincoln* (New Brunswick: Rutgers University Press, 1953).

38. Carl Kaestle, *Pillars of the Republic: Common Schools and American Society, 1780–1860* (New York: Hill and Wang, 1983), pp. 166–67.

39. See Molly O'Brien and Amanda Woodrum, "Symposium: The Ohio Constitution Then and Now: An Examination of the Law and History of the Ohio Constitution on the Occasion of its Bicentennial: The Constitutional Common School," *Cleveland State Law Review* 41 (2004), pp. 581–642.

40. Cited by O'Brien and Woodrum, "The Ohio Constitution," p. 617.

41. Marie Carolyn Klinkhamer, "The Blaine Amendment of 1875: Private Motives for Political Action," *Catholic Historical Review* 42 (1957), p. 21.

42. Jorgenson, *State and Non-Public School*, pp. 103–4.

43. Jorgenson, *State and Non-Public School*, p. 100.

44. Jorgenson, *State and Non-Public School*, pp. 104–6.

45. See Erie, *Rainbow's End*, pp. 25–66.

46. This section on the development of the "Blaine amendment" is drawn generally from Joseph P. Viteritti, "Blaine's Wake: School Choice, the First Amendment, and State Constitutional Law," *Harvard Journal of Law and Public Policy* 21 (Summer 1998), pp. 657–718; and Viteritti, *Choosing Equality*, pp. 151–56. The story is also well told in Steven K. Green, "The Blaine Amendment Reconsidered," *American Journal of Legal History* 36 (1992), pp. 38–69.

47. A. D. Mayo, "What Does the Bible Represent in the American Common School?" *Universalist Quarterly and General Review* 12 (1874), p. 272.

48. The new states affected included North Dakota, South Dakota, Washington, Montana, Utah, Oklahoma, New Mexico, Arizona, Idaho, and Wyoming.

49. See Joseph P. Viteritti, "Choosing Equality: Religious Freedom and Educational Opportunity under Constitutional Federalism," *Yale Law and Policy Review* 15 (1996), pp. 113–92; Joseph P. Viteritti, "Davey's Plea: Blaine, Blair, *Witters*, and the Protection of Religious Freedom," *Harvard Journal of Law and Public Policy* 27 (Fall 2003), pp. 299–338; Mark Edward DeForrest, "An Overview of State Blaine Amendments: Origins, Scope, and First Amendment Concerns," *Harvard Journal of Law and Public Policy* 26 (Spring 2003), pp. 551–626; Kyle Duncan, "Secularism's Laws: State Blaine Amendments and Religious Persecution," *Fordham Law Review* 71 (December 2003), pp. 493–593.

50. William G. Ross, *Forging New Freedoms: Nativism, Education and the Constitution, 1917–1927* (Lincoln: University of Nebraska Press, 1994), p. 61.

51. Ross, *Forging New Freedoms*, pp. 48–49.

52. Meyer v. Nebraska, 262 U.S. 390, 401 (1923).

53. Farrington v. Tokushige, 273 U.S. 283 (1927).

54. Jorgenson, *State and Nonpublic School*, p. 207. See generally David B. Tyack, "The Perils of Pluralism: The Background of the Pierce Case," *American Historical Review* 74 (October 1968), pp. 74–98.

55. Pierce v. Society of Sisters, 268 U.S. 510, 535 (1925).

CHAPTER FIVE: POLITICS, EDUCATION, AND RELIGION

1. Frances Fitzgerald, *America Revised: History Schoolbooks in the Twentieth Century* (Boston: Little, Brown, 1979). See also Elson, *Guardians of Tradition*, p. 76.

2. Paul Vitz, *Censorship: Evidence of Bias in Our Children's Textbooks* (Ann Arbor: Servant Books, 1986). See also Warren A. Nord, *Religion and American Education: Rethinking a National Dilemma* (Chapel Hill: University of North Carolina Press, 1995), pp. 138–59.

3. Diane Ravitch, *The Language Police: How Pressure Groups Restrict What Students Learn* (New York: Knopf, 2003), p. 22.

4. For a more realistic rendering of the Pilgrim story and their relationship with the indigenous population near Plymouth, see Nathaniel Philbrick, *Mayflower: A Study of Courage, Community and War* (New York: Viking, 2006).

5. Ravitch, *The Language Police*, p. 52. See also Joan DelFattore, *What Johnny Shouldn't Read: Textbook Censorship in America* (New Haven: Yale University Press, 1992).

6. Gilbert Sewall, "Religion in the Classroom: What the Textbooks Tell Us," American Textbook Council, 1995.

7. See Charles Haynes, *Religion and American History: What to Teach and How* (Alexandria Va.: Association for Supervision and Curriculum Development, 1990); Warren A. Nord and Charles C. Haynes, *Taking Religion Seriously across the Curriculum* (Alexandria, Va.: Association for Supervision and Curriculum Development, 1998).

8. See C. John Sommerville, *The Decline of the Secular University: Why the Academy Needs Religion* (New York: Oxford University Press, 2006); George Marsden, *The Soul of the American University: From Protestant Establishment to Established Nonbelief* (New York: Oxford University Press, 1996); Julie Reuben, *The Making of the Modern Univer-*

sity (Chicago: University of Chicago Press, 1996); William Buckley, *God and Man at Yale* (New York: Regnery, 1978).

9. Sean Cavanagh, "Teachers Torn over Religion, Evolution," *Education Week*, February 2, 2005, p. 18.

10. "Public Divided on Origins of Life," Washington, D.C., Pew Forum on Religion and Public Life, August 30, 2005.

11. Cornelia Dean, "Evolution Takes a Back Seat in U.S. Classes," *New York Times*, February 1, 2005, sec. F, p. 1. See also Cavanagh, "Teachers Torn over Religion, Evolution," pp.1, 18.

12. "Afraid to Discuss Evolution," *New York Times*, February 4, 2005, sec. A, p. 18.

13. Cavanagh, "Teachers Torn."

14. See J. Ronald Oakley, *God's Country: America in the Fifties* (New York: Dembner Books, 1986); Martin Marty, *Modern American Religion*, vol. 3, *Under God Indivisible, 1941–1960* (Chicago: University of Chicago Press, 1996); David Halberstram, *The Fifties* (New York: Villard, 1993); David Castronovo, *Beyond the Grey Flannel Suit: Books from the 1950's That Made American Culture* (New York: Continuum, 2004).

15. Cited in William R. Hutchison, *Religious Pluralism in America: The Contentious History of a Founding Ideal* (New Haven: Yale University Press, 2003), p. 198. See generally pp. 196–218.

16. Oakley, *God's Country*, pp. 318–27.

17. Will Herberg, *Protestant—Catholic—Jew: An Essay in Religious Sociology* (Garden City, N.Y.: Doubleday, 1956).

18. See also Oakley, *God's Country*, p. 325.

19. Jonathan Zimmerman, *Whose America? Culture Wars in the Public Schools* (Cambridge: Harvard University Press, 2002), p. 135.

20. Richard B. Dierenfield, *Religion in American Public Schools* (Washington, D.C.: Public Affairs Press, 1962), pp. 77–78.

21. Zimmerman, *Whose America?* pp. 144–45.

22. See Vashti Cromwell McCollum, *One Woman's Fight* (Boston: Beacon Press, 1961). Compare with Bates, *Battleground: One Mother's Crusade, the Religious Right, and Their Struggle for Our Schools.*

23. McCollum v. Board of Education, 333 U.S. 203 (1948).

24. The "division" concept would subsequently become a significant consideration in First Amendment jurisprudence. See Richard Garnett, "Religion, Division and the First Amendment," *Georgetown Law Journal* 94 (2006), pp. 1666–1724.

25. "Manifesto of Protestants and Other Americans United for the Separation of Church and State," in Joseph Dawson, ed., *Separate Church and State Now* (New York: Richard R. Smith, 1948), p. 208.

26. Paul Blanshard, *American Freedom and Catholic Power* (Boston: Beacon Press, 1949), pp. 303–5.

27. Quoted in John T. McGreevy, "Thinking on One's Own: Catholicism in the American Intellectual Imagination, 1928–1960," *Journal of American History* 97 (June 1997), p. 98.

28. Arthur Hayes Sulzberger, letter to *Christian Herald*, May 18, 1949.

29. Paul Blanshard, *Communism, Democracy, and Catholic Power* (Boston: Beacon Press, 1951).

30. Zorach v. Clauson, 343 U.S. 306, 313–14 (1952).

31. Frank J. Sorauf, "*Zorach v. Clauson*: The Impact of a Supreme Court Decision," *American Political Science Review* 53 (1959), p. 782.

32. Dierenfield, *Religion in American Public Schools*, p. 92.

33. William M. Beaney and Edward N. Beiser, "Prayer and Politics: The Impact of *Engel* and *Schempp* on the Political Process," *Journal of Public Law* 13 (1964), p. 486.

34. West Virginia State Board of Education v. Barnette, 319 U.S. 624 (1943).

35. David Fellman, *Religion in American Public Law* (Boston: Boston University Press, 1965), pp. 88–89.

36. Joan DelFattore, *The Fourth R: Conflicts Over Religion in America's Public Schools* (New Haven: Yale University Press, 2004), pp. 69–70.

37. Engel v. Vitale, 370 U.S. 421 (1962).

38. See DelFattore, *The Fourth R*, pp. 82–94.

39. William J. Murray, *Let Us Pray: A Plea for Prayer in Our Schools* (New York: William Morrow, 1995).

40. School District of Abington Township v. Schempp (No. 142), Murray v. Curlett (No. 119), 374 U.S. 203 (1963).

41. See Beaney and Beiser, "Prayer and Politics," 475–503, revised in Robert Sikorski, ed., *Prayer in Schools and the Constitution, 1961–1992* (New York: Garland, 1993), pp. 411–39.

42. Cited in Beaney and Beiser, "Prayer and Politics," *Journal of Public Law*, p. 483.

43. John Herbert Laubach, *School Prayers: Congress, the Courts, and the Public* (Washington, D.C.: Public Affairs Press, 1969), p. 49. See generally pp. 47–97.

44. Laubach, *School Prayers*, p. 93.

45. Laubach, *School Prayers*, p. 86.

46. ADL, "Report on Reactions in Public School Districts throughout the Country to the Supreme Court's Decisions on Bible Reading and Prayer," fall 1963, cited in Beaney and Beiser, "Prayer and Politics," p. 490.

47. Kenneth M Dolbeare and Phillip E. Hammond, *The School Prayer Decisions: From Court Policy to Local Practice* (Chicago: University of Chicago Press, 1971), p. 5.

48. McGowan v. Maryland, 366 U.S. 420, 448–49 (1961). See also Gallagher v. Crown Kosher Meat Market 366 U.S. 617 (1961); Braunfeld v. Brown, 366 U.S. 599 (1961); Two Guys From Harrison-Allentown Inc. v. McGinley, 366 U.S. 582 (1961).

49. Torasco v. Watkins, 367 U.S. 488 (1961).

50. Sherbert v. Verner, 374 U.S. 398 (1963).

51. Laubach, *School Prayers*, pp. 141–54.

52. See DelFattore, *The Fourth R*, pp. 164–71.

53. Wallace v. Jaffree, 472 U.S. 38 (1985).

54. Lynch v. Donnelly, 465 U.S. 668 (1984).

55. DelFattore, *The Fourth R*, p. 176.

56. Marsh v. Chambers, 463 U.S. 783 (1983).

57. Lee v. Weisman, 505 U.S. 577, 596 (1992).

58. Santa Fe v. Doe, 530 U.S. 290 (2000).

CHAPTER SIX: FREE EXERCISE, VACATED AND DENIED

1. See generally Kathryn M. Daynes, *More Wives Than One: The Transformation of Mormon Marriage, 1840–1910* (Urbana: University of Illinois Press, 2001); Lawrence Foster, *Religion and Sexuality: Three American Communal Experiments of the Nineteenth Century* (New York: Oxford University Press, 1981), pp. 123–80; Carol Weisbrod, *The Boundaries of Utopia* (New York: Pantheon, 1980), pp. 16–33.

2. Linda King Newell and Valeen Tippets Avery, *Mormon Enigma: Emma Hale Smith* (Urbana: University of Illinois Press, 1994), pp. 12–13.

3. Sarah Barringer Gordon, *The Mormon Question: Polygamy and Constitutional Conflict in Nineteenth Century America* (Chapel Hill: University of North Carolina Press, 2002), pp. 103–6.

4. Jill Mulvay Derr, " 'Strength in Our Union': The Making of Mormon Sisterhood," in Maureen Beecher and Lavina Anderson, eds., *Sisters in Spirit: Mormon Women in Historical and Cultural Perspective* (Urbana: University of Illinois Press, 1987).

5. Reynolds v. United States, 98 U.S. 145 (1879).

6. See Gordon, *The Mormon Question*, pp. 63–76, 132–45.

7. The law authorized the federal government to confiscate church property not used exclusively for religious purposes. See Carol Weisbrod and Pamela Sheingorn, "Reynolds v. United States: Nineteenth-Century Forms of Marriage and the Status of Women," *Connecticut Law Review* 10 (Summer 1978), pp. 828–58.

8. Mormon Church v. United States, 136 U.S. 1, 49 (1890).

9. Permoli v. Municipality No. 1, 44 U.S. 589, 609 (1845).

10. Vidal v. Girard's Executioners, 2 Howard 125 (1844).

11. Pierce v. Society of Sisters, 268 U.S. 510 (1925).

12. Meyer v. Nebraska, 262 U.S. 390 (1923).

13. Church of Holy Trinity v. United States, 143 U.S. 457, 471 (1892).

14. Bradfield v. Roberts, 175 U.S. 291 (1899).

15. Quick Bear v. Leupp, 210 U.S. 50 (1908).

16. Cochran v. Board of Education, 281 U.S. 370 (1930).

17. Gobitis v. Minersville, 310 U.S. 586 (1940).

18. See James Hitchcock, *The Supreme Court and Religion in American Public Life: The Odyssey of the Religion Clauses*, vol. 1 (Princeton: Princeton University Press, 2004), pp. 43–60.

19. Cantwell v. Connecticut, 310 U.S. 296 (1940).

20. West Virginia State Board of Education v. Barnette, 319 U.S. 624, 634 (1943).

21. Marshall wrote, "The Constitution was ordained and established by the people of the United States for themselves, for their own government, and not for the government of the individual states." Barron v. Mayor of Baltimore, 32 U.S. 243–47 (1833).

22. It reads, "No State shall make or enforce any law which shall abridge the privileges or immunities of citizens of the United States; nor shall any state deprive any person of life, liberty or property, *without due process of the law*; nor deny to any person within its jurisdiction *the equal protection of the laws*." See William E. Nelson, *The Fourteenth Amendment: From Political Principle to Judicial Doctrine* (Cambridge: Harvard University Press, 1988).

23. See Lucas A. Powe Jr., *The Warren Court and American Politics* (Cambridge: Harvard University Press, 2000); Rosemary C. Salomone, *Equal Education under Law: Legal Rights and Federal Policy in the Post-Brown Era* (New York: St. Martin's Press, 1986), pp. 43–44.

24. Everson v. Board of Education, 330 U.S. 1 (1947).

25. "New Jersey cannot hamper its citizens in the free exercise of their own religion. Consequently, it cannot exclude Catholics, Lutherans, Mohammedans, Baptists, Jews, Methodists, Non-Believers, Presbyterians, or the members of any other faith, because of their faith or lack of it, from receiving the benefits of public welfare legislation." *Everson*, 330 U.S., at 16.

26. "The 'establishment of religion clause' of the First Amendment means at least this: neither a state nor the federal government can set up a church. Neither can pass

laws which aid one religion, aid all religions, or prefer one religion over another. Neither can force nor influence a person to go to or remain away from church against his will or force him to profess a belief or disbelief in any religion. No person can be punished for entertaining or professing religious beliefs or disbeliefs, for church attendance or nonattendance. No tax in any amount, large or small can be levied to support any religious activities or institutions, whatever they may be called, or whatever form they may adopt to teach or practice religion. Neither a state nor the Federal government can, openly or secretly, participate in the affairs of any religious organizations or groups, and *vice versa*. In the words of Jefferson, the clause against establishment of religion by law was intended to erect 'a wall of separation between church and state.' " *Everson*, 330, U.S., at 15–16.

27. See, for example, Philip Hamburger, *Separation of Church and State* (Cambridge: Harvard University Press, 2002), pp. 422–34; Michael W. McConnell, "Religious Freedom at the Crossroads," in Geoffrey Stone et al., eds., *The Bill of Rights in the Modern State* (Chicago: University of Chicago Press, 1992), pp. 121–27.

28. Roger K. Newman, *Hugo Black: A Biography* (New York: Pantheon, 1994), pp. 71–121, 233–63.

29. John C. Jeffries Jr. and James E. Ryan, "A Political History of the Establishment Clause," *Michigan Law Review* 100 (November 2001), p. 287–88.

30. Jeffries and Ryan, "Political History," p. 337. See generally pp. 328–38.

31. Ronald James Boggs, "Culture of Liberty: History of Americans United for the Separation of Church and State, 1947–1953," Ph.D. dissertation, Ohio State University, 1978, cited in Jeffries and Ryan, "Political History," p. 314.

32. "An Open Letter," *New York Times*, March 8, 1948, cited in Jeffries and Ryan, "Political History," p. 315.

33. Board of Education v. Allen, 392 U.S. 236 (1968).

34. Lemon v. Kurtzman, 403 U.S. 602 (1971).

35. Walz v. Tax Commission, 397 U.S. 664 (1970).

36. "Special tax benefits . . . cannot be squared with the principle of neutrality established by the decisions of the court." Committee for Public Education v. Nyquist, 413 U.S. 756, 793 (1973).

37. Sloan v. Lemon, 413 U.S. 825, 830, 832 (1973).

38. For citations of cases mentioned in the last two paragraphs, see Viteritti, "Davey's Plea," pp. 329–30.

39. Yoder v. Wisconsin, 406 U.S. 205 (1972). See Salomone, *Visions of Schooling*, pp. 85–96; William Bentley Ball, *Mere Creatures of the State? Education, Religion and the Courts* (Notre Dame, Ind.: Crisis Books, 1994), pp. 59–76.

40. See Allen D. Hertzke, *Representing God in Washington: The Role of Religious Lobbies in the American Polity* (Knoxville: University of Tennessee Press, 1988), pp. 161–93; DelFattore, *The Fourth R*, pp. 199–222.

41. Widmar v.Vincent, 454 U.S. 263 (1981). See Rosemary C. Salomone, "From *Widmar* to *Mergens*: The Winding Road of First Amendment Analysis," *Hastings Constitutional Law Quarterly* 18 (1981), pp. 295–323.

42. The Equal Access Act prohibits "any public secondary school which receives Federal financial assistance and which has a limited open forum to deny equal access or fair opportunity to, or discriminate against, any students who wish to conduct a meeting within the limited open forum on the basis of the religious, political, philosophical or other content of the speech at the meetings."

43. Westside Community Board of Education v. Mergens, 496 U.S. 226 (1990).

44. Lamb's Chapel v. Center Moriches Union Free School District, 508 U.S. 384 (1993).

45. Good News Club v. Milford Central School, 533 U.S. 98 (2001).

46. Mueller v. Allen, 463 U.S. 825 (1983).

47. Marsh v. Chambers, 463 U.S. 783, 792 (1983).

48. The data in this paragraph is referenced in Jeffries and Ryan, "Political History," pp. 336–37.

49. Cited in Patrick Allitt, *Religion in America since 1945: A History* (New York: Columbia University Press, 2003), p. 186.

50. See Jeffries and Ryan, "Political History," pp. 343–50.

51. Witters v. Washington Department of Services for the Blind, 474 U.S. 481 (1986). See Jesse Choper, "The Establishment Clause and Aid to Parochial Schools—An Update," *California Law Review* 75 (1987), pp. 5–14.

52. See Viteritti, "Davey's Plea," pp. 301–23.

53. Bowen v. Kendrick, 487 U.S. 589 (1988).

54. Zobrest v. Catalina Foothills School District, 509 U.S. 1 (1993).

55. Rosenberger v. Rector and Visitors of the University of Virginia, 515 U.S. 819 (1995).

56. Agostini v. Felton, 521 U.S. 203 (1997).

57. Mitchell v. Helms, 530 U.S. 793 (2000).

58. Zelman v. Simmons-Harris, 536 U.S. 639 (2002).

59. See Viteritti, *Choosing Equality*, pp. 180–208.

60. See Joseph P. Viteritti, "School Choice: How an Abstract Idea Became a Political Reality," in Diane Ravitch, ed., *Brookings Papers on Education Policy, 2005* (Washington, D.C.: Brookings Institution Press, 2005), pp. 137–56.

61. See generally Viteritti, "Reading Zelman."

62. Employment Division v. Smith, 494 U.S. 872 (1990). For critical appraisals of the decision, see Michael W. McConnell, "Free Exercise Revisionism and the *Smith* Decision," *University of Chicago Law Review* 57 (1990), pp. 109–53; Douglas Laycock, "The Supreme Court's Assault on Free Exercise, and the *Amicus* Brief that Was Never Filed," *Journal of Law and Religion* 8 (1990), pp. 99–114; Steven D. Smith, "Free Exercise Doctrine and the Discourse of Disrespect," *University of Colorado Law Review* 65 (1994), pp. 519–76.

63. Church of Lakumi Babalu Aye, Inc. v. City of Hialeah, 508 U.S. 520 (1993). See David M. O'Brien, *Animal Sacrifice and Religious Freedom: Church of Lakumi Babalu Aye v. City of Hialeah* (Lawrence: University Press of Kansas, 2004).

64. City of Boerne v. Flores, 521 U.S. 507 (1997).

65. See Viteritti, "Davey's Plea," pp. 310–23; Viteritti, "Blaine's Wake."

66. Locke v. Davey, 540 U.S. 807 (2004).

67. See Viteritti, "Choosing Equality."

68. For further analysis of these conceptual tensions see Jesse H. Choper, *Securing Religious Liberty: Principles for Judicial Interpretation of the Religion Clauses* (Chicago: University of Chicago Press, 1995).

CHAPTER SEVEN: AGELESS WISDOM

1. For lively portraits of the key actors, see John Ferling, *Setting the World Ablaze: Washington, Adams, Jefferson and the American Revolution* (New York: Oxford Univer-

sity Press, 2000); Joseph E. Ellis, *Founding Brothers: The Revolutionary Generation* (New York: Random House, 2000); Gordon S. Wood, *Revolutionary Characters: What Made the Founders Different* (New York: Penguin, 2006).

2. See Thomas J. Curry, *The First Freedoms: Church and State in America to the Passage of the First Amendment* (New York: Oxford University Press, 1986); Leonard W. Levy, *The Establishment Clause: Religion and the First Amendment* (Chapel Hill: University of North Carolina Press, 1994), pp. 1–78; Patricia U. Bonomi, *Under the Cope of Heaven: Religion, Society and Politics in Colonial America* (New York: Oxford University Press, 1986); Michael W. McConnell, "The Origins and Historical Understanding of Free Exercise of Religion," *Harvard Law Review* 103 (May 1990), pp. 1421–30; Edwin Gaustad and Leigh Schmidt, *The Religious History of America* (San Francisco: Harper San Francisco, 2002), pp. 1–118.

3. See Edmund S. Morgan, *Roger Williams: The Church and the State* (New York: Norton, 1967); Mark DeWolfe Howe, *The Garden and the Wilderness: Religion and Government in American Constitutional History* (Chicago: University of Chicago Press, 1965), especially pp. 5–39.

4. Roger Williams, "Mr. Cotton's Letter Lately Printed, Examined and Answered," cited in Howe, *Garden and Wilderness*, pp. 5–6.

5. See Ellis Sandoz, *A Government of Laws: Political Theory, Religion, and the American Founding* (Baton Rouge: Louisiana State University Press, 1990); Daniel L. Dreisbach, Mark D. Udall, and Jeffrey H. Morrison, eds, *The Founders on God and Government* (Lanham, Md.: Roman and Littlefield, 2004); Shain, *Myth of American Individualism*; West, *Politics of Revelation and Reason*.

6. McConnell, "Origins and Historical Understanding," pp. 1430–36; Bernard Bailyn, *The Ideological Origins of the American Revolution* (Cambridge: Harvard University Press, 1992), pp. 22–59; Jerome Huyler, *Locke in America: The Moral Philosophy of the Founding Era* (Lawrence: University Press of Kansas, 1995); and more generally, Gordon S. Wood, *The Creation of the American Republic, 1776–1787* (New York: Norton, 1969); Gordon S. Wood, *The Radicalism of the American Revolution* (New York: Random House, 1993).

7. John Locke, "Two Tracts on Government" (1660). For an excellent discussion of Locke's views on religion and their influence during the founding, see Barbara A. McGraw, *Rediscovering America's Sacred Ground: Public Religion and the Pursuit of the Good in a Pluralistic America* (Albany: State University of New York Press, 2003), pp. 23–106.

8. John Locke, "A Letter Concerning Toleration," in David Wootton, ed., *Political Writings of John Locke* (London: Mentor, 1993), p. 394.

9. John Locke, *First Treatise of Government*, cited in McGraw, *Rediscovering America's Sacred Ground*, p. 403.

10. Locke, "Letter Concerning Toleration," p. 403.

11. See Harvey J. Kaye, *Thomas Paine and the Promise of America* (New York: Hill and Wang, 2005), pp. 81–84.

12. See H. W. Brands, *The First American: The Life and Times of Benjamin Franklin* (New York: Doubleday, 2000); Gordon S. Wood, *The Americanization of Benjamin Franklin* (New York: Penguin, 2004); Walter Isaacson, *Benjamin Franklin: An American Life* (New York: Simon and Schuster, 2003); Edmund S. Morgan, *Benjamin Franklin* (New Haven: Yale University Press, 2002).

13. Benjamin Franklin, "Speech of June 28, 1787," in Max Farrand, ed., *The Records of the Federal Convention*, rev. ed. (New Haven: Yale University Press, 1966), , vol. 1, p. 451.

14. See Isaac Kramnick and R. Lawrence Moore, *The Godless Constitution: The Case against Religious Correctness* (New York: Norton, 1996).

15. On the improbability of the Revolution succeeding, see John Ferling, *A Leap in the Dark: The Struggle to Create the American Experiment* (New York: Oxford University Press, 2003).

16. Quoted in Brands, *The First American*, p. 707.

17. See Joseph J. Ellis, *His Excellency: George Washington* (New York: Knopf, 2004); John Ferling, *The First of Men: A Life of George Washington* (Knoxville: University of Tennessee Press, 1988).

18. Paul F. Boller, *George Washington and Religion* (Dallas: Southern Methodist University Press, 1963).

19. George Washington, Farewell Address (September 19, 1796), in John C. Fitzpatrick, ed., *The Writings of George Washington*, vol. 1, 35 (Washington, D.C.: Government Printing Office, 1931–44), p. 229.

20. Michael Novak and Jana Novak, *Washington's God: Religion, Liberty, and the Fathers of Our Country* (New York: Basic Books, 2006), p. 243.

21. George Washington, Speech to the Delaware Chiefs (May 12, 1779), in *Writings of George Washington*, vol. 15, p. 55.

22. George Washington, Circular to the States (June 8, 1783), in *Writings of George Washington*, vol. 26, p. 496.

23. George Washington, Letter to Marquis de La Fayette (August 15, 1787), in *Writings of George Washington*, vol. 29, p. 259.

24. George Washington, Letter to the United Baptist Churches of Virginia (May 1789), in *Papers of George Washington*, vol. 2, p. 424.

25. George Washington, Letter to the Hebrew Congregation of Newport, Rhode Island (August 18, 1790), in *Papers of George Washington*, vol. 6, p. 285.

26. See Joseph J. Ellis, *Passionate Sage: The Character and Legacy of John Adams* (New York: Norton, 1994); David McCullough, *John Adams* (New York: Simon and Schuster, 2001).

27. John Adams, Letter to James Warren (January 9, 1787), quoted in McCullogh, *John Adams*, p. 373.

28. Abigail was the only woman profiled in Ellis, *Founding Brothers*. But also see Carol Berkin, *Revolutionary Mothers: Women in the Struggle for America's Independence* (New York: Knopf, 2005).

29. John Witte Jr., "One Public Religion, Many Private Religions: John Adams and the 1780 Massachusetts Constitution," in Dreisbach, Hall, and Morrison, *Founders on God*, pp. 23–52.

30. Quotations in this and the preceding paragraph are from Witte, "One Public Religion," pp. 25, 38, 41, 42.

31. For an excellent portrait, see Joseph J. Ellis, *American Sphinx: The Character of Thomas Jefferson* (New York: Random House, 1996).

32. Thomas Jefferson, Letter to James Madison (September 6, 1789), in Merrill D. Peterson, ed., *The Portable Thomas Jefferson* (New York: Penguin, 1975), p. 445.

33. See Sheldon, *Political Philosophy of Jefferson*; Matthews, *Radical Politics of Jefferson*; Jean Yarbrough, *American Virtues: Thomas Jefferson on the Character of a Free People* (Lawrence: University Press of Kansas, 1998).

34. See generally, Ralph Ketcham, *James Madison: A Biography* (Charlottesville: University Press of Virginia, 1990); Jack N. Rakove, *James Madison and the Creation of the American Republic* (New York: Longman, 2002).

35. See Jack Rakove, *Original Meanings: Politics and Ideas in the Making of the Constitution* (New York: Random House, 1996).

36. Thomas Jefferson, A Bill for Establishing Religious Freedom (1777), in *The Portable Thomas Jefferson*, 251–53.

37. Thomas Jefferson, A Letter to Nehemiah Dodge and Others, A Committee of the Danbury Baptist Association, in the State of Connecticut (January 1, 1802), in *The Portable Thomas Jefferson*, p. 303.

38. In an earlier section of the bill, Jefferson wrote more pointedly, "To compel a man to furnish contributions of money for the propagation of opinions which he disbelieves and abhors, is sinful and tyrannical."

39. See Sheldon and Dreisbach, *Religion and Political Culture.*

40. Hamburger, *Separation of Church and State*, pp. 1–9, 144–89; Daniel L. Dreisbach, *Thomas Jefferson and the Wall of Separation of Church and State* (New York: New York University Press, 2002), pp. 1–54.

41. See generally, Akhil Reed Amar, *The Bill of Rights: Creation and Reconstruction* (New Haven: Yale University Press, 1998), pp. 3–133.

42. Thomas Jefferson, First Inaugural Address (March 4, 1801), in *The Portable Thomas Jefferson*, pp. 292, 295.

43. Quotes from Jefferson's first and second messages to Congress are taken from Dreisbach, *Thomas Jefferson and the Wall of Separation*, p. 58.

44. James Madison, "Memorial Remonstrance against Religious Assessments" (June 20, 1785), in Jake N. Rakove, ed., *Writings* (New York: Library of America, 1999), pp. 30–31. See also Vincent Blasi, "School Vouchers and Religious Liberty: Seven Questions from Madison's Memorial and Remonstrance," *Cornell Law Review* 87 (March 2002), pp. 783–818.

45. James Madison, "Detached Memoranda" (1817), in *Writings*, p. 763.

46. Jack N. Rakove, "Once More into the Breach: Reflections on Jefferson, Madison, and the Religion Problem," in Diane Ravitch and Joseph P. Viteritti, eds., *Making Good Citizens: Education and Civil Society* (New Haven: Yale University Press, 2001), pp. 233–62.

47. Cited by Rakove in Madison, *Writings*, p. 10.

48. James Madison, Speech in Congress Proposing Constitutional Amendments (June 8, 1789), in *Writings*, p. 442.

49. See David F. Epstein, *The Political Theory of the Federalist* (Chicago: University of Chicago Press, 1984); Herert J. Storing, *What the Anti-Federalists Were For* (Chicago: University of Chicago Press, 1981).

50. James Madison, "The Federalist No. 51" (February 6, 1788), in *Writings*, p. 324.

51. Cited in Ketcham, *James Madison*, p. 633.

52. James Madison, Letter to William Bradford (April 1, 1774), in *Writings*, p. 7.

53. James Madison, "Vices of the Political System of the United States" (April 1787), in *Writings*, p. 78.

54. James Madison, Letter to Frederick Beasley (November 20, 1825), in Robert S. Alley, ed., *James Madison on Religious Liberty* (Buffalo, N.Y.: Prometheus, 1985), p. 85.

55. See Lance Banning, *The Sacred Fire of Liberty: James Madison and the Founding of the Federal Republic* (Ithaca, N.Y.: Cornell University Press, 1995); Drew R. McCoy,

The Last of Our Fathers: James Madison and the Republican Legacy (New York: Cambridge University Press, 1989).

56. James Madison, "The Federalist No. 10," in *Writings*, p. 161.

CHAPTER EIGHT: AMERICAN LANDSCAPE

1. Robert D. Putnam, *Bowling Alone: The Collapse and Revival of American Community* (New York: Simon and Schuster, 2000), p. 79. See generally pp. 65–79.

2. See Norman Nie, Jane Junn, and Kenneth Stehlik-Barry, *Education and Democratic Citizenship in America* (Chicago: University of Chicago Press, 1996); Ravitch and Viteritti, *Making Good Citizens*; Viteritti, *Choosing Equality*, pp. 180–208.

3. Mark Chaves, *Congregations in America* (Cambridge: Harvard University Press, 2004), p. 3.

4. See Putnam, *Bowling Alone*, pp. 31–67; Thomas E. Patterson, *The Vanishing Voter: Public Involvement in an Age of Uncertainty* (New York: Knopf, 2002), pp. 3–22.

5. Roger Finke and Rodney Stark, *The Churching of America, 1776–1790: Winners and Losers in Our Religious Economy* (New Brunswick, N.J.: Rutgers University Press, 1992), p. 16. See also Philip E. Hammond, *Religion and Personal Autonomy: The Third Disestablishment in America* (Columbia: University of South Carolina Press, 1992), p. xiv.

6. "Many Americans Uneasy with Mix of Religion and Politics," Washington, D.C., Pew Forum on Religion and Public Life, August 24, 2006.

7. Robert Wuthnow, "Mobilizing Civic Engagement: The Changing Impact of Religious Involvement," in Theda Skocpol and Morris P. Fiorina, eds, *Civic Engagement in American Democracy* (Washington, D.C.: Brookings Institution Press, 1999), pp. 336–41.

8. Chaves, *Congregations in America*, pp. 24–25.

9. Herberg, *Protestant—Catholic—Jew*. See David K. Yoo, ed., *New Spiritual Homes: Religion and Asian Americans* (Honolulu: University of Hawaii Press, 1999).

10. See generally Robert Wuthnow, *America and the Challenges of Religious Diversity* (Princeton: Princeton University Press, 2005), pp. 38–72.

11. Wolfe, *Transformation of American Religion*, 226–36. See also Yvonne Yazbeck and John L. Esposito, eds., *Muslims on the Americanization Path?* (New York: Oxford University Press, 2000).

12. Hutchison, *Religious Pluralism in America*.

13. Wuthnow, *Challenges of Religious Diversity*, p. 72.

14. Wuthnow, *Challenges of Religious Diversity*, pp. 90, 205, 215, and, generally, 190–229.

15. Alan Wolfe, *One Nation after All: What Middle-Class Americans Really Think about God, Country, Family, Racism, Welfare, Immigration, Homosexuality, Work, the Right, the Left, and Each Other* (New York: Viking Penguin, 1998), pp. 39–87.

16. "Pragmatic Americans Liberal and Conservative on Social Issues," Washington, D.C., Pew Forum on Religion and Public Life, August 3, 2006.

17. Wolfe, *Transformation of American Religion*, p. 41.

18. Wolfe, *Transformation of American Religion*, p. 47.

19. Sonya Gais, "Latino Catholics Increasingly Drawn to Pentecostalism," *Washington Post*, April 30, 2006, sec. A, p. 3.

20. Wolfe, *Transformation of American Religion*, p. 216.

21. Joseph Gremillion and Jim Castelli, *The Emerging Parish: The Notre Dame Study of Catholic Life since Vatican II* (New York: Harper and Row, 1987). See also Jay Dolan, *In Search of American Catholicism* (New York: Oxford University Press, 2002).

22. Wolfe, *Transformation of American Religion*, p. 255.

23. "OMG! How Generation Y Is Redefining Faith in the iPod Era," Washington, D.C., Reboot, April 2005. According to its website (www.rebooters.net), Reboot is an organization dedicated to facilitating an intergenerational conversation about the meaning of Jewish identity. Organizations that supported the research include CIRCLE (University of Maryland), the Walter and Elise Haas Foundation, Carnegie Corporation, Sundra Foundation, Andrea and Charles Bronfman Philanthropies, Nathan Cummings Foundation, Pew Charitable Trust's Project MAPS.

24. Other studies have found a negative correlation between religiosity and adolescent sexual activity. See "The Association between Parent, Family and Peer Religiosity and Teenagers' Sexual Experience and Contraception Use," National Campaign to Prevent Teen Pregnancy, November 2005, www.teenpregnancy.org.

25. Dennis Gilbert, "The Hamilton College Hot Button Issues Poll: An Analysis," Hamilton, N.Y., Arthur Levitt Public Affairs Center at Hamilton College, in cooperation with Zogby International, January 2006.

26. Chaves, *Congregations in America*, p. 8.

27. Chaves, *Congregations in America*, pp. 17–21.

28. Chaves, *Congregations in America*, p. 47.

29. See generally Chaves, *Congregations in America*, pp. 47–106.

30. See Jeffries and Ryan, "Political History," pp. 336–37.

31. Robert Wuthnow, *Saving America: Faith-Based Services and the Future of Civil Society* (Princeton: Princeton University Press, 2005), pp. 28–42.

32. Wuthnow, *Saving America*, pp. 102–4.

33. Wuthnow, *Saving America*, pp. 219–50.

34. Wuthnow, *Saving America*, p. 277. See generally pp. 276–85.

35. Wuthnow, *Saving America*, pp. 150–55.

36. See Charles Glenn, *The Ambiguous Embrace: Government and Faith-Based Schools and Organizations* (Princeton: Princeton University Press, 2000), pp. 212–40.

37. See Chaves, *Congregations in America*, pp. 108–26.

38. Chaves, *Congregations in America*, p. 117.

39. Wuthnow, *Saving America*, p. 293.

40. Sidney Verba, Kay Lehman Schlozman, and Henry Brady, *Voice and Equality: Civic Voluntarism in American Politics* (Cambridge: Harvard University Press, 1995).

41. See also Lawrence R. Jacobs and Theda Skocpol, eds., *Inequality and American Democracy: What We Know and What We Need to Learn* (New York: Russell Sage Foundation, 2005).

42. Verba, Schlozman, and Brady, *Voice and Equality*, pp. 75, 243–47, 264, 282–83, 320–22, 383–85.

43. See also Fredrick C. Harris, *Something Within: Religion in African-American Political Activism* (New York: Oxford University Press, 1999).

44. Verba, Schlozman, and Brady, *Voice and Equality*, p. 519.

45. Verba, Schlozman, and Brady, *Voice and Equality*, p. 317.

46. Morris P. Fiorina, *Culture War? The Myth of a Polarized America* (New York: Longman, 2004).

47. Fiorina, *Culture War?* p. 8. See also Wayne Baker, *America's Crisis of Values: Reality and Perception* (Princeton: Princeton University Press, 2005), pp. 64–109.

48. "Pragmatic Americans Liberal and Conservative on Social Issues," Washington, D.C., Pew Forum on Religion and Public Life, August 3, 2006.

49. See Patterson, *The Vanishing Voter*, pp. 63–98; Joseph N. Capella and Kathleen Hall Jamieson, *Spiral of Cynicism* (New York: Oxford University Press, 1997); E. J. Dionne, *Why Americans Hate Politics* (New York: Touchstone, 1991).

50. Patterson, *The Vanishing Voter*, pp. 23–62. Patterson's portrait of the American center is confirmed in a later book by Hacker and Pierson. However, the latter focus on how Republican leaders manipulate a moderate electorate and have little to say about the disconnection between Democrats and the same electorate. Jacob S. Hacker and Paul Pierson, *Off Center: The Republican Revolution and the Erosion of American Democracy* (New Haven: Yale University Press, 2005).

51. "Public Divided on Origins of Life: Religion a Strength and a Weakness for Both Parties," Washington, D.C., Pew Forum on Religion and Public Life, August 30, 2005. See also Christine Todd Whitman, *It's My Party Too: The Battle for the Heart of the GOP and the Future of America* (New York: Penguin, 2005).

52. "Many Americans Uneasy with Mix of Religion and Politics," Washington, D.C., Pew Forum on Religion and Public Life, August 24, 2006.

53. Alan Wolfe, "Schooling and Religious Pluralism," in Ravitch and Viteritti, *Making Good Citizens*, p. 285.

54. Phillips, *American Theocracy*, p. viii.

55. Phillips, *American Theocracy*, p. 389.

56. Robert Toner and Kate Zernike, "For Incoming Democrats, Populism Trumps Ideology: New Class Promises End to Partisan Tone," *New York Times*, November 12, 2006, A1; Carl Hulse, "New Mosaic of Democrats Is Challenge for Leaders," *New York Times*, November 9, 2006, P1.

Chapter Nine: Conscience and Compromise

1. Lemon v. Kurtzman, 403 U.S. 602 (1971).

2. Zelman v. Simmons-Harris, 536 U.S. 639 (2002). See Viteritti, "Reading Zelman."

3. Locke v. Davey, 540 U.S. 807 (2004).

4. Employment Division v. Smith, 494 U.S. 872 (1990).

5. Harris, *The End of Faith*.

6. Carter, *The Culture of Disbelief*, p. 23.

7. For another iteration of this point based on a case involving restrictions imposed by a secular cemetery in Boca Raton, Florida, see Winnifred Fallers Sullivan, *The Impossibility of Religious Freedom* (Princeton: Princeton University Press, 2005).

8. Gonzales v. O Centro Espirita Beneficiente Uniao Do Vegetal, 126 S.Ct. 1211 (2006). Justice Alito did not participate in the case.

9. City of Boerne v. Flores, 521 U.S. 507 (1997).

10. See, for example Marci A. Hamilton, *God vs. the Gavel: Religion and the Rule of Law* (New York: Cambridge University Press, 2005), pp. 203–37 (though she does not address this particular case).

11. The medical treatment and pedophile cases are discussed at length in Hamilton, *God vs. the Gavel*, pp. 12–49.

12. My notion of freedom here is not unlike that espoused by Coons and Brennan, who define human equality as "the capacity of every rational person to advance in moral self-perfection through diligent intention of correct behaviors toward other per-

sons." John E. Coons and Patrick M. Brennan, *By Nature Equal: The Anatomy of a Western Insight* (Princeton: Princeton University Press, 1999), p. 13.

13. Perry, *Under God?* pp. 20–52; Michael Perry, *Religion in Politics: Constitutional and Moral Perspectives* (New York: Oxford University Press, 1999).

14. Linda Gordon, *Woman's Body, Woman's Right: A Social History of Birth Control in America* (New York: Grossman, 1976), pp. 21–25.

15. See generally John W. Johnson, *Griswold v. Connecticut: Birth Control and the Constitutional Right of Privacy* (Lawrence: University Press of Kansas, 2005), pp. 5–20.

16. Griswold v. Connecticut, 381 U.S. 479 (1964). See generally Johnson, *Griswold v. Connecticut*.

17. Eisenstadt v. Baird, 405 U.S. 438 (1972).

18. Roe v. Wade, 410 U.S. 113 (1973).

19. See Edward S. Corwin, *The "Higher Law" Background of American Constitutional Law* (Ithaca, N.Y.: Cornell University Press, 1955).

20. See Hamilton, *God vs. the Gavel.*

21. The forthcoming analysis of cases is derived from Gerald Gunther, *Constitutional Law*, 12th ed. (Westbury, N.Y. Foundation Press, 1991), pp. 1586–89.

22. United States v. Seeger, 380 U.S. 163 (1965).

23. The Court said as much in 1943 in the *Barnette* case when it found that the Pledge of Allegiance case brought by the Jehovah Witnesses raised free speech claims that were not necessarily grounded in religion. See chapter 6, note 20.

24. Welsh v. United States, 398 U.S. 333 (1970).

25. According to one estimate, only 70 percent of American high school students graduate in four years. Graduation rates among minorities are especially low: 51.6 percent for African-Americans and Native Americans, 55.6 percent for Hispanics. For boys, the graduation rates are 44.3 percent for African-Americans, 42.7 percent for Native Americans, 50.1 percent for Hispanics. "Diplomas Count: An Essential Guide to Graduation Policy and Rates," *Education Week*, June 22, 2006, p. 6.

26. See William A. Galston, *Liberal Purposes: Goods, Virtues, and Diversity in the Liberal State* (New York: Cambridge University Press, 1991), pp. 251–55.

27. For example, in 2000 the Modesto, California, school district started offering a required course for ninth graders on "World Religions." An evaluation of the course completed in 2006 found that students not only increased their knowledge of various religious traditions, but they developed more tolerant attitudes towards all religious groups. See Emile Lester and Patrick Roberts, *Learning about World Religions: The Impact on Student Attitudes and Community Acceptance* (Arlington, Va.: First Amendment Center, 2006). See also the new high school textbook, Cullen Schippe and Chuck Stetson, *The Bible and Its Influence* (Fort Royal, Va.: BLP Publishing, 2006).

28. See especially Kent Greenawalt, *Does God Belong in Public Schools?* (Princeton: Princeton University Press, 2005). Noah Feldman takes the matter further. Although he opposes the adoption of publicly supported vouchers for children to attend religious schools, Feldman encourages voluntary school prayer in public schools, and argues that Americans should be more accepting of religious symbolism in the form of holiday decorations displayed on public property. Feldman, *Divided by God: America's Church-State Problem—And What We Should Do about It* (New York: Farrar, Straus and Giroux, 2005). See also Robert Kunzman, *Grappling with the Good: Talking about Religion and Morality in Public Schools* (Albany: State University of New York Press, 2006).

29. See John E. Coons and Stephen D. Sugarman, *Education by Choice: The Case for Family Control* (Berkeley and Los Angeles: University of California Press, 1978).

30. See also Rosemary C. Salomone, "Common Schools, Uncommon Values: Listening to the Voices of Dissent," *Yale Law and Policy Review* 14 (1996), pp. 169–235.

31. See, for example, Amy Gutmann, *Democratic Education* (Princeton: Princeton University Press, 1987).

32. Patrick J. Wolfe, "School Choice and Civic Values," in Julian Betts and Tom Loveless, eds., *Getting Choice Right: Ensuring Equity and Efficiency in Education Policy* (Washington, D.C.: Brookings Institution Press, 2005).

33. I understand that a legitimate argument could be made for subsidizing all families that choose, as a matter a conscience, to place their children in a private or religious schools, therefore relieving all the potential burdens inherent in forgoing a public school education. However, as I have argued elsewhere, the policy issues are more complex. Given the limited amount of space available in private and religious schools and the compelling educational reasons for providing more attractive options to the poor, I remain persuaded that a needs-based system of publicly supported choice is the fairer approach at this time. See Viteritti, *Choosing Equality*, pp. 209–24.

34. Walz v. Kurtzman, 403 U.S. 664 (1970).

35. See generally Mark Schneider, Paul Teske, and Melissa Marschall, *Choosing Schools: Consumer Choice and the Quality of American Schools* (Princeton: Princeton University Press, 2002).

36. Bowen v. Kendrick, 487 U.S. 589 (1988).

37. Corp. of Presiding Bishop v. Amos, 483 U.S. 327, 341 (1987). See Douglas Laycock, "Towards a General Theory of the Religion Clauses: The Case of Church Labor Relations and the Right to Church Autonomy," *Columbia Law Review* 81 (1981), pp. 1373–1413.

38. Boy Scouts v. Dale, 530, U.S. 640 (2000).

39. For example, there may be an educational justification for hiring teachers of a particular gender in single-sex schools created to address the specific needs of one gender or the other.

INDEX